EDUCATION FOR CITIZENSHIP AND DIVERSITY IN IRISH CONTEXTS

Edited by
Gerry Jeffers and Una O'Connor

IPA
INSTITUTE OF PUBLIC
ADMINISTRATION

First published in 2008
by the Institute of Public Administration
57–61 Lansdowne Road
Dublin 4
Ireland

www.ipa.ie

ISBN: 978-1-904541-77-6

British Library cataloguing-in-publication data
A catalogue record for this book is available from the British Library

Cover design by Alice Campbell, Dublin
Typeset by Computertype, Dublin
Printed in Ireland by ColourBooks Ltd, Dublin

Education for Citizenship and Diversity
in Irish Contexts

Contents

Foreword

This is not a collection of dry, academic papers on a worthy if difficult topic. It is a book of lively and provocative essays that should engage anyone interested in how people in societies divided by religion, national allegiance, race, class, ability and disability – that is, societies everywhere, not just in Ireland – can start to learn to live better together by using the great and wonderful process of educating children.

And before you begin to educate children, you have to educate their teachers. That is a theme that runs through many of the contributions in this book. It is depressingly clear, for example, that after a decade and a half of schooling, most of the young Northern Irish people aiming for a career in teaching have engaged in little or no learning across traditional cultural barriers and are ill-fitted to pass on the responsibilities and skills of citizenship to a new generation. Several decades of community relations, multiculturalism and education for mutual understanding initiatives have not merely failed – for the most part they haven't even been properly tried.

In Northern Ireland the choice for a still deeply segregated society is a stark one: it is between managing separatism – what some people have called 'benign apartheid', as if apartheid could ever be benign – or building a shared, interconnected future. If it is going to be the latter, education for shared citizenship will be vital to this small society's well-being. That doesn't make it any more important in the eyes of the school authorities, for whom individual academic achievement remains the *ne plus ultra* of educational attainment. Citizenship education will never rate highly in a world that is obsessed with target setting and examination results, and maybe it is time to find other ways to help teachers in this pioneering area to overcome their isolation, e.g. by building effective networks between them.

Building networks – and in particular, cross-border networks – is another common theme in this book. SCoTENS, which sponsored the conference that spawned these essays, is one example of a remarkably successful all-Ireland network of teacher educators emerging from a sector not previously known for either its intellectual dynamism or interest in happenings on the other side of the border. The Education for Reconciliation project for secondary schools – which the Centre for Cross

Border Studies helped to evaluate – provides another example of building an innovative North-South network around teacher development.

Another recurrent theme is that the only way to teach children citizenship and democracy is for them to see it at work in their own schools. I am reminded of a Dublin secondary school in my own recent experience, where sixth-formers had reached a painstakingly negotiated agreement with the senior teachers about an event close to their hearts, only to find the arrangement undermined at the last minute by executive *fiat*. How can that help build trust and confidence in educational, social and political institutions among young people? One essayist notes survey evidence that open and honest dialogue in the classroom is one of the most important factors leading to positive civic outcomes among teenagers.

There are lessons to be learned from every single one of the 18 fascinating chapters in this book. Two more are the need for a more holistic approach to teaching immigrant children rather than a concentration on English language learning, and for new ways of allowing Ireland's young disabled people to express their active citizenship. Much of the strength of these essays lies in the knowledge that their writers are the very opposite of detached academics. These *engagé* intellectuals and practitioners are striving hard to follow Gandhi's exhortation 'to be the change you wish to see in the world'. More power to them.

Andy Pollak
Director, Centre for Cross Border Studies
Secretary, Standing Conference on Teacher Education North and South
(SCoTENS)

Contributors

Maria Barry is Head of Education with Trócaire, the overseas development agency of the Catholic Church in Ireland, based in Maynooth, Co. Kildare.

Tony Gallagher is Professor of Education and Head of School at the School of Education, Queen's University, Belfast.

Mary Gannon is co-ordinator of the Equality and Diversity Project managed by the Curriculum Development Unit of the City of Dublin VEC.

Jim Gleeson is Senior Lecturer in the Department of Education and Professional Studies at the University of Limerick.

Conor Harrison is National Co-Ordinator of the Support Service for Civic, Social and Political Education (CSPE) of the Second-Level Support Service (SLSS) and is based in the Curriculum Development Unit of the City of Dublin VEC.

Tom Healy is Senior Statistician at the Department of Education and Science and Research Associate at the Policy Institute at Trinity College Dublin as well as, formerly, a consultant to the Taskforce on Active Citizenship in 2006.

Daniel Holder is the Racial Equality Policy and Research Officer at Dungannon and South Tyrone Borough Council.

Gerry Jeffers is a Lecturer in Education (Innovation and Development in Schools) at the Education Department, National University of Ireland, Maynooth.

Alan McCully is a Lecturer in Education (History and Citizenship) at the School of Education, University of Ulster, Coleraine.

Majella McSharry is a lecturer in the School of Education Studies at Dublin City University.

Deirdre A. Murphy is a teacher at St John's Secondary School, Bally-fermot, Dublin.

Una O'Connor is a Lecturer in Education (Children and Young People) in the UNESCO Centre, University of Ulster, Coleraine.

Chuck Richardson is Director of The Spirit of Enniskillen Trust, a youth-focused, non-governmental organisation based in Belfast.

Norman Richardson teaches Religious Studies and education for diversity and mutual understanding to student teachers at Stranmillis University College, Belfast.

Marie Rooney is co-ordinator of Research and Policy Development with County Dublin Vocational Educational Committee and a former co-ordinator of the Education for Reconciliation Project.

Michael Shevlin is Head of the School of Education at Trinity College, Dublin.

Paul J. Smyth is Director of Public Achievement (Northern Ireland), based in Belfast.

Máirín Wilson is a lecturer in the Church of Ireland College of Education, Rathmines, Dublin and External Chief Examiner of Civic, Social and Political Education in the Junior Certificate Examination.

Introduction

To enter the arena of 'Education for Citizenship' is to visit a challenging and contested space. In a global context, new perspectives on citizenship education have been triggered by such diverse happenings as the ending of the apartheid system in South Africa, the literal and metaphorical demolition of the Berlin Wall, the genocide in Rwanda and events associated with what has become known as '9/11'.

Within individual nations, voiced concerns, including perceived loss of trust between citizens, decline of positive social capital, elevated levels of violence and law-breaking and reduced civic participation, often shine a spotlight – at times momentarily – on the value of education for citizenship.

Within formal and informal education, the strengthening of respect for basic freedoms and the adoption of the discourse of human rights have led to fresh perceptions about specific programmes and learning experiences that educate for democratic citizenship. An emphasis on the uniqueness of each learner invites new approaches to the teaching and learning of what it means to be a citizen.

To complicate matters further, the understanding of citizenship itself is far from static. The discourse of neo-liberalism elevates economic calculations and the power of 'the market' to regulate relationships to levels that undermine values such as rights, solidarity, inclusion and participation. Politicians and media commentators frequently place economic considerations centre-stage, with wider societal concerns and implications relegated to the wings; increasingly people are spoken of as 'consumers' and 'customers' rather than as 'citizens'. Bottery's (2003) analysis of forces that threaten current conceptions of citizenship deserves attention. He asks whether the nation state will be able to call upon the loyalty of its inhabitants and be the primary focus for a commitment to a form of citizenship in the future.

Latterly, the ideal of a 'common citizenship' has underlined the divisive nature of this concept. Whilst it invokes shared solidarity and respect for diversity there is little doubt that personal and group identities – whether these are religious, cultural or political – continue to impact on the way in which people see themselves as individuals and as members of a community (Kymlicka and Norman, 2000; Waldron, 2000).

On the island of Ireland, recent history presents fresh opportunities and challenges for citizenship education. The arrival and settling of migrants from diverse backgrounds presents a new lens through which we can view our evolving development. In schools and youth groups from Antrim to Kerry, from Tipperary to Tyrone, learning about one's identity as 'Irish' is further nuanced when parents or grandparents have their roots, for example, in Lithuania or Nigeria, Poland or China. Growing respect for the rights of the full spectrum of young learners, including those with special educational needs, adds a distinct perspective to how we understand 'diversity'.

Origins

This book was born out of a recognition of the need for those concerned with education for citizenship to share their experiences. Prompted by the supportive structure of the Standing Conference on Teacher Education, North-South (SCoTENS), a selection of interested people from Northern Ireland and the Republic of Ireland attended a conference in Ballyconnell, Co. Cavan, in late 2004. It was a stimulating and encouraging learning experience and some of the chapters that follow began life as papers at the Ballyconnell event. Of course our world has moved on in many ways since then and citizenship education practitioners now face additional opportunities and challenges. Winds of economic, cultural and political change are reshaping our everyday social landscapes. The restoration of the Northern Ireland Assembly in May 2007 represents a particularly significant development. Some consequences of this change find their way into a wide range of relationships throughout the island and beyond.

Within schools, the on-going experiences with curriculum implementation under the 'education for citizenship' banner continue to offer instructive insights, not least about school as organisations, about the difficulty of innovation and about the robust resistance of established patterns and cultures. The emergence of fresh thinking, for example the proposed introduction of a new subject Politics and Society into senior cycle education in the Republic of Ireland (Tormey, 2006; NCCA, 2007), the statutory introduction of Local and Global Citizenship within a revised Northern Ireland Curriculum (CCEA, 2007) and the Report from the Taskforce on Active Citizenship (2007) are further reminders that the conversation about 'education for citizenship' takes place in this constantly shifting environment.

Wider contexts

Citizenship education initiatives on this island find resonances in many other countries. Developments at grass-root level are often complemented and supported by policy emphases at international levels. For example, the Council of Europe recommends, *inter alia*, that member states 'make education for democratic citizenship a priority objective for educational policy-making and reforms' (Council of Europe, 2002). Furthermore, a core belief running through the Council of Europe's 'Education for Democratic Citizenship' project (see www.coe.int) is that individuals learn to be citizens through active participation. For formal and informal educators, this perspective leads to promoting the development of reflective and creative actors. Active participation and questioning is valued more than passive acceptance and conformity. Among the key competencies identified for learning to live in a democratic society is the ability to:

- settle conflicts in a non-violent manner
- argue in defence of one's viewpoint
- listen to, understand and interpret other people's arguments
- recognise and accept differences
- make choices, consider alternatives and subject them to ethical analysis
- shoulder shared responsibilities
- establish constructive, non-aggressive relations with others
- develop a critical approach to information, through patterns and philosophical, religious, social, political and cultural concepts, at the same time remaining committed to the fundamental values and principles of the Council of Europe.

Structure

Each contributor to this volume, in her or his own way, has been engaged in advancing 'education for citizenship and diversity' in a variety of settings on the island of Ireland. The chapters reflect a diversity of experiences and perspectives. However, they are united by a belief among the contributors that 'education for citizenship and diversity' is an important matter that needs to be discussed within and beyond formal and informal education. A great value of these contributions is that they clarify our vision of what we think we are about when we talk about 'educating young people for twenty-first century citizenship'. While such conversations always seem to struggle against being marginalised within wider educational discussions, our hope is that the diverse richness of contributions in this book will nurture and sustain these conversations and lead to meaningful action to improve practice.

In the opening chapters, **Alan McCully** and **Gerry Jeffers**, both engaged in the education of teachers of 'citizenship', introduce some of the challenges facing education for citizenship and diversity in the different contexts of Northern Ireland and the Republic of Ireland.

Identifying good practice in the citizenship education arena has to be a key concern for practitioners, educational leaders and policy makers. **Tony Gallagher** poses a series of insightful and probing questions that provide an engaging and promising map of discovery. His questions can be applied to both the formal and informal sectors, and collaboration between the two arenas is a recurring theme throughout the book. A central belief informing the collection is that school-based education must reach beyond the confines of the traditional classroom. In practice this involves young people and their teachers going out to the wider community and the wider community being invited in to schools as collaborators in the educational enterprise. Thus, examples of co-operation between schools and non-governmental organisations follow.

Chuck Richardson recounts how an initiative with its origins outside formal education is being integrated into regular classrooms. As with a number of other chapters, this chapter reminds us of the centrality of students' voices in citizenship education. **Maria Barry's** account of how an NGO with a global perspective devised a project that captures the everyday social concerns of teenagers is instructive and exemplary. Its inclusion underlines a distinct feature of citizenship education on this island: the extent to which agencies whose primary mission is concerned with development in poorer countries promote and support citizenship education.

To engage successfully with young people in this contested arena of citizenship education, practitioners – whether youth workers or teachers – need to be competent and confident in their approaches, strategies and pedagogies. The European Union funded *Education for Peace and Reconciliation* project prompts **Marie Rooney's** account of a cross-border initiative with a focus on teachers' professional development.

Norman Richardson makes the case well for the fundamental foundations of education for citizenship and diversity being an essential dimension in primary education.

This is followed by a number of chapters that look at policies and practices in second-level schools, north and south. **Jim Gleeson** takes a critical perspective on Civic, Social and Political Education (CSPE), locating it in its historical, socio-cultural and policy contexts. He sounds important warnings for practitioners and policy makers. His concerns resonate with the findings of practices in the five schools that **Deirdre Murphy** investigated and on which she reports in the subsequent chapter.

Within schools, classrooms are key sites for citizenship education. The basic premise that active citizenship requires active teaching and learning methodologies informs the next chapter. **Conor Harrison** identifies some important challenges faced by classroom practitioners and also raises questions for teacher educators.

Changing classrooms invite some re-thinking about diversity among student populations and our growing appreciation of diversity manifesting itself in different ways. **Mary Gannon** offers a well-thought-out framework for responding to diversity in schools. With a Northern Ireland case study, **Daniel Holder** illustrates how the persistent issue of equity in education manifests itself with new migrant communities.

The chapter by **Una O'Connor** demonstrates how citizenship education both is challenged by and can offer opportunities to young people with learning difficulties. She invites citizenship educators to respond imaginatively to the diversity of learners in classrooms. The chapter by **Michael Shevlin** that follows reinforces this need for imaginative responses. His capturing of the voices of young people with disabilities makes compelling reading.

The chapter by **Paul Smyth** offers a practical example of education for active citizenship. *Public Achievement* is based in Minnesota in the United States and has a particular propensity to action. This chapter describes how this organisation manifests itself in the context of Northern Ireland. In the Republic of Ireland, Action Projects in CSPE represent a genuine breakthrough in regard to pedagogy and assessment. **Máirín Wilson's** analysis of trends within CSPE projects in the Junior Certificate Examination provides a unique map that will be of value to every teacher of the subject.

Standing back from individual classrooms, **Majella McSharry** poses some uncomfortable questions about schools and their priorities. As we hope is evident throughout this book, a commitment to education for citizenship and diversity demands serious reappraisal of how schools operate. It is our belief that in the re-conceptualising of schools for the twenty-first century, schools that are truly 'learning schools' will put education for citizenship at the heart of their enterprise and build strong links with their immediate communities.

Finally, **Tom Healy** frames some questions arising from the work of the Republic of Ireland's Taskforce on Active Citizenship (2007). His reference to the forthcoming International Civics and Citizenship Education Study is a timely reminder that comparative data on the knowledge and attitudes of 14-year-olds are likely to stimulate further debate – and action – on education for citizenship.

One of the recommendations arising from the Taskforce was the establishment of an all-island Observatory on Active Citizenship. Such an enterprise is to be welcomed and this present volume offers some signposts to the value of sharing insights relating to education for citizenship and diversity.

Gerry Jeffers, Una O'Connor
NUI Maynooth and the University of Ulster, Coleraine

References

Bottery, M. (2003), 'The End of Citizenship? The Nation State, Threats to its Legitimacy and Citizenship Education in the Twenty-First Century', *Cambridge Journal of Education,* 33:1,101-122

Council of Europe (2002), *Draft Recommendations of the Committee of Ministers to member states on education for democratic citizenship,* Strasbourg, 16th October www.coe.int

CCEA (Council for Curriculum, Examinations and Assessment) (2007), *The statutory curriculum at Key Stage 3. Rationale and detail,* Belfast: CCEA   www.ccea.org

Kymlicka, W. and Norman, W. (2000), 'Citizenship in culturally diverse societies: issues, contexts, concepts', in W. Kymlicka and W. Norman (eds), *Citizenship in diverse societies,* Oxford: Oxford University Press, pp 1-41

Tormey, R. (2006), *Social and Political Education in Senior Cycle, A Background Paper,* Dublin: National Council for Curriculum and Assessment

NCCA (National Council for Curriculum and Assessment) (2007), *Senior Cycle Developments: Report on Consultation on Social and Political Education in Senior Cycle, A Background Paper,* Dublin: NCCA

Waldron, J. (2000), 'Cultural identity and civic responsibility', in W. Kymlicka and W. Norman (eds), *Citizenship in diverse societies,* Oxford: Oxford University Press, pp 155-174

Taskforce on Active Citizenship (2007), *Report of the Taskforce on Active Citizenship,* Dublin: Secretariat of the Taskforce on Active Citizenship. Available at www.activecitizenship.ie

Reflections on the Local and Global Citizenship Programme in Northern Ireland

Alan McCully

Thirty years ago, in my first year teaching, I had the privilege of being involved in the Schools Cultural Studies Project (SCSP) (Robinson, 1983), initiated by Professor Malcolm Skilbeck and based at the then New University of Ulster. The project engaged twelve post-primary schools in the North and West of Northern Ireland in a social studies programme based on a social reconstructionist philosophy that was a direct curricular response to the spiralling violence in the Province in the 1970s. At one of the early teacher workshops the project was nearly blown asunder before it properly became established. As preparation for a first-year module on *difference*, participants were asked to bring along pictures that represented different individuals within society. Someone arrived with a picture of a black beauty queen and others with images of a traveller woman and a skinhead. Then, someone produced 'the smiling policewoman' as she became known, a picture of a female RUC officer. All hell broke loose. To some present it was a smiling policewoman while to others the picture represented a deliberate attempt to introduce propaganda into the project.

The fall-out convinced one or two that the initiative was not for them, but the majority worked through the differing perceptions and emerged with a new understanding and a deeper commitment to the potential of education to make a positive contribution to the clarification of young people's thinking on the 'troubles'. Certainly, at the beginning of my career the incident had made me aware of two things. First, that addressing issues of citizenship in a divided society presents particular challenges. Second, that as a pre-condition for working in the field it is crucial that practitioners themselves first work through issues before they attempt to work with young people.

Given this long association with educational activity in the community relations field, it has often struck me that despite, or maybe even because of, the considerable resources that have been put into the area over the years, there has been a tendency for practice to be re-invented or re-cycled with successive initiatives. Retrospectively, SCSP continues to stand out favourably as a project characterised by conceptual rigour and innovative methodologies. Unfortunately, its social studies orientation failed to find a place in the traditional curricular structures of the 1980s and, while it may have had some influence in the emergence of the cross-curricular themes of Education for Mutual Understanding (EMU) and Cultural Heritage, the cutting edge of its approach was largely lost by the 1990s. Therefore, it is both salutary and pleasing to recognise that the Local and Global Citizenship provision that has emerged in Northern Ireland, and is now a part of the statutory provision of the revised curriculum from September 2007, is, however unwittingly, re-establishing many of the stronger features of SCSP. It advocates allocated timetabled space, has a similar conceptual framework, places emphasis on active methodologies and has a commitment to address controversial and sensitive issues in the classroom.

Achievements and challenges

By way of introduction to the Local and Global Citizenship programme, and as a companion article to Gerry Jeffers' reflections on CSPE in the Republic of Ireland (Chapter 2), this account seeks to identify, from a personal perspective, some of the achievements to date and the issues that need to be addressed if citizenship education is to become fully embedded in the structures of education in Northern Ireland and, more importantly, have a significant impact on the experience of young people. So that we can see the similarities and differences in the challenges faced in each jurisdiction, I present my reflections under a similar set of headings to those used by Jeffers (some of which I have extended) and add a few more from my own perspective. They include:

• The conceptual challenge (and the contribution of research)

• The cross-curricular challenge (and the challenge of specific provision)

• The curricular location challenge

• The time challenge

• The community challenge

• The institutional challenge of democracy in action

• The training challenge.

The conceptual challenge – the contribution of research

During the 'troubles' many socially-orientated educators sought ways by which the formal education system might contribute to the reduction of community tension and division. Initially, the statutory authorities were reluctant to formally promote such initiatives. This was one reason for the failure of SCSP to gain widespread recognition. With Circular 82/21 the Department of Education began to more explicitly support community relations orientated work (Richardson, 1992). This included cross-community contact schemes, integrated schools and, with the introduction of the Northern Ireland Curriculum in the early 1990s, statutory support for the cross-curricular themes of EMU and Cultural Heritage.

The strengths and limitations of EMU have been well documented (Smith and Robinson, 1996; DENI, 2000; Gallagher, 2004), particularly the lack of clarity of its curricular provision in practice and the fragility of the cross-curricular model by which the conjoined themes were to be implemented. It was also argued that EMU placed too great an emphasis on building positive relationships and not enough on addressing sensitive issues and the structural imbalances within society. In following up this assessment Smith argued for the necessity of a curriculum which ensured that young people had opportunities to explore the following:

- Identity (including language, culture and religion)
- The contemporary history of Northern Ireland
- The media (developing a critical awareness of how media function within a divided society)
- Justice and the law
- Civic education, rights and responsibilities
- Equality of opportunity (including the rights of minorities)
- Politics (decision-making and concepts of democracy within the civil society)
- Violence and sectarianism within society (Smith, 1997).

Since the inception of the Social, Civic and Political Education pilot project at the University of Ulster in 1997 (Arlow, 1999, 2004), and then the incorporation of Local and Global Citizenship into the Northern Ireland Curriculum Review by the Council for Curriculum, Examinations and Assessment (CCEA), considerable progress has been made in fulfilling Smith's criteria. In common with the citizenship programme adopted in England, Local and Global Citizenship seeks to balance the classical liberal emphasis on the rights of the individual with the communitarian values of civic republicanism (Lockyer, 2003). Advocates of critical pedagogy would no doubt dismiss it as doomed to perpetuate social inequalities. However, as Smith (2003) points out, developing citizens in a divided society presents special challenges. In that context, the radical aspects of the Northern Ireland programme should not be under-estimated in that it seeks to move beyond disputed national identities to define citizenship in terms of rights and responsibilities.

If that fundamental premise is accepted as legitimate (Smith, himself, recognises that it is problematic; see also McEvoy, 2007), then the Local and Global Citizenship programme has a logical purpose and coherent structure. The programme is enquiry-based and issues-orientated so, potentially, it gives teachers and students the flexibility to examine current areas of concern (including those issues on Smith's list) from a range of perspectives. Yet, the programme is underpinned by a conceptual frame-work (Diversity and Inclusion, Equality and Social Justice and Democracy and Active Participation, all in the context of Human Rights and Social Responsibilities) that promotes rigour and provides reference points for investigation and comparative study.

The evolution of the global dimension alongside the local during the CCEA phase of development facilitates the latter. The examination of conflict situations removed in distance (and time) from Northern Ireland was an important tool in the SCSP strategy to enable students to gain greater insight into emotionally charged issues closer to home. Using the core concepts to probe issues, both locally and internationally, can provide ways in to sensitive topics but also safeguards against the relentless introspection which has sometimes been a 'turn-off' for young people engaged in community relations work in Northern Ireland.

The cross-curricular challenge – and the challenge of specific provision

Structurally, Local and Global Citizenship, as envisaged, has advantages. EMU's impact was restricted by the emphasis the Northern Ireland Curriculum placed on established subject provision. Its proposed cross-curricular delivery through the subject areas in reality placed it on the periphery of learning, with little opportunity for development even when the will was there. No specific model of delivery has been identified for Local and Global Citizenship but there is a pointed expectation by the Department of Education (DENI) and CCEA that the work will be taken seriously by schools. The preferred option is that specific time-tabled space be allocated, but by placing social values at the core of the reformed curriculum and making the fostering of these compulsory at all key stages, it is envisioned that young people will have the opportunity to investigate, and clarify their thinking, on key contemporary issues both within and beyond formal citizenship classes.

If citizenship is to be effective, creating this space for young people is crucial, though structures alone will not ensure success. That is where the advocacy of active and experiential learning approaches, a key principle of the citizenship programme, comes in to play. Engaging teaching methods are vital if young people are to perceive the citizenship classroom as offering something qualitatively different to the provision offered in other subject areas. Interestingly, CCEA's interim evaluation (CCEA, 2006:3) of the pilot phase has identified that even when time-tabled space is provided, this must be in long enough time blocks to allow active learning to be pursued to a deliberative conclusion. The citizenship class should be seen as the place where issues relevant to young people are tackled, where opinions are heard and where action can be initiated that has the potential to have an impact beyond the classroom and school.

Curricular initiatives outside the confines of established subject boundaries are difficult to embed. The SCSP experience typifies that. Such initiatives struggle for resources, time-tabling space and the attention of teachers, who often perceive their main subject as the vehicle for career advancement. However, potentially, the position of Local and Global Citizenship is a strong one. Within the core framework of the reformed NI curriculum it has been allocated a central position and thus can be a catalyst towards change. Further, by committing extensive financial resources between 2003 and 2007 the Department of Education has signalled its commitment to developing teacher competence in the citizenship field.

This four-year roll-out, resulting in three teachers from each post-primary school receiving six days of citizenship training prior to its statutory introduction, aimed at providing a critical foundation of informed practitioners. The training was carried out by the Education and Library Boards (ELBs) and, by engaging the ELB advisers responsible in the creation of core materials for each of the Key Stage Three years, this facilitated a direct and creative relationship between training, resources and practice. In contrast to the situation in England, a uniformly sound platform was being sought for implementation.

All in all, then, I am greatly reassured that the Local and Global Citizenship programme, as it emerges, has identified, through accident and design, the core structural, curricular and pedagogical strengths of previous practice. However, that does not mean that the future of citizenship education is secure. There are several concerns around policy and curriculum, provision and training that deserve attention.

The curricular location challenge

My first worry concerns the association of Local and Global Citizenship with the nomenclature of 'Learning for Life and Work' within the revised curriculum. This has both short-term and longer-term dangers.

The short-term first. Here, I believe mistakes were made at an early stage of implementation. Having put detailed planning and resources into establishing a firm foundation for the introduction of citizenship at Key Stage Three, the CCEA then introduced a new Key Stage Four syllabus in Learning for Life and Work (including a discrete citizenship strand) and made it open to schools, teachers and students who had not yet experienced the roll-out programme. Anecdotal evidence suggests that this resulted in some teachers feeling conscripted and ill-prepared. The subsequent decision to locate citizenship within a similar designation at Key Stage Three may have damaged the credibility of citizenship education by association.

The longer-term concerns towards the inclusion within the Learning for Life and Work area of study (alongside Personal Development, Home Economics and Employability) are more philosophical. This is not the place for a detailed analysis but it can be said that, whereas Local and Global Citizenship appeals to our communitarian instincts, Personal Development and Employability place emphasis on individual agency. Is there not a clash of underlying values here? While such tensions could possibly be held in check when each of the strands is taught by practitioners committed to the specific rationales of each component (as was envisaged by CCEA at the proposal stage) there is increasing evidence from job advertisements that new staff are being employed under the broad Learning for Life and Work nomenclature. I would contend that those appointed from Personal Development and Employability backgrounds, while possibly having the pedagogical approaches necessary, are less likely to share the communitarian value base that will make them the transformative practitioners envisaged by the architects of the original citizenship initiative (Arlow, 1999).

The time challenge

The second concern relates to how the revised curriculum is operating in practice. Placing the values of citizenship at its core requires more than policy statements. The impact of Local and Global Citizenship will be greatly restricted if its exposure to students is confined to an hour a week in citizenship classes. Indeed, one of the expressed aims of the curriculum review was to address pupil criticisms (Harland *et al,* 2000) that current provision lacks any overall connectedness and coherence. It will not be enough for other subject departments to carry out paper audits of their work that indicate vague relevance to citizenship education. Real coherence can be established through teachers re-discovering the professional skills of curriculum development by articulating the relationships between their subject and citizenship and, particularly, the overt contribution their subject can make to inform debate in citizenship classes. In doing so, the latter can create the 'space' in which the issues raised by the subjects of the curriculum are given voice and contemporary relevance.

The community challenge

The third concern addresses the relationship of citizenship education to wider community relations issues. Concerns have been expressed that citizenship education, with its broad-ranging agenda, will deflect attention from addressing the deep-seated community divisions in Northern Irish society. Undoubtedly, the culture of avoidance of difficult issues that exists in society also operates amongst educators (Smith and Robinson, 1996; Arlow, 2004; Gallagher, 2004). Unless the aims of citizenship are explicit there is a danger that teachers will shy away from more contentious material. CCEA's interim evaluation (CCEA, 2006) has indicated that this tendency is still present. It has already been argued that inter-relating the local and global has great benefits in helping understanding in Northern Ireland, if structured properly. Similarly, those seeking better community relations must take into account, alongside sectarianism, the instances of racial abuse directed against the expanding ethnic minority groups that have been a feature of the post-Belfast Agreement situation.

Through citizenship education the underlying sources of this 'culture of intolerance' (OFM/DFM, 2005:8), whether sectarian or racist, can be targeted, without losing sight of the core division in society. When sign-posting future aspirations for the education service the Foreword to the DENI report (1999), *Towards a Culture of Tolerance: Education for Diversity,* argued for:

> a new beginning … a new and better basis on which we may live together, not merely without community violence, not merely 'tholing' one another, but respecting, appreciating, understanding and celebrating our distinctive cultures.

For Local and Global Citizenship to contribute it is necessary to clearly articulate its relationship with what is understood as community relations work. Recent research indicates that even at policy level there is uncertainty and mistrust as to the connections (Henderson, 2005). Teachers (and students) should be under no illusions that effective citizens in Northern Ireland are those who face up to sensitive community issues but also address them by drawing on learning from other contexts. Further, citizenship educators must not assume that a programme that, unproblematically, advocates a pluralist or multi-cultural future for the Province will be easily accepted.

The Government's post-Agreement assessment of 'Good Relations' (OFM/DFM, 2004, 2005:7-16) acknowledges that there are those who would be quite comfortable with pursuing, as far as possible, a path of separate development, a benign form of apartheid, as an alternative to contemplating radical change. Such alternatives must be examined seriously if citizenship is to be inclusive of all. Teachers must have confidence in the rigour of the conceptual framework of the programme as a basis for challenging students to think through the implications of their positions. For example, how can diversity as represented by the growing ethnic communities find a place in a society dominated by two monolithic groups that merely 'thol' each other?

The institutional challenge of democracy in action

The fourth concern relates to Local and Global Citizenship in the wider school context. Diversity and interdependence, equality, social justice, human rights, and democracy cannot be isolated in one curricular area. Those concepts should not only be modelled in practice within the citizenship classroom but also be reflected in the ethos and relationships of the whole school. Students will quickly see through an institution that advocates one approach and practises another. Similarly, students will soon tire of a programme that encourages debate but does not provide opportunities to engage with issues beyond the classroom. The inclusion of an action project was an integral part of the original pilot proposal. This has been diluted to an optional element within the statutory provision, particularly at Key Stage Three.

Surely some form of action component is essential to establishing the authenticity of Local and Global Citizenship by demonstrating its relevance in young people's eyes. Its sphere of influence should extend beyond the school gates. This includes tapping in to expertise in the community. For instance, the educational system in Northern Ireland has failed to explore the benefits of the potential interface between teachers and youth workers, despite both sets of professionals being employed by the same organisations (McCully, 2006).

Youth workers have considerable experience in the field of social education, not least in the context of community relations work. Co-operation around the action dimension of citizenship has the potential to enhance practice in both the formal and non-formal sectors. Engagement with issues in the community, again, lifts citizenship education beyond the normal horizons of curricular provision. This also provides opportunities for the common experience of citizenship education to become the medium for purposeful joint-work focused on community relations across communities. New technologies have a role in facilitating this.

The training challenge

Finally, there is the training agenda. While applauding the in-service roll-out put in place at the behest of DENI there is no room for complacency, again as suggested in the interim evaluation study (CCEA, 2006:6). Research indicates that whatever the institutional support structures the key to effective practice in citizenship/ community relations is the relationship that exists between practitioner and young person. The characteristics necessary for an effective practitioner to work in a divided society are formidable ones (McCully, 2006:60-63). At their core are the capacity for trust-building and the willingness to take risks.

Ultimately, the success of the Local and Global Citizenship programme will depend on the quality and skill of the teachers it recruits. Such teachers are exceptional rather than typical. Their subject background is less important than their willingness to engage with young people on issues of relevance, and this desire often emerges from the realisation that their role as a subject specialist is failing to meet, as fully as they might wish, the needs of the young people they teach. Initial teacher education has a role to play in introducing student teachers to citizenship education and broadening their cultural awareness through encounter, but it is possible that the majority of teachers are best positioned when they have overcome the insecurities of their first few years and are relishing the challenge of taking their students into contested territory.

In conclusion, in keeping with Arlow's aspiration that Local and Global Citizenship should, unashamedly, appeal to the idealism and optimism of young people (Arlow, 1999), I am hopeful that the formal education sector has moulded an initiative of potential to help address Northern Ireland's considerable social and political divisions. On the other hand I am under no illusions as to the capability of the educational sector to subvert its intentions in practice.

References

Arlow, M. (1999), 'Citizenship education in a contested society', *The Development Education Journal,* 6:1

Arlow, M. (2004), 'Citizenship education in a divided society: the case of Northern Ireland', in S. Towel and A. Harley (eds), *Education, Conflict and Social Cohesion,* Geneva: International Bureau of Education, UNESCO, pp 255-314

CCEA (Council for Curriculum, Examinations and Assessment) (2006), *Local and Global Citizenship at Key Stage 3: Preliminary Evaluation Findings,* Belfast: CCEA

DENI (Department of Education, Northern Ireland) (1999), *Towards a Culture of Tolerance: Education for Diversity,* Report of the Working Group on the Strategic Promotion of Education for Mutual Understanding, Bangor: DENI

DENI (Department of Education, Northern Ireland) (2000), *Report of a Survey of Provision for Education for Mutual Understanding (EMU) in Post-Primary Schools,* Bangor: Education and Training Inspectorate, DENI

Gallagher, A.M. (2004), *Education in Divided Societies,* Basingstoke: Palgrave-Macmillan

Harland J., Moor, H., Kinder, K. and Ashworth, M. (2000), *Is the Curriculum Working? The Key Stage Three Phase of the Northern Ireland Cohort Study,* London: NFER

Henderson, H. (2005), 'Exploring the relationship between citizenship and community relations in the context of education in Northern Ireland', MSc Dissertation, University of Ulster, unpublished

Lockyer, A. (2003), 'Introduction and Review', in A. Lockyer, B. Crick and J. Annette, *Education for Democratic Citizenship: Issues of Theory and Practice,* Aldershot: Ashgate Publishing

McCully, A. (2006), 'Practitioner perceptions of their role in facilitating the handling of controversial issues in contested societies: a Northern Irish experience', *Educational Review,* 58:1

McEvoy, L. (2007), 'Beneath the Rhetoric: Policy Approximation and Citizenship Education in Northern Ireland Education', *Citizenship and Social Justice,* 2(2), pp 135-158

OFM/DFM (Office of the First Minister/ Deputy First Minister) (2004), *A Shared Future: Consultation, Executive Summary,* http://www.asharedfutureni.gov.uk/exsummary.htm

OFM/DFM (Office of the First Minister/ Deputy First Minister) (2005), *A Shared Future,* Belfast: Community Relations Unit, OFM/DFM

Richardson, N. (1992), *Roots if not wings! Where did EMU come from?* Belfast: Churches' Peace Education Centre

Robinson, A. (1983), *The Schools Cultural Studies Project: a contribution to peace in Northern Ireland,* Coleraine: University of Ulster

Smith, A. (1997), 'The Future of EMU', Internal paper, Coleraine: UNESCO Centre, School of Education, University of Ulster

Smith, A. (2003), 'Citizenship Education in Northern Ireland: beyond national identity?', *Cambridge Journal of Education,* 33:1

Smith, A. and Robinson, A. (1996), *Education for Mutual Understanding: The Initial Statutory Years,* Coleraine: University of Ulster

2

Some challenges for citizenship education in the Republic of Ireland

Gerry Jeffers

The 1990s is increasingly described as a decade of curricular change when imaginative and innovative programmes were introduced in schools in the Republic of Ireland. Greater attention to 'education for citizenship' can be identified as one of the common strands running through the Social, Personal and Health Education (SPHE) component of the revised curriculum for Primary Schools (DES, 1999), the Transition Year Programme (TYP) (DoE, 1993) and the Leaving Certificate Applied (LCA) (DoE, 1994). Above all, the arrival of the new subject Civic, Social and Political Education (CSPE) as a compulsory feature of the Junior Certificate marked a significant breakthrough. Indeed, in a school system that rates examination achievement very highly, the first ever assessment of CSPE as part of the Junior Certificate Examination in 1999 – particularly the 'action project' component – can be seen as a landmark event in curricular developments in the Republic of Ireland. At the end of the century there were indicators to suggest that, eventually, the State was adopting a more considered and committed approach to education for citizenship.

However, while undoubted progress has been made in citizenship education in recent years, there are also signs that the dominance of certain attitudes within the formal education system continues to marginalise the subject and disconnect it from a broader community-based citizenship education. Welcoming a more focused and structured curricular provision should not preclude a realistic appraisal of the challenges that continue to face those involved in education for citizenship. While many challenges arise from the social changes occurring within the wider society, some emanate from the education system itself.

This chapter seeks to explore some of these challenges, especially as they manifest themselves within schools. The urgency of the discussion arises partly from the perennial concerns that surround notions of national identity, partly from the impact of a new economic prosperity and partly from the increasingly visible diversity among the citizenry. For those working in classrooms the overt and covert manifestations of xenophobia, for example, as well as undoubted confusion about living in a rapidly changing society, add to the immediacy and centrality of ensuring that there is meaningful and relevant education for citizenship and diversity.

Ambiguities

Official attitudes to education for citizenship have been characterised by a certain ambiguity. One of the first lessons this young teacher of civics learned in the 1970s was that there was an obvious mismatch between the formal Syllabus (DoE, 1966) and the pamphlet *Notes on the Teaching of Civics* (DoE, undated). The structure of the former implied a vision of citizenship education that involved accumulating knowledge about various state organisations and institutions and, not unreasonably, was seen by many – students and teachers – as dull, boring and conformist. The latter document, by contrast, with its insistence, for example, that 'the teaching method we use must be essentially an active one', was liberating and empowering. One was never quite sure who believed in which emphasis, though the fact that the pamphlet remained as a set of poorly duplicated pages is probably significant.

There seems to be general acceptance that the old Civics syllabus was a major disappointment if not a total failure. Hyland (1993:4) noted that 'in many schools, Civics gradually came to be ignored …' and former Education Minister Martin (1997:5) described the subject as 'a token and an inconvenient add-on'. Against such a backdrop, the CSPE syllabus with its emphasis on key concepts, on active participation and on a 'comprehensive exploration of the civic, social and political dimensions of their lives at a time when pupils are developing from dependent children into independent young adults'(DoE, 1996:1), offers scope and hope. Furthermore, the Leaving Certificate Applied (DoE, 1994) includes a module on 'Social Education', and within Transition Year programmes many schools avail of the flexibility offered (DoE, 1993) to explore numerous strands of education for citizenship and diversity. Within initial teacher education programmes, citizenship education has become more established, usually with distinct methodology classes, a significant indicator of being mainstreamed. And yet there are reservations.

Research

Three pieces of research in particular suggest that citizenship education continues to struggle in many schools. Shannon (2002) looked at the implementation of CSPE in twelve schools, including the views of 72 students and 37 teachers and the relevant school leaders. Murphy (2003) charted the attitudes to the subject's implementation in five schools. Redmond and Bulter (2003) conducted a baseline postal survey for the NCCA that elicited 188 responses from principals (63 per cent) and 530 from teachers (33 per cent) (sometimes referred to in this chapter as the NEXUS Report). Among the many insights to emerge from these three investigations are the following:

- CSPE has a low status in many schools.
- Teachers with little interest in the subject are often conscripted to teach it.
- There is a very high turnover rate of CSPE teachers from year to year.
- Many teachers express discomfort with 'active methodologies'.
- Where leadership shows interest and commitment to the subject and where teachers volunteer for and participate in in-service education, the subject can flourish.
- Seventy hours over three years is regarded as insufficient time to do justice to the subject, especially when timetabled on the basis of a single period per week.
- Teachers are often confronted with negative attitudes to, among others, Refugees, Asylum Seekers and members of the Traveller Community and unsure about educationally appropriate responses.
- The lack of a sufficiently structured follow-up into senior cycle further weakens the status of the subject.

In its commentary on the Redmond and Butler report, the NCCA (2003b) highlights six major areas of challenge to CSPE. They are:

- the allocation of teachers to CSPE
- the amount of time allocated to the subject
- the level of assessment
- teacher support and professional development
- resourcing of the subject
- management support.

Despite indicators that there are very particular problems for the 'new' subject, the NCCA stated: 'It is not envisaged that the survey would lead to significant review of CSPE at this early stage of its implementation' (NCCA, 2003b:2). Some encouragement can be taken from the Taskforce on Citizenship recommending 'the expansion of education for citizenship in the school system', in particular:

Strengthen the status and role of the CSPE programme in the junior cycle and introduce a citizenship programme as an exam subject at senior cycle[1] (Taskforce on Active Citizenship, 2007:21).

Emerging challenges

CSPE does need to face, imaginatively, the six areas of challenge set out by Redmond and Bulter (2003) if it is to thrive as a subject. The proposal here is that, in addition, such challenges need to be located in a broader context and so five, specific, interrelated challenges are presented. Furthermore, some attempts are made to point to creative responses to these challenges. The challenges can be described as:

- the syllabus challenge
- the time challenge
- the turnover challenge
- the cross-curricular challenge
- the community challenge.

The syllabus challenge

If politicians have traditionally been wary of citizenship education, there have been occasional exceptions. Garret FitzGerald (2003) described the CSPE syllabus as 'remarkably timid in relation to its political component' and suggested that 'it is a fair bet that this document must have been written by an exceptionally cautious civil servant'.

It appears that the former Taoiseach may have missed the concept-focused nature of the syllabus, even if he was more complimentary about some of the CSPE textbooks. But the accusation that the syllabus may err on the side of caution is worth exploring. Back in 1987 there was a widespread expectation that the Curriculum and Examinations Board (CEB) was going to give citizenship education a much needed boost. A syllabus was drafted (CEB, 1987) and its fate is an instructive lesson in educational policy-making. The draft syllabus proposed framing students' learning around key concepts. As this approach is also a distinctive feature of the current syllabus, a comparison between the two sets of concepts does indicate a shying away from overtly political components.

---

[1] The NCCA, to its credit, had already published a valuable background document (Tormey, 2006) on a proposed new subject. Following public consultation, the thrust of the responses, albeit relatively few, were positive and encouraging (NCCA, 2007).

1987 Draft Syllabus	*1996 Syllabus*
Interdependence	Interdependence
Peace/Conflict	Law
Development	Development
Power/Participation	Democracy
Human Rights/Justice	Rights and Responsibilities
Environment/Culture	Human Dignity
	Stewardship

In particular, the omission of explicit reference to 'power' as a key concept may be seen as a serious weakness within the current CSPE programme. In practical terms, one cannot help wondering, for example, whether action projects involving fundraising would be so popular if students were exploring the concept of power. At a broader level, the question has to be posed whether the absence of 'power' in the syllabus is part of what Lynch (2000) refers to as a 'deepening consensualism governing political discourse' in Ireland. This she sees as 'a thinly disguised mask for the perpetuation of the political status quo and the inequalities and silences that go with it' (Lynch, 2000:8).

The incorporation of the European Convention on Human Rights into Irish law prompts important questions for CSPE. Discussions at meetings of the Dublin-based Citizenship Education Network (CEN) focused on how well equipped the syllabus is to incorporate such important legislative changes. To some it appeared that the concepts of 'Rights and Responsibilities' and 'Law' are sufficiently flexible to mean that the Convention has effectively become part of the syllabus. Others were less sure. This brings us close to the heart of a major tension: as a broad, almost skeletal framework for exploring issues of citizenship and diversity the flexibility of the syllabus is a major strength because it offers the potential for responsiveness, growth and development; at the same time its broad conceptual nature may be read as vague and general and lead to practitioners taking a minimalist view of its demands.

Trends in action projects identified by Máirín Wilson in Chapter 16 give some indication of how this tension manifests itself in practice. She notes a growing popularity of projects directed towards visiting speakers and fundraising. While these are potentially empowering activities, the trend may be indicative of a tendency to adopt a safe, minimalist approach to the syllabus rather than a creative, developmental one. The former approach, what might be labelled as a 'we have cracked the formula' one, is perhaps partly inevitable given the kind of school culture that results from an examination-dominated school system. At the same time there is also evidence each year of new, imaginative interpretations of action projects where students respond to issues that have arisen in the classroom and teachers 'facilitate the provision of real opportunities for involvement and participation, seeing this not only as a logical outcome of the learning process, but as a significant means of reinforcing new knowledge, skills and attitudes' (DES, 1998:10).

Hence, effective education for citizenship and diversity requires teachers to develop further not just the potential of action projects, but of the total syllabus. To realise this teachers need courage, confidence, imagination and support.

Furthermore, the current syllabus can be thought of as a foundation on which the senior cycle subject 'Politics and Society' (NCCA, 2003a, 2007) can be built. Lynch (2000:10) remarks when commenting on the three basic models of curriculum development – the academic, the utilitarian and the pedagogic – '… it would be almost impossible for CSPE to survive within the traditional Leaving Certificate System without a core academic dimension'. As already evident in the responses to the NCCA background paper (NCCA, 2007 and Tormey, 2006), the CSPE syllabus will come under further scrutiny, with its strengths and weaknesses identified through analysis of practice rather than potential.

The time challenge

Student-teachers of CSPE as well as more established enthusiasts come back, time and time again, to the flawed thinking that implies that any subject can flourish within the present Junior Cycle curriculum with a single class period per week. Forty minutes of CSPE time per week, they point out, offer insufficient time to engage seriously and systematically with active methodology. Such provision, they say, creates an impression that, no matter what the rhetoric, the subject cannot be very important. This is a major source of frustration among interested students and teachers.

Within this debate, policy-makers and administrators point to an already overcrowded curriculum. In the context of the review of the Junior Cycle, subject specialists, perhaps understandably, tend towards a territorial perspective, a 'what we have, we hold!' position. The voices for increased time provision for citizenship education, when not silent, tend to be occasional and muted. And yet, if one was to embark on a fresh start – on an imaginary *tabula rasa* – devising the most appropriate core curriculum for 12- to 15-year-olds, citizenship education would command, I suggest, a centre stage position with at least three and probably four or more periods each week.[2]

---

[2] The subject focus here is to highlight the marginalisation of CSPE. The case for moving away from a subject focus on curriculum construction is desirable. The competency approach advocated by RSA (Bayliss, 1999) and the emphasis on key skills currently being promoted by the NCCA offer attractive possibilities for education for citizenship.

However, trends in public discourse about living 'in an economy' rather than 'in a society' often resonate with educational practice. For example, it is worth noting that 60 per cent of Junior Cycle students now opt for the subject Business Studies within Junior Cycle (SEC, 2007). Typically these students spend about four class periods per week over their three years studying 'business' and its values. The message about what is perceived to be really important is not lost on them as they contrast this experience with the single period provision for CSPE.

This and other tensions between the aspirational rhetoric surrounding 'education for citizenship' and actual practice prompts questions about how strongly policy-makers in the DES and the NCCA actually value CSPE or the wider citizenship education agenda. The time challenge also extends to teacher education, both initial and on-going; citizenship education needs dedicated time and resources during initial teacher education, during the induction stage, especially within schools and as a central feature within continuing professional development. While the emergence of 'Politics and Society' at Leaving Certificate level will enhance the status of citizenship education, CSPE will, in future, find itself also competing for time with its 'more grown up' sister/brother.

The cross-curricular challenge

The CSPE syllabus states that 'the Civic, Social and Political Education course provides unique opportunities and greater potential for cross-curricular work in schools'. There is little evidence yet of any such cross-curricular thinking, planning or implementation in schools. The NEXUS report and the accompanying NCCA commentary barely refer to it. Yet, as the syllabus asserts, each day, across a range of subjects, pupils study topics and issues, encounter concepts and practise skills which are common both to those subjects and to CSPE. Hence, it can be argued, every teacher is a citizenship educator.

For example, there are clear links between the CSPE concepts of Development and Interdependence within parts of the JC Geography syllabus. Stewardship as a concept resonates loudly with aspects of the Science syllabus. Teachers of Religious Education devote extensive time to issues close to the CSPE concepts of Rights and Responsibilities, Human Dignity and Law. Much of what is studied in English and other languages can be read as developments of the concept of Human Dignity. The core concepts also link in various ways with subjects such as Art, Materials Technology (Wood) and (Metal), History, Home Economics. It can be more challenging to make direct links between CSPE and Business Studies, mainly due to the lack of a critical social awareness perspective in that particular syllabus. Furthermore, the general organisation of the school and specific structures such as Students' Councils present powerful opportunities for students to appreciate concepts such as Democracy and Law.

And yet the coherence is not there. In many schools, the price of a strong ethos of teacher autonomy can be a culture of teacher isolation. Similarly, emphatic subject identities and independence can contribute to curriculum fragmentation. The strength of such traditions is encountered even in programmes that ostensibly aim for greater cross-curricular coherence than the Junior Cert. Despite encouraging guidelines, the Transition Year Programme continues, in many schools, to be a collection of individual subjects and modules rather than one that displays coherent cross-curricular themes and links (Jeffers, 2007).

It appears that the lack of cross-curricular work is primarily a cultural issue within schools and within the teaching profession. Perhaps school leaders and subject co-ordinators fear that the amount of time and effort that would be required to bring about genuine collaborative, cross-curricular work could be better spent. While not wishing to impose unnecessary further demands on already stretched teachers of CSPE, the case for such teachers forging alliances with colleagues in other subjects is strong. Indeed, a more explicit citizenship focus on the whole Junior Certificate programme could both extend the learning opportunities for students and enhance the status of CSPE. Such cross-curricular collaboration requires CSPE teachers who have a strong commitment to citizenship education, see its possibilities across a number of subjects and have the confidence to invite colleagues to work collegially.

The turnover challenge

The NEXUS study discovered that a large number of teachers do not choose to teach CSPE but often find it like an uninvited guest on their timetables at the start of the school year (Redmond and Bulter, 2003:24). If one were setting out deliberately to undermine a subject, this would seem like a good starting strategy. School leaders, in their defence and with justification, will point to the NEXUS finding that 41 per cent of principals report 'difficulty in finding staff willing to teach CSPE' (Redmond and Bulter 2003:6). The NCCA (2003b:7) acknowledges the high turnover of CSPE teachers as 'a significant indicator of the problematic nature of current provision'.

A range of responses is required to improve this situation. The task of giving status to a school subject should begin within the DES, followed by agencies such as the State Examinations Commission and the NCCA.

Teacher unions and the subject association (ACT – Association of CSPE Teachers) can also play their parts in profiling CSPE positively. The active pursuit of 'good news stories' relating to citizenship education in the media would help. The withholding of CSPE results by the DES in 2002 was followed by what some saw as 'negative' press coverage. Headlines in newspapers of 12 September 2002 included the following:

- Some Results in CSPE Withheld to Allow for Copying Checks (*The Irish Times*)
- Department Launches Exam Cheat Investigation (*Examiner*)
- 600 Junior Cert Kids in Exam Cheat Probe (*The Sun*).

However, as an enquiry into the suspected plagiarism revealed, one can hardly blame the media:

> A free press is a feature of democratic societies and most of those interviewed accepted the media's right to report on exam results etc., even though in some cases such coverage brought unwelcome attention to the subject and to certain schools. There was a marked similarity in the newspaper reports of 12 September with identical phrases occurring in *The Irish Times*, *The Sun, The Star,* the *Irish Independent* and the *Examiner*. Having spoken with some of the journalists who wrote the stories, it appears that the newspaper reports were all based on a press release from the Department of Education and Science. This was confirmed by the Department's communications office.
>
> While one can appreciate the need for the Department to highlight the rigorous standards associated with public examinations, what might be called the 'collateral damage' done to CSPE as a subject by focusing on the 'cheating' dimension has been considerable (Jeffers, 2003:15).

As with other curricular initiatives of the 1990s, the DES has provided on-going support for CSPE implementation with a dedicated support team of seconded teachers. Undoubtedly such teams, made up of practitioners who are familiar with classroom practices and highly committed to change, carry credibility with colleagues, and the strategy has the potential to support real change. But invariably these teams get stretched to the point of trying to service unrealistic numbers of schools. Perhaps, in addition to supporting individual teachers, the identification and development of a 'citizenship education co-ordinator', who would be an unapologetic advocate for citizenship education within each school, is needed. Building a cohort of such leaders within schools should serve to reduce the high turnover rate.

Initial teacher education programmes also have a key role to play in strengthening citizenship education, and while many such programmes now offer specific courses for those wishing to teach CSPE, the inclusion of a more explicit emphasis on 'education for citizenship' throughout these programmes is a bigger challenge. A reduced turnover of CSPE teachers is more likely when the status of the subject rises and teachers teaching the subject are adequately prepared for such work. The arrival of 'Politics and Society' may enhance the status of CSPE.

The community challenge

CSPE presents schools with opportunities to connect with local communities in new ways. Unit 2 of the course is entitled 'The Community' and community involvement is a strong thread running through the thinking on action projects, which are among the most distinguishing features of CSPE. This emphasis is effectively challenging many schools' traditional isolation and lack of meaningful connections with their immediate local communities. In practice, there is the possibility that schools will work with a plethora of local organisations, seeing them as partners in a wider process of community development, bringing schools closer to the hearts of communities.

While collaborative links with sports clubs, credit unions, citizen information bureaus, heritage centres and others are worth forging, the potential of schools and youth organisations working together seems particularly promising. Many young people already encounter significant experiences that contribute to their sense of citizenship through youth organisations. In fact, some youth organisations have a distinguished track record in citizenship education. Two examples will illustrate this. Firstly, many CSPE teachers find their classes greatly enriched by using development education material devised by Johnny Sheehan and his colleagues in the National Youth Council and available at www.youth.ie. Secondly, even a cursory analysis of Foróige's philosophy and programmes should enable teachers to realise that schools do not have a monopoly on education for citizenship. The Foróige mission statement is as follows:

> The purpose of Foróige is to enable young people to involve themselves consciously and actively in their own development and in the development of society. Foróige challenges young people to develop themselves, to be more self-reliant, to seek ways to help others and to improve their communities (Foróige website).

In relation to a specific programme on citizenship, one can see how that youth organisation's vision resonates with how CSPE teachers might see their task.

Citizenship is also about creating what ought to be rather than adapting to what is. The present world with its justice and injustice, its love and its lack of love, its strengths and its weaknesses is what people have made it. The future world is not predetermined. The essential task of citizenship is not to predict the future, it is to create it (Foróige website).

The possibilities of new partnerships between schools and other groups (community groups, youth organisations, other non-governmental organisations), spearheaded through citizenship education, need greater exploration. In the first instance schools need to see the local community as a resource. Enriched by such experiences one would hope that the school would emerge as a vital centre for the development of civic society. The Taskforce on Citizenship tends to underplay such possibilities though, as already stated, it does advocate expanding education for citizenship within the school system. It also suggests that:

> … better use should be made of schools at evening and weekend time to act as community hubs – facilitating, for example, adult education, literacy programmes, various community activities and services (Government of Ireland, 2007:20).

The disappointment here is with the implicit assumption that outside 'the evening and weekend' time all is well with schools' relationships with their local communities.

Conclusion

The introduction of the new subject of CSPE into Irish schools in the final stages of the twentieth century presents challenges and possibilities. Without wanting to minimise the restrictions that arise from the syllabus, the chronically limited amount of time, the rapid turnover of teachers, the almost absence within schools of a cross-curricular approach or the traditional isolation of schools from their local communities, we do need to focus on what is possible. The vision of citizenship as genuinely active and participatory, the vibrant emphasis on active ways of learning, especially through action projects, the course structure that highlights concepts and so gives a flexibility that invites everyday social and political realities into classrooms, the consistent openness to young people's own experiences, all offer great possibilities for meaningful learning experiences. The realisation of such possibilities and visions depends greatly on the quality of the interactions in CSPE classes up and down the country. That, as we well know, hangs on the commitment and competencies of teachers, the common strand running through all the challenges mentioned here.

There are also some specific structural initiatives that schools might take to strengthen education for citizenship and diversity. Designating a citizenship education co-ordinator, preferably with dignity and status, could bring greater coherence. Specifically, such a staff member might work in five main areas:

- as a teacher of CSPE and as a co-ordinator of CSPE teaching within the school
- as a leader who would work with colleagues in advancing the capacity within the school to promote education for citizenship and diversity – continuous professional development and resource gathering being two obvious areas
- as a designated link person with responsibility for promoting cross-curricular links in relation to citizenship and diversity
- as the staff member with primary responsibility for promoting and liaising with the Student Council
- as the school's main link person with local youth organisations, NGOs and community organisations.

References

Bayliss, V. (1999), *Opening Minds, Education for the 21st century,* London: Royal Society of Arts

CEB (Curriculum and Examination Board) (1987), *Civic and Political Studies, Syllabus Document,* April 14 1987, Unpublished

DoE (Department of Education) (1966), *Rules and Programmes for Secondary Schools,* Dublin: Department of Education

DoE (Department of Education) (undated), *Notes on the Teaching of Civics,* Dublin: Department of Education (duplicated notes)

DoE (Department of Education) (1993), *Transition Year Programme – Guidelines for Schools,* Dublin: Department of Education

DoE (Department of Education) (1994), *Leaving Cert Applied Programme – Guidelines for Schools,* Dublin: Department of Education

DES (Department of Education and Science) (1998), *Civic, Social and Political Education, Taking Action, A Guide to Action Projects and their Assessment,* Dublin: DES and NCCA

DES (Department of Education and Science) (1999), *Primary School Curriculum,* Dublin: DES and NCCA

FitzGerald, G. (2003), 'Putting Politics on the Educational Agenda', *The Irish Times,* 17 May 2003

Government of Ireland (1999), *Primary School Curriculum: Social, Personal and Health Education,* Dublin: Stationery Office

Hyland, Á. (1993), 'Address to the first meeting of the teachers involved in the Pilot Scheme for the introduction of Civic, Social and Political Education at Junior Cycle level', paper delivered at the joint NCCA/Department of Education In-Service course, Dublin Castle, 9 December

Jeffers, G. (2003), *Some Issues and Concerns arising from the Assessment of Junior Certificate CSPE in 2002*, A report to the Department of Education and Science. Unpublished

Jeffers, G. (2007), *Attitudes to Transition Year, A Report to the Department of Education and Science*, Maynooth: Education Department, NUI Maynooth

Lynch, K. (2000), 'Education for Citizenship: The Need for a Major Intervention in Social and Political Education in Ireland', Paper presented at the CSPE Conference, Bunratty, Co. Clare, 29 September

Martin, M. (1997), 'Educating for Citizenship in a Changing Democracy', lecture by Minister for Education and Science, NUI Maynooth, 4 December.

Murphy, D. (2003), 'Civics Revisited? An Exploration of the Factors Affecting the Implementation of CSPE in Five Post-Primary Schools', Unpublished MEd Dissertation, Education Department, NUI Maynooth

NCCA (National Council for Curriculum and Assessment) (2003a), *Developing Senior Cycle Education, Directions for Development*, Dublin: NCCA

NCCA (National Council for Curriculum and Assessment) (2003b), *Civic, Social and Political Education, NCCA response to NEXUS report on survey of principals and CSPE teachers*, Dublin: NCCA

NCCA (National Council for Curriculum and Assessment) (2007), *Senior Cycle Developments, Report on Consultation on 'Social and Political Education at Senior Cycle, a background paper'*, Dublin: NCCA

NEXUS Report: see Redmond, D. and Butler, P. (2003)

Redmond, D. and Bulter, P. (2003), *Civic, Social and Political Education, Reports on Survey of Teachers and Principals to NCCA*, Dublin: NEXUS Research Co-Operative

Taskforce on Active Citizenship (2007), *Report of the Taskforce on Active Citizenship,* Dublin: Secretariat of the Taskforce on Active Citizenship

Shannon, M. (2002), 'Curriculum Implementation: Theory and Practice and the Role of Leadership, A case study: Civic, Social and Political Education', unpublished MEd (School Leadership) dissertation, Education Department, NUI Maynooth

SEC (State Examination Commission) (2007), *Junior Certificate Examination 2004, Business Studies, Chief Examiner's Report*, Athlone: SEC

Tormey, R. (2006), *Social and Political Education at Senior Cycle, a background paper,* Dublin: NCCA

Websites

Foróige: www.foróige.ie
Student Councils: www.studentcouncil.ie
National Children's Office: www.nco.ie
Joint CRA, CPA, EA and SVP site www.cspe.ie
Citizenship teachers: www.act.ie

3

Good practice in citizenship education

Tony Gallagher

The purpose of this chapter is to examine some principles which we might use to inform the development of citizenship education in Northern Ireland. I offer these thoughts in order to provoke debate and discussion. They are based on my reflections of the experience we have gained over the years through various initiatives in education and beyond to promote better understanding and reconciliation in Northern Ireland. I have no doubt others would give different emphases or priority to some of these issues, or might want to include issues that I do not raise at all. The important point, I think, is that we have this discussion.

There have been many initiatives designed to meet these aims over the past thirty years and there are some extraordinary examples of inspirational work. Despite this, however, any reasonable assessment of the different initiatives that have occurred would suggest that the gains have been somewhat limited: the reality has never quite lived up to the expectation or hope invested in these programmes. If only for this reason it is important that we embark on the roll-out of the citizenship education programme with this realistic assessment of past experience in mind. We do not want to wonder in ten or twenty years time why the Local and Global Citizenship programme was not as successful as it might have been. If we can have that critical and hard-headed examination of the lessons of the past now, perhaps we can ensure that we achieve the best gains we can from what is yet to come. It is in that spirit that these thoughts and suggestions are offered.

The chapter is organised around nine general principles that should be kept in mind as we extend and develop citizenship education in Northern Ireland. There is nothing particularly significant in the fact that nine principles are offered.

Principle 1: It is too soon to tell exactly what good practice in classrooms actually is – we are still in the process of discovering it

In the specific context of the Local and Global Citizenship programme it is still too soon to stand up and identify best practice. Some exemplary experience has come out of the various stages of the pilot project and we await the results of the evaluation with great interest. We need to remember, of course, that the pioneers in any initiative are almost always likely to invest immense energy, enthusiasm and imagination, so we need to attend to the more challenging circumstance the programme will face as it moves beyond the pilot schools across the system more generally.

It is also true that we have much to learn from the experience of colleagues in other parts of the UK and, perhaps even more particularly, from colleagues in the Republic of Ireland. Despite this, however, we should always attend to the particular challenges presented by the idiosyncrasies of Northern Ireland, with an education system that is replete with divisions, political discourses that seem to thrive on sectarian verities and an enduring legacy of a quarter century of political violence.

Principle 2: We will discover that good practice if we (that is people involved in teacher education and the other support systems) consciously try to co-create with teachers – work out together how to do it

This is a particularly important point, i.e. that the discovery of good practice has to be a joint enterprise between those working in schools and those supporting that work. In fact, one of the strengths of the Local and Global Citizenship programme is that this principle has been followed in many of the support projects we have seen so far. This is true of the exemplary cases of the pilot programme run by the UNESCO Centre in Coleraine, the approach taken in the CDU Education for Reconciliation project which has linked teachers North and South and significantly enhanced teacher capacity, and the Education and Library Board training programme for post-primary teachers. There is plenty of evidence to support this particular principle and the example of these recent and on-going projects simply reinforces that conviction.

Principle 3: Make a conscious effort to do no harm

This principle may seem to be very obvious, but it is worth mentioning because the capacity of education to do harm is underestimated. This is particularly so if we consider, for example, the shocking events in Beslan. I was reminded of this when I participated in the 2004 annual conference of the British Association of International and Comparative Education (BAICE). The terrible massacre in Beslan occurred while the conference was underway and while we, like most people, were shocked and horrified at the carnage, a speech given by one of the conference organisers provided a more chilling commentary on these terrible events. We were reminded that the people who planned, prepared and carried out this atrocity had themselves gone to school, followed a curriculum and been taught by teachers. What effect, we were asked, did their educational experience have on their later actions: did it invest in them the fires of hatred, or did it seek to douse these flames if their source lay elsewhere?

We were jolted again the next day in a presentation by John Rutayisire, head of the curriculum development unit in Rwanda (see Tawil and Harley, 2004). John Rutayisire has been scouring the world to learn from the experience of others as he seeks to develop a curriculum that will enable schools in Rwanda to help young people deal with the legacy of the genocide. This would be a compelling experience in its own right, but Rutayisire placed the issue on a different scale when he identified one of the problems as being that many of the school managers and teachers in Rwanda had themselves participated in the genocide.

For reasons that are laudable and understandable, we often assume that education is a self-evident good and that young people will almost always benefit from more education, rather than less. But we need also to remember the negative potential of education. It is a vehicle for enlightenment, but it can also be a vehicle for the promulgation of hatred and intolerance. So, while encouraging the aspiration for education to be a force for good, let us guard against the risk that we consciously or unconsciously do harm.

Principle 4: While making sure we do no harm, do not assume that doing nothing is okay
And while we should endeavour to do no harm, let me suggest that there is no virtue in doing nothing. The sense of this was probably best captured in John Hewitt's poem *The Coasters* in which he critiques the comfortable complacency of so many in Northern Ireland, even where they maintained their liberal sense of self through friendship, of a sort, with 'the other sort' (Ormsby, 1991). All along, he suggested, the 'old lies festered' as they 'coasted along ... [and] never noticed', but avoidance, he suggests, cannot be sustained:

> The cloud of infection hangs over the city,
> a quick change of wind and it
> might spill over the leafy suburbs.
> You coasted too long.

One suspects that there are many in Northern Ireland, within education and without, who feel little or no responsibility for the terrible tragedies of the past three decades, largely on the basis that they did not do anything wrong. But, as Hewitt so eloquently reveals, there are sins of omission as well as sins of commission. So, when we work in schools, or support those who do, let us not absolve ourselves too readily. And rather than focusing on the fact that we did no wrong, let us be strong enough to wonder what more we can do.

Principle 5: We should be alarmed that so many people outside education have such high expectations on what we can deliver
This point has been a factor of significance for some time, and those of us who work in education may not have fully appreciated its importance. In the late 1960s and early 1970s many looked to schools to ameliorate the growing violence in Northern Ireland. Indeed, when we look back at the blizzard of books and reports that emerged at the time, we are struck by, not only the extent to which many commentators believed that schools should do something, but also the extent to which they felt that schools *would* do something and that this would be socially effective. The evidence of the last thirty years would offer a more pessimistic assessment of the capacity of education to deliver on such lofty social goals. Despite this, the expectations held by the public on the possibilities of education remain extraordinarily high.

The example that brought all of this forcibly to mind arose at a recent meeting of the Northern Ireland Race Forum. This special meeting had been called to discuss the rise in racist attacks in Northern Ireland: indeed, a presentation from the PSNI suggested that the level of racist attacks has increased four-fold over the past five years, while the representatives of the minority ethnic communities on the Forum insisted that even this was an underestimate of the actual levels of attack and harassment experienced by members of their communities. For the present purposes, however, the most striking feature of the meeting was that in the general discussion of the problem, speaker after speaker suggested that schools and teachers would 'solve' the problem by introducing appropriate programmes on to the curriculum. It had to be pointed out that our track record in dealing with sectarianism, never mind racism, is not at all good, so people should be wary of placing too much expectation on the shoulders of our schools.

As part of the consultation on Hate legislation for Northern Ireland, the Hansard Society ran an online discussion forum to allow as many people as possible to offer ideas and suggestions (see http://www.tellparliament.net/hatecrime/). Even a cursory glance at some of the comments on the forum reveals the same high expectation that schools and teachers should and could contribute significantly to ameliorating the problem of racism.

Postman (1996) offers a cautionary note on a similar theme when he states that teachers are 'not competent to serve as priests, psychologists, therapists, political reformers, social workers, sex advisers, or parents … [U]nprepared teachers are no substitute for ineffective social institutions'. But he then goes on to add: 'It should be clear, by the way, that in this argument the phrase "unprepared teachers" does not mean they cannot do *their* job. It means they cannot do *everyone's* job.'

Citizenship education is the latest in a long line of initiatives aimed at allowing education to make a socially positive contribution to key aspects of our society in Northern Ireland. And it is precisely because the expectations of society on what education can deliver are so high that we constantly remind the wider public on the limitations of that contribution. That said, it is important that we do not use this as an excuse and that we seek to maximise that contribution.

Principle 6: We should continue to wonder (and worry) why the gulf between teachers and youth workers remains so wide
I have been privileged to see the work of a number of NGOs over recent years, including Public Achievement,[1] Spirit of Enniskillen[2] and St Columbs Park House. There is no doubt that there is enormous energy and commitment in the sector and a wonderful capacity to seek innovation when trying to tackle new, and sometimes old, problems. And much of this happens in a context where maintaining the very existence of an organisation is often a key and ever-present priority. In higher education we often complain about the imposition of systems of accountability, but for the NGO sector, constantly having to justify yourself and your work to funders is a level of accountability we in third-level education have rarely experienced.

However, it is also true that there are many advantages in the stability and history and tradition available to teachers and schools, and in the wider infrastructure of support and organisation that is available to support the work of teachers. Teachers have training, experience, curriculum, history, stability, a massive infrastructure to support what they do. Youth workers often feel they themselves are better able to engage with young people, are more committed to work in active learning, less constrained by the weight of bureaucracy and tradition. Yet despite the examples of such work as the *Speak Your Piece* project, which show the value of engagement between

[1] See Chapter 16
[2] See Chapter 4

teachers and youth workers, the problem persists and the learning achieved across the groups is less than it might be.

It reminds me of the Sufi story of the three blind men who came across a monster in the jungle and reported their find in very different ways: one thought he had come across a massive bird, the second thought the monster was a massive snake, while the third thought it was a gigantic tree that moved. In fact the 'monster' was an elephant, but each of the men had only experienced a bit of the overall picture: each was truthful in his account, but each account provided only a part of a wider whole. I suspect it is the same with teachers and youth workers. It is often said in Northern Ireland that one of our main problems is that too many people think that 'listening' means 'waiting your turn' and that we need to learn to really listen. The same may be true in this relationship between teachers and youth workers.

Principle 7: We need to pay more attention to language
We should worry about the casual use of language in Northern Ireland, particularly where this language is invested with sectarian consequences. For example, when we talk about 'nationalist' or 'unionist' areas we ascribe a common political purpose to a community – what we may mean is that the communities are predominantly Protestant or predominantly Catholic areas, but to assume political homogeneity is to fix everyone within the straitjacket of the political conflict. As a general principle we should be trying to encourage people to think outside the box, not reinforcing the walls of the boxes. So we should think a little more carefully about the language we use, because language helps to construct social reality and we sometimes take aspects of the process of social construction too much for granted.

Indeed, we may wish to consider ways in which we can actively promote language that encourages the notion of a 'common good' in education in Northern Ireland. One is struck by the challenge involved in such an enterprise when reading Postman's (1996) identification of a list of texts that he felt all teachers in US public schools should know in order to help young Americans engage in the great conversation on what the United States is or might be. Most of the items on his 11-item list will be very familiar to us: Thomas Paine's Rights of Man, John F Kennedy's Inaugural speech, Martin Luther King's 'I have a dream' speech in Washington DC, the Declaration of Independence, the Emancipation Proclamation, etc. A few of the items would be less familiar, but the main point is that Postman can identify a fairly succinct list of items which would receive a high degree of consensus as being appropriate for the task.

Given this example, I carried out a little exercise some years ago with an email discussion list to build on Postman's example and seek views on an analogous list of texts that people thought all teachers in Northern Ireland should know if they are to help young people play an active role in the construction of a new society.

After many suggestions, the circulation of lists, ideas on additional items or suggestions that some items should be removed, I was eventually able to narrow down the Northern Ireland list to a little over 250 items! It was obviously striking that it was not possible to narrow down the list any further, but the really interesting feature was the way in which the 'list' actually seemed to comprise a number of different lists. Items that were seen as unambiguously obvious to some were totally unfamiliar to others. It did not, in other words, have the sense of recognition or familiarity evident in Postman's shorter list. It is a reminder that Northern Ireland is a place with few grand narratives, rather a place of many narratives, and that this may also make much harder the task of trying to build a sense of a shared future. It may be why the debate over the Shared Future report seemed to break down into those who sought to advocate for a very explicit sense of a shared future and those who seemed to argue that we could develop a form of apartheid that would be benign.

The insanity of this latter position was highlighted by Duncan Morrow, Director of the Community Relations Council, at a conference on the Shared Future consultation held in Queen's University when he said:

> To live in Northern Ireland is to live in a place haunted by its own memories of violence and discrimination or fears of destruction or massacre to come. ... The predicament of Northern Ireland is that we *will* share the future: the only question is what kind future we will share (Morrow, 2004).

The experience of the ethnic minorities in Northern Ireland, he argued, suggests we have developed a culture 'which has grown too tired to be shocked by violence and tolerant of ideas that protection means excluding those who are different rather than looking for renewal to those who bring fresh perspectives'.

Citizenship education can be about many things, but as Morrow said in his speech, essentially it is about 'communities and their relationship to each other and to the state'. As in the Shared Future consultation, the options appear to be either managing separatism or building a shared, interconnected future. The communities, by virtue of circumstance, are in an interdependent relationship and we will have to learn to live with that interdependence. The question is whether we will choose a form in which that relationship is positive or negative.

Principle 8: We still need to decide how best we can engage with the policy system, and think realistically on the limits of that engagement

For many years we have struggled to achieve a higher status and priority for work in education aimed at promoting reconciliation. Over recent years, and not without some success, many of us have tried to raise the priority attached to the opportunity provided by citizenship education. Despite all these efforts, however, I'm not sure that we are using this energy to best effect. The problem is that, in an abstract sense, these issues are important to the education system. What is less clear is just *how* important they are, or rather, how important they are in relation to other priorities for education. As long as schools are held to account primarily for academic achievement, through base-lining, targets, inspection and development planning, citizenship education is always going to come lower down, perhaps much lower down, the pecking order.

Up to now much effort has been expended on trying to build supportive structures within schools as a way of getting the system as a whole to raise the priority attached to this type of work. But if the *relative* priority of this is likely to remain low, perhaps we need to think of other ways of strengthening and supporting the work of the teachers who are committed to this work. Perhaps now we need to expend some of that effort in a different way, by tackling the potential isolation of citizenship education teachers not within schools, but between schools. Maybe it is time we tried to build effective networks among the committed teachers, rather than hoping that the system will catch up with us. Let us not abandon the attempt to raise the relative priority of this work, but let us not focus on that to the neglect of other tasks.

Principle 9: Remember Lance Armstrong's adage – it's not about the bike

No matter how good the programmes we devise, it is all about how they are delivered. One is reminded of the story of Lance Armstrong, the US cyclist who survived cancer to go on to win the Tour de France for a record six times. His autobiography, *It's Not About the Bike*, recounts his struggle with illness and the rebuilding of his professional career as a cyclist. It is a spectacular story. The title is taken from his notion that winning the Tour de France is not just a matter of having the best bike, it's about the team, the training, the individual will and dedication, the preparation, the support, and so on – it's not just about the bike.

This would seem to serve as an appropriate and important final principle for this chapter. No matter how good the curriculum we devise, it is all about how it is delivered. Therefore, while we properly invest significant time and energy to the task of devising the best curriculum we can, we need to plan to invest time and energy in the implementation of that curriculum, the training and support of teachers, the critical evaluation and discussion on what works and what does not work. It's not about the curriculum, it's about the curriculum and a whole lot more, so let us make sure we save some energy for the 'whole lot more'.

Postscript: In 2005, Lance Armstrong won the Tour de France for a record seventh time.

References

Armstrong, L (2001), *It's Not About the Bike: my journey back to life*, London: Yellow Jersey Press

Morrow, D. (2004), 'On the far side of revenge: presentation to the Shared Future conference', Queen's University Belfast, 27 January available at: www.community-relations.org.uk/about_the_council/speeches/

Ormsby, F. (ed.) (1991), *The Collected Poems of John Hewitt*, Belfast: Blackstaff Press

Postman, N. (1996), *The end of education: redefining the value of school*, New York: Vintage

Tawil, S. and Harley, A. (eds) (2004), *Education, Conflict and Social Cohesion*, Geneva: International Bureau of Education, UNESCO

4

The Spirit of Enniskillen

Chuck Richardson

The purpose of this chapter is to outline the introduction of a programme for citizenship in the formal school sector using strategies more commonly employed in informal educational settings. The *Schools Together* programme has been developed and delivered by young people working with the Spirit of Enniskillen (SOE). The evolution of the programme is a two-fold progression: firstly, it is representative of the complementary nature of formal and non-formal education; and secondly, it is reflective of the capacity of outside agencies to support schools in the implementation of citizenship education as part of the revised curriculum.

Perhaps the defining characteristic of the revised curriculum is the importance attached to providing a meaningful educational experience that prepares young people for life in an increasingly diverse society. This is reflected in the overall curricular aim: 'to empower young people to achieve their potential and to make informed and responsible decisions throughout their lives' (CCEA, 2003). The philosophy of SOE offers a corresponding position that is grounded in the transformative potential of participative learning environments 'that enable young people from all backgrounds to reach across barriers, build relationships and make their own contribution towards a peaceful and shared future' (SOE, 2006). Importantly, this includes an approach grounded in the practice of dealing with difference together to help young people 'clarify what their contribution might be and develop their capacity to meet this potential' (SOE, 2006).

Background

The Spirit of Enniskillen Trust was established in 1989 following the *Remembrance Day* bombing in Enniskillen in which eleven people died and many more were injured. Within the divided society of Northern Ireland, SOE advocates that 'while we are not responsible for Northern Ireland, we are responsible for our own contribution'. The aim of the organisation is to create improved relationships and better communication between all traditions. Specifically, this has focused on direct engagement with young people from all backgrounds through a series of peer-learning programmes[1] that encourage and support better understanding and a shared future through a process of 'dialogue, learning and good relations'.

Historically, the work undertaken by SOE has been more closely aligned with the informal education sector. Latterly, however, partnerships with formal education have been forged through a *Dealing with Difference Together* programme, involving groups of sixth-form (Year 13) pupils. The rationale for this programme is based around two defining principles: that the positive legacy of work undertaken within non-formal education can be usefully applied within the formal education sector; and that peer-led dialogue can make a significant contribution to the learning process. The programme was officially launched in 2004 as *Schools Together*. To date, well over 2,000 sixth-form pupils (including many from schools in Oldham) have taken part. During 2007-2008, 21 schools from across Northern Ireland (comprising controlled, maintained and integrated) participated in the programme.

Context

The complementary combination of informal approaches to learning in a formal setting has been a relatively unexplored area of school culture and practice and, in approaching schools, the SOE worked to ensure that the *Together* programme was viewed as a source of help and support – making the teacher's life easier rather than more complex. Teacher confidence was also helped in that many schools who signed up for *Together* came with a history of sixth-form participation in the SOE *Explore* core leadership programme and a consequent awareness of the change in skills and maturity of these young people. It was the expressed interest in the underlying non-formal methodology that paved the way for school workshops based on peer-led learning from dialogue on contentious and contemporary issues.

Though grounded in informal education, in an emerging field where theory and practice are constantly changing and informing each other, SOE working approaches have evolved through review and refinement over 20 years of the *Explore* programme.

The basis of informal youth work practice proposes a critical developmental need for young people to be supported into taking on responsibility, and to learn from doing this (Smith, 1982). The underlying framework for dialogue is informed by intergroup contact theory, which proposes conditions under which positive constructive intergroup contact

[1] See www.soe.co.uk

can take place; positive and constructive in the sense that individuals from both sides leave the contact experience with more understanding and a more positive view of the opposite group as well as of individuals in that group (Allport, 1954). Whilst the central approach is to support learning through discussion of contemporary and contentious issues, engaging well in the *process* of discussion – with the necessary blend of understanding, awareness and skills – is also developed in individuals through feedback and reflection. As their confidence and skills grow, young participants are gradually encouraged to take on the responsibility of leading a workshop, and many show a real ability and talent in doing this.

Over the years SOE young volunteer leaders from all backgrounds have emerged to give significant amounts of their time and energy into supporting similar learning for others – particularly when they see their own organisation and delivery being successful. As the adult/young people partnership and participative culture of the organisation has deepened, this has been accompanied by a parallel and increasing rise in the capacity, facilitation skills and confidence of the organisation.

Developing partnerships with schools, to explore how approaches from the informal sector might be adapted for practical use within formal settings, is the latest stage of evolution for the SOE.

The *Schools Together* Programme

The *Schools Together* programme (also referred to as *Together*) offers non-formal learning within formal education settings. It has been developed to complement the Local and Global Citizenship curriculum in schools whilst advocating the overall good relations aspirations of *A Shared Future* (OFM/DFM, 2005). The programme is delivered voluntarily by trained young peer-facilitators who lead *dealing with difference* dialogue, learning workshops, residentials and conferences.

The aim of the *Together* programme is: 'to develop the capacity of sixth-form pupils, from differing backgrounds and traditions, to engage, on an inter-school basis in dialogue that explores the commonalities and differences of life in Northern Ireland and in working together for a shared future in a fair and pluralist society' (SOE, 2006). It encourages a philosophy of working together through a developmental process of non-formal learning and active citizenship and through 'discussions exploring commonalities and differences and to develop the blend of skills, understanding and attitudes needed to lead others through a similar process of learning' (SOE, 2006). This is achieved through the sequential construct of participative, mutual and transferable learning situations that engender ownership within and across the school environment; and includes teachers as well as pupils.

Perhaps the most distinctive characteristic of the *Together* programme is the utilisation of past participants as facilitators in all dialogue and leadership activities. Importantly, the facilitators represent a balance of backgrounds and traditions; they have been suitably trained to introduce the subject matter of the programme and to direct discussion on sensitive and/or contentious issues. In addition, the age range of the facilitators establishes them as peers (albeit slightly older) of the pupils with whom they are working. SOE currently has 60 volunteers working in facilitator roles across all projects, with a further 30-40 engaged in community work. At present, there are over 50 volunteers available for work in schools.

Key findings

The reported findings represent the collective outcome of a recent evaluation of the *Schools Together* programme. Drawing on interviews with participating pupils, teachers, senior management and SOE staff, the evaluation sought to review the impact of the programme to date and to consider the various options for its future development and/or sustainability.

Format of the programme

The *Together* programme represents a strategically innovative approach to diversity and good relations than currently exists within the formal education sector. It is developed around a common conceptual framework that can be adapted to address specific school needs as necessary. Importantly, although the experimental nature of the work is both creative and aspirational, its aim is compatible with the overall objectives of the revised curriculum and with the content of Local and Global Citizenship.

School participation

School participation in the *Together* programme has been largely motivated by a commitment to offer pupils a teaching and learning opportunity that would introduce, explore and challenge understandings of diversity and provide them with the key skills to assume their place as informed and inquisitive participants in an increasingly diverse society. There was a common appreciation amongst pupils and teachers for the relevance and timeliness of the programme, and a corresponding acknowledgement of occasional personal and institutional tendencies towards avoidance or superficiality in dealing with certain issues.

Pupils

Contact encounters are a central element of the programme. These were reported as extremely positive experiences for participating pupils, many of whom had developed an understanding of social, cultural and political issues within community, local, national and international contexts. Similarly, pupils were fluent in the language of diversity and good relations, and were willing to engage in reflective dialogue on their personal capacity for prejudicial and stereotypical behaviours within their own community and the wider society.

Teachers

The centrality of teachers' learning is intended to be an integral component of school participation, and there was little doubt of the commitment of co-ordinating teachers and senior management. To date, the SOE has supported approximately 100 staff members who are engaged in this area, but it is intended that training options for teaching staff will assume increased priority within the developmental strategy of the *Together* programme.

The value of facilitation

The merit of using external facilitators and the expertise that they provide was acknowledged as a crucial factor in the success of the programme. Notably, the age profile of the facilitators was perceived to provide a pivotal backdrop – as validation of their credentials as past participants; as a touchstone against which pupils could explore contemporary issues affecting young people today; and as acknowledgement that corresponding discussions were often conducted with greater openness and honesty than would be possible with teachers.

The rules of engagement

The intervention strategies applied during the course of the programme offered opportunities for sustained discussion and reflection that would not have been possible within the structured regime of the school environment. For this reason, pupils appreciated opportunities to explore their own and others' opinions, and considered that the composition of mixed groups effectively informed and challenged opinions, encouraged the articulation of latent or unexplored viewpoints, and often prompted an internal reflective dialogue.

The way forward

The *Together* programme has offered schools a unique opportunity to engage in innovative approaches to diversity that otherwise may not have been possible within existing institutional and community cultures. The development and sustainability of *Together* is dependent on a number of factors, not least the commitment of schools. In considering the future direction of the programme, the findings of the evaluation have highlighted several factors that could contribute to its duration in the formal sector. These relate to institutional commitment; partnership potential; and expansion.

Institutional commitment
Participation in the programme has given schools a certain freedom within the systemic parameters of the formal curriculum so that teachers and pupils have experience of less formal approaches to teaching and learning. The transfer of skills and expertise between the formal and non-formal sector has been advocated within successive education policy reform; it follows, therefore, that the application of alternative and complementary methodologies should be actively encouraged as a key criterion of schools' work in diversity and good relations.

The institutional longevity of the programme would not be possible without the strategic contribution of core staff, in particular senior management and/or the co-ordinating teacher. Clearly, the co-ordinating teacher has a pivotal role in the development of the programme, whilst support from senior management is a crucial indicator for the status of the programme within institutional culture and practice, and within the wider community. However, the recruitment of additional staff members is essential for long-term sustainability. To date, citizenship teachers have had little engagement with the programme. Although this has been ascribed, in part, to staff availability and time constraints, the citizenship teacher (and/or co-ordinator) has a potentially integral role – as a member of a core school team and as a key link for the adaptation and dissemination of the programme to younger pupils.

Partnership potential
A valid by-product of the programme has been the potential for inter-school collaboration. Whilst the findings suggest that the programme has potential sustainability in participating schools, this should not be sustainability in isolation. The scope for collaborative practice not only facilitates collaborative networks of teacher-pupil engagement, but also is an exemplar of recommended good educational practice. It is an arrangement that offers possibilities, e.g. the establishment of cluster schools; professional partnerships; reciprocal opportunities for shared expertise and/or staff development; cascading expertise and peer mentoring; and facilitating the participation of new schools.

The premise of partnership also extends to the relationship between SOE and schools. In particular, lack of staff engagement in the development of the programme has the potential to minimise its status as a school commitment and conveys a limited representation of shared ownership. Identification of core staff – to include, for example, the citizenship co-ordinator, form tutors, heads of year – represents an opportunity to create a dedicated team of teachers within the school. The benefits for the programme are two-fold: it dispels the perception of individually responsible staff members, and it reinforces the profile of the programme as a whole-school, cross-curricular initiative.

As a model of sustainability, teacher development is crucial. Although there is clear evidence of the depth of work achieved by the young facilitators, it is also acknowledged that, with appropriate training, this can be effectively undertaken by teachers. It is a developmental approach that offers teachers the opportunity to refine and/or acquire the skills and confidence to undertake similar work, to motivate and support the learning of others, and to contribute to a revised institutional vision. It is an arrangement that can be negotiated with SOE and delivered individually or in a cluster basis.

Expansion

The benefits to those pupils who have participated have been demonstrably significant, although the number of pupils who progress to the residential remains limited.

The *Together* programme is currently offered to sixth-year pupils only – most commonly Lower sixth pupils. In a few instances, the programme had been previously offered to Upper sixth pupils. However, it was considered that its introduction to Lower sixth offered greater longevity, since participants would be present for a further year and could act as ambassadors for the programme both inside and outside the school.

Expansion of the programme was most commonly referenced to include pupils coming into the school in Year 8 and pupils in Year 12 who may be leaving school on completion of GCSE exams. This decision was informed by two factors: firstly, a consideration that dissemination of a suitably adapted and age-appropriate programme to younger pupils could address potentially prejudiced behaviours at an early stage; secondly, pupils leaving school after Year 12 could not benefit from the current remit of *Together*.

The public face of the project is important in raising the profile of the programme in the community. So far, publicity has been limited and largely confined to articles in the local press and occasional meetings with the business community. Senior management and external stakeholders agreed that increased publicity in the local community and within the education sector should be a key feature of any future development strategy.

Conclusion

The strength, energy and commitment of the current pool of young SOE volunteers working to support others is an indicator of the wider societal potential to be realised when young people are helped to develop their leadership capacity.

A recent UK government document (DFFCS, 2008) has indicated a key policy shift towards unlocking the leadership capacity of young people to make their own impact for change in society, including peer-led learning and citizenship initiatives in schools. In setting out a new national body to promote this, a key vision is that by 2018 *every* young person in the UK should have the chance to develop his/her leadership skills.

The *Together* programme has begun to tap into an interest in schools to support their own potential sixth-form leaders in facilitating the non-formal learning of their peers and younger pupils. So far, two pilot programmes have already shown promise, with experienced sixth formers in one school delivering key concepts of the Local and Global Citizenship curriculum for over 100 Year 11 pupils, and a joint pupil grouping facilitating critical interschool collaboration across the separate religious and cultural traditions of two others.

The present 'Facilitative Leadership' culture of SOE continues to grow and evolve. It is important that the concurrent synergy of citizenship in the revised curriculum and the potential motivation of young people should be nurtured. To do so, investment in the education of young citizens needs to be matched by a political will and resources that will sustain the long-term prospects.

References

Allport, G.W. (1954), *The Nature of Prejudice*, Cambridge, Mass.: Addison Wesley
CCEA (Council for Curriculum, Examinations and Assessment) (2003), *Proposals for the Curriculum and Assessment at Key Stage 3, Part 1: Background Rationale and Detail*, Belfast: CCEA
DFFCS (Department For Families, Children and Schools) (2008), *Young People Leading Change*, available at http://publications.everychildmatters.gov.uk
OFM/DFM (Office of the First Minister and Deputy First Minister) (2005), *A Shared Future. Policy and strategic framework for good relations in Northern Ireland*, Belfast: OFM/DFM

Smith, M. (1982), *Creators not Consumers*, London: NAYC Publications, downloadable at www.infed.org.uk

SOE (Spirit of Enniskillen) (2006), *Together: Dealing with difference together*, Belfast: Spirit of Enniskillen Trust. www.soetrust.co.uk

5

Trócaire's development education programme: a case study of NGO involvement in citizenship education

Maria Barry

This chapter looks briefly at the experiences of one NGO in the Republic of Ireland that has been involved in citizenship education in recent years. It will explain why Trócaire, an agency for overseas development, might be involved in citizenship education in Ireland and will then move on to outline the different levels of that involvement.

Much of Trócaire's work is associated with the provision of financial and technical support to local communities in the developing world, utilising their own development initiatives. While this is very much the key focus of Trócaire's work, the organisation's mandate also states that:

> ... at home, [Trócaire] will try to make us all more aware of the needs of these [developing] countries and of our duties towards them. These duties are no longer a matter of charity but of simple justice.

With such a mandate and focus on social justice, Trócaire has been able to pursue education and campaigns work in Ireland and, more specifically, be involved in citizenship education. This involvement has occurred at many levels and, for Trócaire, has afforded opportunities and encouraged valuable contributions.

Opportunities

1 A platform for development issues
Central to Trócaire's development education work is the imperative to raise awareness of development issues and ultimately to motivate and encourage people to act for positive global change. In a world faced with many challenges, causes and issues, finding avenues through which to achieve

such a goal is not always easy. Add to this the increasingly loaded education curricula and the task is even greater. Given its foundations and background, Trócaire's traditional point of entry into the formal education sector has been through the religious education subject area. Primary schools and religious education teachers were, and still are, a major stakeholder and target in our work. We continue to enjoy a successful partnership with them.

However, the evolution of citizenship education from the margins to a now established part of school programmes, through such subject areas as SPHE at primary level and CSPE and LCA at secondary level, has provided a new and broader platform for development issues. Through this, Trócaire can raise the current challenges faced by millions in the developing world. The formal framework for exploring such issues has been expanded thanks to citizenship education and, in highlighting development and global issues, Trócaire can at the same time fulfil teachers' and students' needs.

2 Access to schools

One of the effects of this curricular change has been the expansion of Trócaire's access to schools. Whether in a positive or a negative sense, the portfolio of citizenship education is taken up by many teachers. It is estimated that currently there are approximately 3,000 CSPE teachers around the country. In second-level schools, there is generally a greater number of citizenship education teachers than religious education teachers. A large number of the former are in need of support in terms of resources, subject content and pedagogical approaches. In addition, the action project component within CSPE has seen the number of Trócaire visits to schools increase dramatically over the past number of years.

These factors combined have meant that Trócaire has had the opportunity of meeting with many of these teachers and students and now enjoys a sustained relationship with them and their schools. Currently the organisation has approximately 600 named teachers on its citizenship education teacher databases. This reflects more than a 50 per cent increase in terms of Trócaire's access to secondary schools.

3 Support base for campaigns

Trócaire is firmly committed to a vision of education that is directed not only towards educating people about the countries in which the organisation is involved, but essentially towards education for action and for change on the issues and challenges that face the world we all share. For this reason Trócaire views education and campaigns as being fundamentally linked. They are the two pieces of a jigsaw that together provide the tools of analysis and knowledge, involvement and action.

Trócaire also recognises that the key to any successful public campaign is the mobilisation of large numbers under a united message. To this extent, one of the primary objectives of its education work is to build support for current and relevant campaigns while at the same time empowering people to actively participate in bringing about change. One of the strongest support bases for this work within the past few years has undoubtedly come from the students and teachers of citizenship education. The methodologies and action components integral to citizenship education have afforded Trócaire the opportunity to motivate and encourage a wide spectrum of young people to become campaigners for such issues as fair trade, the abolition of slavery, gender issues in Malawi, the Millennium Development goals and Climate Change.

4 Deeper understanding of Trócaire's work
When eliciting from a group of young people what words or phrases they associate with Trócaire, it is common to hear terms such as 'charity', 'poor people' and of course the perennial 'Trócaire box'. Citizenship education provides the opportunity for Trócaire education officers and citizenship education teachers to facilitate students to move beyond this level of understanding. The very language of citizenship education accommodates this. In recent times, student familiarity with and understanding of such terms as 'human rights', 'human dignity', 'development' and 'inter-dependence' has deepened significantly. In turn, this allows students to develop a deeper understanding of the work of Trócaire and the challenges it faces. In addition, it equips them with the skills to engage with the wider world, to question the structures of the organisation and to begin to realise that they have a role to play in bringing about change.

Ultimately, it offers students possibilities to move beyond the traditional responses to an NGO or a charity, that of fundraising. While all NGOs, including Trócaire, depend on fundraising to allow them to carry out their work, a deeper level of understanding of that work presents alternative and further actions for long-term change. The root causes of poverty and injustices are highlighted and this, in turn, raises the need for structural change through public campaigning and lobbying.

Contributions

1 Research, analysis and policy
Trócaire's education work is driven by a strategic plan. Apart from carrying out day-to-day work, the organisation also recognises the need for research, analysis and policy documentation. This rationale has led to a

long and continuing partnership with the Curriculum Development Unit of the VEC in Dublin. Indeed, the Human Rights Education project, funded by Trócaire in the early 1990s, which proposed, argued for and made a realistic case for a subject relating to citizenship issues, is considered to be one of the cornerstones of what ultimately became CSPE. In a concrete yet reflective way, this project provided a supportive and practical white paper for citizenship education lobbyists and proponents. This partnership continues to this day as the Citizenship Education Project, looking to the future development of citizenship education at senior cycle.

2 Methodology and pedagogical approaches

Underpinning much of Trócaire's education and campaigns work is a strong theoretical foundation whereby the process through which we educate is as important as the content and the outcome. The world is an ever-changing place, with new challenges every day. New knowledge becomes old knowledge very quickly. To this extent, skills such as critical thinking, analysis of a situation, expressing and listening to opinions and problem solving become the essential tools for global citizens. Development education practitioners, inspired by the teachings of Paolo Freire, educate from this basis. Such an approach also lies at the heart of what citizenship education is about and, while the content of citizenship education work may vary, this approach is a strong common bond between practitioners from the two backgrounds.

Trócaire's experience is that teachers who wish to facilitate the exploration of global development issues with their students are challenged by the fact that, all too often, the issues seem far removed from the lives of young Irish students. The interactive and participatory approach is thus essential, not only as a process, but also to create for the student the sense that global issues are not 'out there' but are part of the student's world in Cavan, Dublin, Belfast, wherever. It could be argued, however, that this pedagogical approach is far removed from the more traditional, teacher-centred approach to education. The former requires a democratic space for learning, whereby the student is central and actively involved in the learning and the enhancement of skills.

At the early stages of the implementation of CSPE in schools, with its vision of actively engaging students in participatory citizenship studies, this approach sometimes created quite a challenge. Trócaire's education team drew on their development education theoretical foundations and expertise to support initial teacher training for CSPE during its pilot phase, in conjunction with the CSPE Support Service. Since then, this partnership has yielded many activities and projects, culminating in workshops around the country involving part-time Regional Development Officers and teachers of CSPE, on a particular approach to global issues. It is here that Trócaire believes it has made a key contribution to citizenship education within the formal sector at second level and one that has been mutually beneficial.

3 Resources

Over the years Trócaire has produced numerous resources in different forms and for different audiences. Examples include activity books ranging from the early years to second-level sectors, school visits and workshops, a website dedicated specifically to CSPE, education and action packs to accompany the Lenten campaign, campaign email actions and updates and CSPE student conferences. Here, collaborative work with other NGOs has occurred. While this does present a certain challenge, given the different motivations of each, it has proven effective and practical for teachers and students. The *Cearta Daona* joint publication between Amnesty and Trócaire was widely used, and the joint workshops with Combat Poverty Agency highlighted the link between poverty local and poverty global. Such an archive and depth of input indicates a long and lasting commitment to global and citizenship education, financially and otherwise. This area of resource production has also proven to be one of the most valuable contributions Trócaire has made to the area of citizenship education in relation to its key stakeholders, the teacher and students.

4 Pamoja Kwa Haki – Together for Rights

Pamoja Kwa Haki is an innovative and unique citizenship education programme established by Trócaire's education team in 2003. In a sense this programme reflects best not only what Trócaire is aiming to achieve in terms of its work but also *how* to achieve it. It is a new schools programme for senior cycle students and teachers.

The piloting of the Pamoja programme was undertaken in two phases and involved 12 schools throughout Ireland, North and South. The chosen schools were invited to take part in the project because of their proven commitment to human rights and peace and justice issues.

Phase One centred around Trócaire's Lenten campaign on Rwanda. For its part, Trócaire provided two training days for four key students from each school where they were introduced in depth to the Lenten campaign and where presentation and campaigning skills were developed and enhanced. During the Lenten period itself, each Pamoja group within the 12 schools launched their own local campaign, organising school awareness days, local radio and press interviews, library displays, public meetings (one attended by the then Minister of State for Overseas

Development, Tom Kitt), and even speaking at Mass in their local churches. The overriding aim of each of these events was to build public support for the Trócaire postcard campaign on the Millennium Development Goals (MDGs).

Phase Two focused on linking with similar groups in Kenya through Trócaire partners during a Human Rights Summer School in August 2004. Forty students from the 12 schools above were selected to attend. In the course of the week, the students explored the MDGs further, particularly the right to education and gender equality and linked up with their Kenyan counterparts each day through a specially created site where they shared their ideas and opinions and exchanged the different perspectives of both countries on the same theme.

Through its aims and actions, Pamoja is very reflective of the work and contribution of Trócaire's education unit. Its aims include the following:

- To build on, extend and support existing work already being carried out in schools under the banner of human rights, peace and justice and citizenship education
- To capitalise on students' learning from CSPE, and enhance their understanding of the seven concepts and the idea of action projects
- To facilitate the development of the knowledge and skills needed to identify human rights issues, to respond to them in an appropriate manner and to use imaginative ways to bring these issues to peers and beyond the immediate school and youth environment
- To help create future advocates who can support each other in working for a just world.

From the outset, the following elements were outlined as appropriate foundations for Pamoja. These have helped to create a unique programme.

- That the projects be student-led and that the programme be a forum for young people with common interests in human rights
- That the process and activities carried out by the students be as central to the programme as any end result
- That there be a fair and equal relationship between all the Pamoja partners in Kenya, Northern Ireland and the Republic
- That the programme would carry on the foundations of CSPE and open up human rights and citizenship education to a space beyond homework, the timetable and the classroom
- That the programme present students with alternative tools to bring about change, thus contributing to the move beyond the mentality of fundraising. To this extent, the action element of Pamoja is firmly rooted in campaigns work and action to bring about structural change

- That the use of technology be exploited to facilitate a link between young people, north and south of the equator, to act as global citizens
- That the link teacher act as a genuine facilitator, allowing the students to carry out the activities and actions themselves, thereby minimising the time and input from that teacher and ensuring that the project is student-led
- That Pamoja fits into the particular needs and structure of each school involved, in both the Republic and Northern Ireland. During Trócaire visits to each of the schools, this was one of the more striking elements of Pamoja. One might describe it as chameleon-like – changing colour to suit the needs of its immediate environment yet, at its essence, never changing. Each school had capable, informed and motivated students participating in a process that facilitated them to act as global citizens for positive change. Pamoja has grown from strength to strength over the years. Hundreds of students have participated in the programme across the island of Ireland and Kenya. In 2008, Pamoja teachers participated in a study visit to Malawi.

Conclusion

Trócaire's work as citizenship educators may take on different colours or indeed shapes at times, affording the organisation a variety of opportunities and the possibility of making a unique contribution. Ultimately, however, at its essence, Trócaire shares with citizenship education a vision of socially concerned and aware future generations, equipped with the knowledge and skills to work together for an equal and just world.

6

Building teacher capacity – Education for Reconciliation project

Marie Rooney

The Education for Reconciliation project is based in the CDVEC Curriculum Development Unit, Dublin and is funded by the EU Peace and Reconciliation Fund. While the overall aim of the project is 'to equip students with the knowledge, skills and attitudes necessary to participate actively in and contribute to the development of peaceful democratic societies', its focus is on 'engaging teachers in a programme of personal and professional development'. The project also aims 'to embed education for reconciliation in schools' and 'to support and strengthen the role of education in the process of reconciliation'. Through building the capacity of teachers to address with their students controversial issues related to diversity, conflict and reconciliation, it aims to progress the process of reconciliation on the island of Ireland. In its focus on cross-border teacher professional development it is also a contextual response to the peace process.

Peace-building in post-conflict communities has many dimensions, including a structural dimension which focuses on physical reconstruction, economic development and negotiating political systems. Equally important is the psycho-cultural or relationships dimension, which encompasses the addressing of social justice issues, acknowledging past hurts, fostering cultural/attitudinal change and mending/building relationships. These elements have much in common with those involved in the process of reconciliation. It is in the psycho-cultural area, particularly in contributing to the processes of cultural/attitudinal change and of mending/building relationships, that Education for Reconciliation has an important role to play.

A focus on teacher professional development is a means of resourcing the educational system in its commitment to promoting peace and reconciliation. Education reflects social change but can also be in itself a strong force for social change and development. Within education, teachers are key agents in the implementation of change. Michael Fullan writes that 'educational change depends on what teachers do and think'.[1] This reflects the project's rationale and is congruent with the CDU's philosophy that teachers must be placed at the centre of any curriculum initiative.

The second phase of the project began in 2003. Its focus, as in Phase I, 1999-2001, is the citizenship education curriculum and citizenship education teachers.

Curriculum context

The newly introduced Local and Global Citizenship curriculum in Northern Ireland has a great deal in common with the CSPE programme in the South. Education for Reconciliation incorporates many of these common concepts as outlined below:

Local and Global Citizenship	Education for Reconciliation	Civic, Social and Political Education
• Diversity and Inclusion • Equality and Social Justice	Diversity, Inclusion and Interdependent Relationships	• Human Dignity • Interdependence
• Democracy and Active Participation	Democracy and Active Participation	• Democracy • Law
• Human Rights and Social Responsibilities	Rights and Responsibilities	• Human Rights and Responsibilities
	Conflict, Change and Reconciliation	
		• Development • Stewardship

Because of this 'fit', Education for Reconciliation would seem to find a natural home in citizenship education. It is of course also relevant in many other curriculum areas, and one of the spin-offs of training citizenship

[1] Fullan, M. (1991), *The New Meaning of Educational Change*, 2nd edition, London: Continuum, p. 117.

education teachers is that they all teach other subjects as well and will bring their learning and development to bear in those areas.

Overall, Education for Reconciliation could be seen as addressing themes of diversity (positive and problematic aspects), conflict, conflict transformation and reconciliation. The diagram below illustrates this as a cycle:

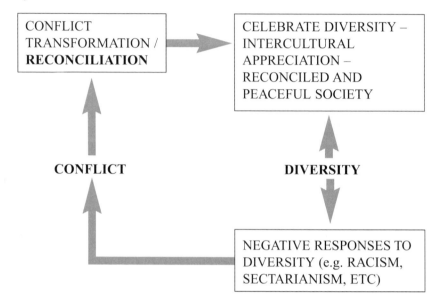

Training

There are 32 schools participating in the project, sixteen from Northern Ireland and sixteen from the Republic (mostly from the border counties). A citizenship education teacher from each of these schools participates in ongoing in-service training, attending three residential workshops (an evening and the following day) over the course of the school year. A group of teachers based in the North-East has been involved in this process over a three-year period, a North-Western group over two years.

The training could be described as having the following characteristics:

- An *active* approach to learning and teaching, as is advocated in citizenship education generally, is modelled during in-service. Participative rather than transmission mode is used, with inputs and presentations kept to a minimum.
- The training aims to be *experiential*, with participants taking part in exercises, then reflecting on the experience and on how they might use the exercises with their students.

- By facilitating exercises and learning activities at adult level and then discussing how they might be adapted for a younger age-group, the project aims to integrate *personal and professional* development as much as is possible within the limits of time available.
- The fact that teachers from *North and South* of the border are working together has a major impact on learning and on the enriching effect of the experience for participants.
- The *ongoing* nature of the training enables participants to plan, carry out, report back on and get support and feedback for teaching and learning activities with their students.
- A *partnership* approach is encouraged, where two teachers plan together and keep in touch. This has a supportive and motivating effect and has also led to some successful student contacts and meetings.
- The fact that training is *residential*, with work beginning on Thursday evening and continuing all day Friday, has a beneficial effect on group dynamics and relationships.
- The training programme is an *evolving* one, constantly developing through consultation with participants and reflection on the part of the project team. The following list summarises understandings and skills addressed to date:

- Theories/concepts/definitions of reconciliation and peace-building
- Exploration of identity
- Diversity
  - positive aspects (celebration of diversity and difference)
  - negative aspects (issues of racism, sectarianism, etc)
- Conflict/ conflict transformation
- Developing understanding of history and politics of Republic and Northern Ireland
- Legal issues involved in partnerships between schools (student exchange visits, use of ICT, etc)
- Partnerships/ sharing of strategies
- Curriculum context
- Facilitation skills
- Active teaching/learning methodologies
- The creation of safe, participative classroom environments
- Raising and dealing with controversial issues
- Materials, resources, lesson plans/schemes
- Knowledge of resources/research skills
- Dealing with minorities in classroom/school

Dissemination/Mainstreaming

The project has the aim, not merely of facilitating the professional development of the teachers taking part in training, but also of bringing Education for Reconciliation to their colleagues on citizenship education teams in their schools. Ideally, through a cascade model, these teachers will share their learning and promote Education for Reconciliation with their colleagues. To assist the teachers in this process, the project has a small support team of three teachers who are released from their schools on Fridays throughout the school year to facilitate in-school workshops in Education for Reconciliation for citizenship education teams. The project meets substitution costs for teachers attending these workshops.

As another means of dissemination, the project is in the process of producing a handbook for teachers. A group of participating teachers has developed a resource entitled *On the Right Track – Peace and Reconciliation education – a handbook for teachers of citizenship education*. In draft form, this is currently being piloted by teachers with a view to publication.

Research

The project employs a full-time Research Officer, who is tracking and documenting learning and teaching activities and will produce a report at the end of this phase of the project.

Challenges

The project faces challenges – many of them common to other education projects and most of them in relation to its aim of dissemination. The first category relates to the cascade model, and another area of difficulty is posed by issues in relation to citizenship education.

Cascade model

Part of the project rationale is that the teachers participating in training will share their learning on Education for Reconciliation with colleagues on citizenship education teams in their schools. This model can work well where there is an effective and working citizenship education team in place in the lead (participating) teacher's school, where there is a collaborative school culture, where management is supportive and where the lead teacher is confident and in a position of influence in the school. This description indeed applies to some of the teachers and schools participating in the project. However, difficulties are encountered where these conditions do not prevail. The workshops run by the project support team in schools can be helpful, both in promoting awareness of Education for Reconciliation and in bringing the citizenship education team together.

Citizenship education

In locating itself within citizenship education and focusing on teachers in this area of the curriculum, Education for Reconciliation is exposed to the many challenges faced by citizenship education itself.

In *CSPE* these could be listed as:

- time allocation
- teacher allocation to subject
- teacher turnover
- professional development/support
- resources
- management support.

In *Local and Global Citizenship* they can be listed as:

- continuity between training and teaching
- perceived threat from new subject
- politics of citizenship education in post-conflict society ('culture of silence' and contested notions of citizenship).

Other challenges facing the project include the following:

- Some schools in Northern Ireland are slow to introduce Local and Global Citizenship, even when their teachers have taken part in the Education and Library Board training.
- There are difficulties in gaining cross-community representation, in that state/Protestant schools are often reluctant to become involved.
- The funding measures impose geographical constraints and preclude significant 'far South' (i.e. non-border counties in the Republic) and East-West (UK) dimensions.

Conclusion

The Education for Reconciliation project is one of only two curriculum-based, teacher-centred cross-border projects at second level on the island of Ireland (the other being the European Studies project). It is unique in its emphasis on teacher development as the way forward in North-South co-operation in education and in its focus on the themes of post-conflict reconciliation. The project also has the advantage of a built-in research element, which will greatly enhance the learning to be gained from the project experience.

The design and facilitation of teacher professional development, along with the team's reflective approach to practice, have resulted in the deepening of understanding of key issues and methods for effective learning in the areas of conflict and reconciliation for teachers north and south of the border. The challenges faced by the project are mainly in the areas of 'mainstreaming' and dissemination in schools. It is to be hoped that it will be possible to apply the learning from this phase of the project to future initiatives in the field of Education for Reconciliation.

7

Laying the foundations: citizenship in the primary school

Norman Richardson

For children to start putting the concepts of citizenship education into practice, the whole-school ethos has to be supportive. Piecemeal tokenism will never replace cynicism and apathy (Claire, 2004:94).

In a recent discussion a primary school principal expressed in fairly vehement terms his criticism of post-primary schools which, in his view, were responsible for neglecting, damaging or even destroying work to promote cross-cultural and cross-community awareness and understanding that had been carried out in primary classrooms and through inter-school activities. This particular principal has a genuine commitment to such work and a very creditable track-record – and indeed good practice in his school is referred to later in this chapter – so his anger came across as more than mere rhetoric. His perspective was striking, however, because so often in recent years we have heard criticisms from those involved with older pupils and young people suggesting that much of the work carried out in primary schools on issues of cultural diversity and mutual understanding is superficial and lacking in depth and progression.

In fact no sector in Northern Ireland can claim very much virtue in this regard. The evidence from research and inspection reports (for example, Smith and Robinson, 1996; NFER, 1999; ETI/DE, 1999 and 2000; O'Connor *et al*, 2002) is that notwithstanding some examples of good work in both primary and post-primary schools the reality has all too often been very disappointing. Indeed this was one of the reasons why the case was forcefully made over the past few years to move away from the educational themes of Education for Mutual Understanding and Cultural Heritage towards a curriculum-based citizenship model.

In Northern Ireland, at the time of writing, we are at the commencement of a process of establishing this firmly into the Revised Curriculum in the form of Local and Global Citizenship (LGC) in post-primary schools and Personal Development and Mutual Understanding (PDMU) in the primary sector (CCEA, 2002; 2003a; DE, 2007a). This chapter will focus on the role of the primary school in this process, particularly in relation to the very important dimension within LGC and PDMU of dealing with diversity. The discussion will be illustrated with reference to the Northern Ireland experience, because of the author's involvement in the preparation and formation of student teachers for the primary sector there, though it is likely that many of the issues are of wider relevance.

'Primary Citizenship' and the Revised Northern Ireland Curriculum

Many educators in Northern Ireland have been committed for more than three decades to finding ways of responding positively to local and global issues of diversity, conflict and community relationships, and for some of that time much effort was put into the Educational Themes approach – the model which set Education for Mutual Understanding (EMU) and Cultural Heritage into the curriculum as the focal points for such work, supported by voluntary involvement in the Schools' Community Relations Programme.[1] The aspirations of this programme were laudable and, at their best, engendered some very creditable work (Richardson, 2001, 2002), but the overall picture left much to be desired in all sectors of education. For this reason many educators have welcomed the sharpening up and strengthening process by which the aspirations of the EMU model are being redirected into the approach that now features in the Revised Curriculum. In pursuing this approach, however, we need to be sure that we have learned from past experience.

It is not unusual to hear some educators referring to citizenship education as though it were a feature of the curriculum in general, despite the fact that as far as school subjects (more correctly 'Areas of Learning') are concerned the actual *terminology* is restricted in Northern Ireland to the post-primary sector – Key Stages 3 and 4. Citizenship education does, in fact, feature throughout all Key Stages as one of several 'Curriculum Objectives', through which children should: 'become aware of some of their rights and responsibilities; ... of some of the issues and problems in society; [and] contribute to creating a better world for those around them'

---

[1] Established in 1987 (as the *Cross-Community Contact Scheme*) the Schools' Community Relations Programme (SCRP) continues to provide funding for schools to engage in inter-school encounter activities, on application according to published criteria. This programme was intended to be supportive of the work done in the Northern Ireland Curriculum through EMU and Cultural Heritage, though many teachers confused the term 'EMU' with this scheme and neglected the (statutory) classroom elements of the work. Many teachers continue to speak of EMU when they actually mean the contact scheme.

(CCEA, 2007:4). Nevertheless, it often seems that many of those who have been active in promoting citizenship education have been focused largely or solely on the post-11 age group. I have sometimes been asked by educational colleagues if the Northern Ireland Curriculum includes citizenship education at the primary stage, and it is still not very common to hear people consciously and overtly linking citizenship education with PDMU even though Strand 2 of this new Area of Learning at Foundation Stage and Key Stages 1 and 2 – Mutual Understanding in the Local and Wider Community – is clearly intended as the primary school avenue into post-primary Local and Global Citizenship. This is indicated in the Guidance Materials which describe PDMU as:

> ... encouraging each child to become personally, emotionally, socially and physically effective to lead healthy, safe and fulfilled lives and to become confident, independent and responsible citizens, making informed and responsible choices and decisions throughout their lives (PMB/CCEA, 2007:3).

In England the citizenship terminology is used at all Key Stages, alongside that of Personal, Social and Health Education (PSHE) (see, for instance, QCA, 2000). Perhaps we would have been wiser to do the same in Northern Ireland. On the laudable initiative of the Department of Education a significant programme of in-service training in LGC was provided for teachers in the post-primary sector in the period just prior to the statutory introduction of the Revised Curriculum, but no comparable initiatives have been made in the primary schools in relation to PDMU. On various occasions it was proposed that there should be representatives of the primary sector involved in the process of developing programmes and materials for citizenship education, and *vice versa*, but this did not materialise.

At the same time there are concerns about the extent to which the link with citizenship education has been perceived from within the primary sector. It has been disconcerting to see some adverts for PDMU posts in the Education and Library Boards predominantly emphasising Health Education. Will we find schools using the 'softer' elements of Strand 1 of PDMU, Personal Understanding and Health, to avoid the potentially more contentious issues inherent in Strand 2, Mutual Understanding in the Local and Wider Community? If we wish not only to learn from, but also to apply, the lessons of the Educational Themes model, we must ensure that the emphasis which is rightly being placed on the various curricular dimensions of citizenship education in secondary schools is not lost or neglected in primary schools (whether or not we are specifically using the language of 'citizenship' at the primary level). The task is surely one of laying solid foundations throughout the primary years and then ensuring that there is proper cross-phase cohesion as well as progression into Key Stage 3 and beyond. One of the main steps in this process is to be sure that we have a solid and well-communicated rationale for what we are doing at the primary stage of education.

Clarifying the rationale

In the early 1980s, after some years as a classroom teacher, I took on a new role as a 'peace education officer' within an NGO. One of the first articles I read was on research in the USA about how racially-aware attitudes were evident in children as young as 3 years of age, how such children showed a capacity to make prejudiced remarks about children of other races, and how, if allowed to continue, such attitudes were seen to harden through later childhood and into adolescence (see, for instance, Brown, 1995:121ff). This was almost two decades before the research carried out by Paul Connolly and others on racist and sectarian attitudes in young children in Northern Ireland (Connolly and Keenan, 2001; Connolly *et al*, 2002), to which I will return.

At that time, in the 1980s, I used the accounts of that research to make the point that attitudinal challenge through education needs to begin in the early years, and this reinforced my long-held belief that learning about other cultures and religions must have a significant place in the primary school. Yet in the period since then I have frequently heard teachers and even student teachers express the view that young children should not be exposed to contentious or sensitive issues; or that such concerns will inevitably lead to conflict in the classroom; or that young children are 'colour-blind'; or that Protestant and Catholic children at primary school should focus on their similarities but need not, or should not, learn about their differences or their divisions; or that, in particular, to learn about 'other religions' (other than Christianity) under the age of 16, will simply make children 'confused'.

My current work in teacher education places me in a position where I can gain a very good impression of the impact of 14 years of school education on the young adults who come to study in our Bachelor of Education programme. Only a few of them appear to have engaged previously in any discussion or learning across traditional cultural barriers, which makes it very difficult when we try to prepare teachers to deal with issues of diversity, equality, inclusion and mutual understanding. Despite over a decade of statutory Education for Mutual Understanding and two more decades of unofficial community relations initiatives in education (in which so many of those who are currently working in the citizenship field have invested so much energy over a long period); despite significant awareness of multicultural and anti-racist work in Britain and elsewhere; and despite much evidence, anecdotal and researched, of the serious impact of sectarianism, racism and other forms of exclusion on children and young people, we seem to have made little impact on the young adults who are now entering initial teacher education, and even on those who will emerge from four years of higher education into the nursery units, schools and colleges. It is not even that most of these approaches have failed – for the most part they have *simply not been implemented*. If we continue in this scenario we preserve for yet another generation a culture of silence or avoidance and contribute to the perpetuation of negative stereotypes or ignorance.

I have sometimes quoted a song from the 1950s Rogers & Hammerstein musical *South Pacific*, which was written around the time of the Little Rock Arkansas race riots:

> You've got to be taught to hate and fear
> You've got to be taught from year to year
> It's got to be drummed in your dear little ear
> You've got to be carefully taught
> You've got to be taught before it's too late
> Before you are six or seven or eight
> To hate all the people your relatives hate
> You've got to be carefully taught.

Babette Brown has suggested that 'between the ages of three and six, most children have developed a deeper understanding of themselves and their world' (Brown, 1998:14) and that in the process children pick up both positive and negative attitudes and behaviour. From a range of research, much of it emanating from the United States, we know that pre-school children can express strong race or difference-related values. Jane Elliot, of the famous *Blue-Eyes, Brown-Eyes* experiment in the late 1960s, is scathing about people who claim that children are colour-blind, and another champion of anti-racism in education, Louise Derman-Sparks, describes it as 'pernicious' and 'analogous to the ostrich's head-in-the-sand strategy' (Derman-Sparks *et al*, nd).

The process appears to begin very early in life as infants learn to categorise objects by appearance and function. Such young children have limited experience on which to base their descriptions of difference, and restricted language with which to express it, but there seems little doubt that the capacity to identify difference is present. There are studies which show that 3- to 5-year-olds are most conscious of physical differences, such as colour, but also of cultural characteristics such as language and dress (Derman-Sparks *et al*, op cit). Studies in Britain have also shown that 3- to 5-year-olds are learning to attach value to skin-colour and that there is a pecking order whereby White is at the top and Black is at the bottom (Milner, 1983). It is clear from other studies that for 3- to 4-year-olds an awareness of gender diversity and stereotyped gender roles also appears to be very strong.

Studies in integrated, all-white and all-black schools in the US have shown how children perceive their racial identity and that children in separate-race schools showed more evidence of dislike of other races (Dutton *et al*, 1998). One study indicated that pre-school children were more likely to mention racial differences when the researcher was of the same race as themselves (Glover and Smith, 1997). Brown's research (1995) revealed that American children had shown a canny awareness of adult attitudes by using respectful language when questioned by a researcher but when they thought no-one was listening had been heard over a concealed microphone using terms that were much more racist in nature.

This was reflected in a recently-completed SCoTENS[2]-sponsored Early Years project in both parts of Ireland (Kenny and McLaughlin, 2004). The researchers noted that some children did not remark on colour at all when shown trigger photographs relating to racial differences. The teachers noted that racist remarks were more likely to erupt in a moment of conflict after years of harmony and seemingly deep friendship:

> One teacher reported that, at the end of her three year cycle with a class, she was astonished to hear a white girl fling racist slurs in a fight with a black girl: they had been seemingly colour-blind best friends in her class from the start. She also noted that children did not need to understand terms in order to use them to hurt (Kenny and McLaughlin, 2004:36).

Derman-Sparks argues that inaccurate stereotypical and caricatured images and information about racial and/or cultural groups – such as those that children may pick up from the media or the home – are particularly harmful in the early years:

> Having not yet fully formed clear concepts of themselves or others, preschoolers are still in the process of learning to determine what is authentic and what is not. Especially when children do not have many

---

[2] SCoTENS is the *Standing Conference on Teacher Education North-South* and is supported by the Centre for Cross-Border Studies.

opportunities for feedback about their ideas through direct interaction with people different from themselves, caricatured images can form the basis of their thinking (Derman Sparks *et al*, op cit).

American studies with older children, in the 5 to 8 age range, have shown that programmes designed to reduce negative racial attitudes can be effective (Singh and Yancey, 1974). Children at this age are more conscious of their peers and able to develop a concept of 'fairness'. Derman-Sparks suggests that 'while prejudice can become a part of children's thinking at this age, it is also possible to utilise their emerging moral sense to help them perceive the "unfairness" of racism and to teach them tools for dealing with expressions of ethnocentrism and prejudice in their immediate world' (op cit).

In Northern Ireland there was little clear local evidence of the impact of the Troubles and sectarianism on very young children until the recent studies of Paul Connolly and his collaborators. Conscious that previous work, usually on older children, had been limited by being based on adult constructs and understandings, Connolly's 2002 study involved a random sample of 352 three-to-five-year-olds. The results show that young children in Northern Ireland are influenced from an early age by cultural and political events and symbols, starting with those associated with their own culture and extending as they grow older to an awareness of the significance of different cultures and their cultural/political associations:

> For a very small number, this developing awareness provides the foundations upon which they have already begun to identify with a particular community and/or develop sectarian attitudes. However, for the majority, it represents the foundations upon which a significant minority tend to develop community identities and prejudiced attitudes over the following few years (Connolly *et al*, 2002:50).

Elsewhere Connolly has suggested that racial prejudice is, in fact, even more prevalent in Northern Ireland than sectarianism, and recent widely publicised racist attacks in the Province have brought a chilling credibility to his findings:

> Interestingly, the data ... clearly suggest that people in Northern Ireland are around twice as likely to be unwilling to accept and mix with members of the minority ethnic communities than they would be with those from the other main tradition to themselves. As regards initial attitudes towards others, therefore, racial prejudice seems to be twice as significant as sectarian prejudice in the minds of the general population in Northern Ireland (Connolly and Keenan, 2000:22).

That Connolly's work has become relatively well known is something for which we should be grateful. It makes the argument that young children should be immured from such considerations much harder to sustain. Taken together with the international research on prejudiced attitudes in young children it helps us to address the issues around education for anti-bias and positive awareness of diversity in primary schools with much greater seriousness and focus.

The researchers in the cross-border Early Years project noted that 'particularly in areas touched by inter-group conflict some children showed elements that could be classed as what Derman-Sparks has called "pre-prejudice", with varied levels of knowledge of racist and other exclusionary terminology' (Kenny and McLaughlin, 2004:29). Amongst very young children this knowledge does not yet appear to inform specific patterns of behaviour, but 'awareness and barriers grow as children get older' (ibid:31). Some interviewed teachers had suggested that 'the difference between younger and older children was not so much in terms of what they knew, but in terms of how they acted on it' (ibid:36). Yet there seemed to be a view, perhaps more prominent among the Northern teachers, that there are no significant issues or problems amongst early years children. 'Religion' – which, of course, may mean a number of things not necessarily to do with spiritual observances – was not seen as a problem in either jurisdiction with this age group (ibid:33). 'Conflict' (which is often used as though it were synonymous with religion!) was similarly not seen as an issue. Does this suggest that other research findings (for example, those of Connolly *et al*) on young children's attitudes are simply wrong? Or is the problem something to do with adult discomfort in certain areas, leading to denial and avoidance?

Teachers in the study indicated considerable wariness about broaching issues of community conflict in Northern Ireland, particularly with young children, and a similar attitude seems often to be taken in relation to the Traveller Community, especially in the Republic. There was a clear preference for dealing only with 'softer' issues, sometimes seeing diversity only in terms of 'the third world' or in its relatively uncontroversial expressions. I have spent much of my own career advocating the importance of the place of world religions in primary religious education, but I take no joy in the teacher who would prefer to send his or her pupils to visit a synagogue or mosque *rather* than a Catholic church! The cross-border Early Years study also indicates that there is still a significant number of teachers who will argue for schools as 'safe havens' or 'sanctuaries' (Kenny and McLaughlin, 2004:36). Children, they suggest, need to feel secure and safe from the nasty expressions of the world outside. The problem is that many people seem to have taken their images of security from what we have seen of the building of defensive walls and barriers rather than the more significant image of building strong, secure, human and community relationships. Schools, as I have argued elsewhere, would do better to see themselves as bridges to the community, not enclosures to keep another community out (Richardson, 2002).

Education for a shared future?

Even where teachers do recognise the importance of dealing constructively with these issues, there remain significant obstacles to progress. Access to appropriate resources has been limited, particularly in relation to locally-based resources on race and ethnicity and on the harder-edged issues of diversity and conflict, especially for young children. There have always been good-quality materials, some of them focused on the local situation such as the materials emanating from the Churches' Peace Education programme (e.g. Hall, 2005; Richardson, 2005) from the early 1980s to the mid-2000s, the *Primary Values* programme (Montgomery and Birthistle, 2001) and the web-based *Stepping Out* (Naylor, 2006), but many schools have been unaware of their existence or of how to make adequate use of them. This situation is improving with the help of initiatives such as the cross-border *Lift-Off* project (Ruane *et al*, 2003-2007), which has been piloting its human rights materials for primary schools steadily over recent years, and the *Media Initiative for Children* developed by Early Years (formerly known as NIPPA – the Northern Ireland Pre-School Playgroup Association), but the key issue remains one of access and willingness to get involved.

Perhaps the resource that will have the greatest potential for impact is the *Living, Learning, Together* series (Hamill and Edgar, 2007ff) which, at the time of writing, is still in development under the auspices of the Northern Ireland Council for Curriculum, Examinations and Assessment (CCEA). The resource will eventually cover each primary year group and will provide guidelines and teaching ideas covering all aspects of the PDMU programme. As an official and attractively presented set of materials provided to all schools, every teacher should have easy access to it, and it is also available in downloadable format. In keeping with the Guidance Material to the PDMU programme itself, as cited above, the introduction to this resource package clearly sets PDMU in the context of citizenship:

> *Living, Learning, Together* is a planned and progressive … programme for 5-11 year olds. It will assist schools in developing children's personal, emotional, social and health needs and in preparing them to contribute to their communities in ways that make a positive and lasting impact (CCEA Introductory booklet:2).

Ultimately a more significant and serious factor, however, is the continuing limited experience of many teachers in dealing with difficult and controversial areas in the curriculum. The insecurity of teachers in this regard reflects their own lack of personal opportunities to discuss issues such as race, ethnicity, culture and religion – a consequence of the normative experience of people in Northern Ireland of separation and avoidance. The best and most attractive materials will not make much difference if those who are expected to use them feel lacking in the key skills associated with the basic ideas.

Training opportunities in this field have clearly been very limited, from Initial Teacher Education right through Continuing Professional Development, although the introduction of PDMU into the Revised Curriculum is helping to create some new opportunities. Research on the attitudes of Catholic and Protestant student teachers towards religious diversity has suggested that there is a willingness to engage with such issues but that it has often been frustrated by lack of awareness and skills and the opportunities to learn them (Richardson, 2003a, 2006). In addition, a study which was undertaken with parents from minority faith communities painted a depressing picture of teachers in all kinds of schools who appeared not to know how to deal with, or respond to, the questions, needs and concerns of members of different faiths and ethnic groups (Richardson, 2003b).

If we are to move forward in relation to laying the foundations of education for citizenship in primary schools the process will involve a holistic values-change in schools and within the system as a whole. Our ethos and values are conveyed both by what we teach and by how we teach. Values are not just about what we expect of the children in our care – they are about what we expect of ourselves. According to Alison Montgomery in the introduction to the original piloting edition of the *Primary Values* programme, if we want children to have a good sense of self-esteem, to think for themselves and to take responsibility for their own lives, we have to value and promote *autonomy*. If we want children to relate well to others and understand their concerns and feelings, we have to value and promote *empathy*. If we want children to develop a sense of fairness, justice and equality and to respect human rights above personal interest, we have to value and promote a sense of *transcendence* (Montgomery and Birthistle, 2001).

These concepts come together in the ideal of promoting a culture of respect for diversity and for each other's human rights. In an increasingly diverse local and global society, where there remain many divisions and injustices, educators have a responsibility to value and play their part in creating such a culture. This is emphasised by the government policy document *A Shared Future*, which recognises the key role of education in building an equitable and cohesive society, especially one that is still emerging from years of turmoil and division:

> All schools should ensure through their policies, structures and curriculae that pupils are consciously prepared for life in a diverse and inter-cultural society (OFM/DFM, 2005:2).

We prepare our children, however young, for life in a diverse world, by what we do and say, and, for that matter, no less by what we do not do or do not say. **By the very nature of the extended contact between primary school teacher and primary school child, the primary classroom becomes a very important hub for the development of the values inherent in the concept of citizenship education.**

Many of these values are evident in the programme which has been developed for Personal Development and Mutual Understanding at Foundation Stage and Key Stages 1 and 2 in Northern Ireland, and particularly in the second strand of the programme, Mutual Understanding in the Local and Wider Community. It tells us that, amongst other things, children should benefit from the development of:

> insights into society, other cultures and the environment, our interdependence and the need for mutual understanding and respect; (and) an ability to use these insights to contribute to relationships, family life, the local and global community and the environment (PMB/CCEA, 2007:4).

Directions for policy and practice

How then, can we achieve this? The place in the curriculum of PDMU is a significant move forward, but past experience should prompt us to recognise that it will need more than this for such work to flourish. If we are to move from expressions of what is desirable to the effective implementation of quality classroom work, the following points need to be kept firmly in mind over the coming years, in policy and in practice:

• The educational system as a whole must adopt a much more pro-active attitude towards the inclusion of diverse cultures in relation to the curriculum, not least in primary schools. This is changing, but some teachers and others still seem to believe that they live in a mono-cultural world. We should recognise, enjoy, celebrate and respect diversity and encourage children to do so too. This is perhaps best described as *interculturalism*, because it emphasises interaction between cultures, not just the benign acceptance that may be implicit in some people's understanding of 'multiculturalism'.

- Multiculturalism, in fact, may be limited in situations of injustice, oppression and unequal power relationships. It should be supplemented by positive action to promote good relations between groups or communities. Some would describe this in terms such as *anti-racism, anti-sectarianism, anti-discrimination* or *anti-bias,* although it is desirable to find a way of saying this positively – what we are *for*, not just what we are against. This is a more critical, committed form of multiculturalism, as Babette Brown puts it: 'embedded in an anti-discriminatory framework' (Brown, 1998:45).

  This is why it is important to go *beyond* basic curriculum requirements in order to make the most of opportunities presented by inter-school cross-community and cross-cultural programmes, such as those funded through the Northern Ireland Schools' Community Relations Programme, or the EU's Comenius and other exchange programmes. These may be costly in terms of time and money, and they will need to be much more uniformly stringent than some of the previous work of this kind, but if well-handled they can support a very valuable dimension of intercultural school activity. Primary schools generally have more flexible timetables which permit work of this kind to be organised more easily than at the post-primary level.

  Some schools have a particularly impressive track record in this regard, including that of the school head teacher who was quoted at the start of this paper. In the context of a quite divided and now increasingly ethnically diverse area of Northern Ireland, he, along with a partner school, has devised a programme involving all the primary year groups in both contact and curriculum programmes which are inter-related and cohesive, and in which staff are closely involved. We need to hear more about holistic models and case-studies of this kind.

- Schools have an ethical and legal responsibility to promote inclusion and respect for equality and human rights. This can only be achieved if it is a holistic concern and is incorporated into the policy and ethos of a school. In bringing PDMU and citizenship education away from the periphery into a wholeheartedly curricular framework we must not lose sight of the whole-school approach which I believe was, at best, one of the strengths of the earlier Educational Themes approach. This may, however, be very challenging in terms of the power relations within and around any school which can often work to sustain discrimination and inequalities.

  A very good example of this holistic consciousness is in the introductory section of the 'Lift Off' materials on human rights in primary schools, where the authors outline what they describe as a 'human rights classroom' (Ruane *et al*, 2003:3-4). This programme as a whole offers a very comprehensive approach to many aspects of the PDMU area of learning, especially in relation to Strand 2 (Mutual Understanding in the Local and Wider Community). The excellent UNICEF scheme whereby schools may be designated as 'Rights Respecting Schools' (of which, at the time of writing, there are several primary schools so designated in Northern Ireland) is also focused on the whole school, not just on selective activities.

- As educators we need to make ourselves more aware of the diversity around us, and learn something of the practical needs of those who are different from us – celebrations, diet, customs, language, expectations. We can also make children more aware of diversity, even in schools or areas that do not seem particularly diverse. The view that 'there's no problem here so we don't need to do anything about it' ignores the realities of how children increasingly perceive their surroundings in a small world. (We should also be very careful about implying that children from different cultural, ethnic, religious or linguistic backgrounds are 'problems'!) Children need to have an awareness of *both* similarities and differences – it is 'both/and', not 'either/or'! Many educators have advocated a creative, cross-curricular approach to such learning – through the media of music, drama, story, the visual arts, dance and so forth.

  There is a wealth of story material which can help to open up children's – and our own – perceptions and contribute towards a positive and informed appreciation of diversity. (The CCEA *Primary Values* resource, cited above, is an excellent example of this. Many other very useful resources are listed in the CCEA's *Living, Learning, Together* programme, which is referred to above.) The younger the age at which this can be commenced, the better, and Paul Connolly's work has highlighted this very effectively. He has proposed that from age 3 onwards children should be encouraged to explore and experience a range of cultural practices and to appreciate and respect differences and cultural diversity (Connolly *et al*, 2002:51).

- In Northern Ireland one of the areas requiring radical change is in the Revised Core Syllabus for Religious Education (DE, 2007b), which is still anachronistically controlled by the Churches without reference to any other faith communities or interest groups. The Department of Education has failed to challenge this position and thus perpetuates a mono-cultural approach to religious learning which patronisingly ignores religious diversity, even between different kinds of Christians, concurring with the Churches' biased and unfounded view that for primary age children to learn about other religions is unsuitable. Such an approach would seem to be fundamentally contradictory to the principles inherent in PDMU and Local and Global Citizenship, and contrary to human rights principles and to government policy on equality and *A Shared Future*. This situation must be challenged if Northern Ireland's education system is to have any credibility in this regard.

- If we ourselves, as educators of all kinds, are to be able to speak comfortably and openly about difference, we must send a clear message to others – student teachers, the children we teach, their parents – that it is possible and appropriate to do so. This is a principle I apply rigorously in my own work as a teacher educator (especially in relation to the sometimes contentious areas of religious diversity), and it is no less important with all age groups, including young children. Appropriate classroom work should therefore focus on talking and listening, with an emphasis on emotional literacy, reinforced through creative and expressive activities. Primary schools present many excellent opportunities in this area.

- Parents can be brought in to discussions about issues of cultural diversity. What do we do about the Muslim child in Religious Education or the Nativity Play? Do we abandon familiar cultural practices in order to avoid 'offending' anyone – a little like the Birmingham City Council's attempt a few years ago to replace Christmas with 'Winterval' – or do we find ways of *including* everyone's special times and of learning from each other? Parents like to feel that their views are heard and valued and will normally respond to openness and the attempt to include them.

- On the basis of our own openness with children and our encouragement to them to articulate their ideas and issues, we must go on to help young children to develop a language of diversity, respect, inclusion, negotiation, openness and peace. If we neglect this in the primary school how can we expect children to gain this when they are older?

- At the same time we do need to be realistic and supportive to those schools and those areas where there may be genuine sensitivities in relation to diversity and equality issues. We have to help teachers to move into and move on in this work; to find a level of entry which can be effective within the distinctiveness of a particular community and enable and encourage them to progress from there.

- The area that continues to need much attention is that of teacher education, not least at the initial stage. At all stages in teacher education there is a need to focus on the personal development of teachers, their own opportunities to engage with the processes involved, to experience and learn from diversity, to develop their skills in appropriate classroom practice and their awareness of resources. Very often we do the last first

– and just hand resources to people who need much more personal preparation. We need to address the issues of equal opportunities and inclusion and help young teachers to deal comfortably and professionally with issues of diversity and discrimination. Until very recently these areas have seemed all too peripheral in our teacher education programmes. This point was clearly addressed in the government policy document *A Shared Future*:

> Teachers influence greatly the lives of our children and young people and have a key role to play in helping to develop an inclusive society built on trust and mutual respect. Consequently, the universities and institutions with responsibility for training new teachers have a key role to play in preparing them to teach about living and working in a shared society and helping children and young people to respect each other's values and differences (OFM/DFM, 2005:2).

• If we are to improve and sustain this consciousness of citizenship as a primary as well as a post-primary concept, we will need to enable much better cross-phase communication and liaison, both in strategic regional curriculum planning and in the practice of individual schools. This is something that has never been done very effectively in our system, so maybe we have to face the task of subverting the existing culture of non-communication!

Conclusion

Primary school classrooms have tremendous potential to develop and extend those desirable qualities which we currently see as represented by the curriculum area of Citizenship/PDMU/PSHE – or whatever other term may be used in different regions or jurisdictions. This recognition is not new, but the opportunities presented by reflection on past experience, new research and ongoing curriculum review in Northern Ireland make this an important moment in the process. One of the educators who did much to establish the importance of this area of learning and experience was the late Jerry Tyrrell, who placed particular emphasis on peer mediation in schools. In the introduction to his posthumously-published work *Peer Mediation in Primary Schools* (2002:12ff), he expressed what for many people must be the essential heart of this discussion:

> There is currently a great deal of talk about citizenship, in the context of changes in the curriculum, and of preparing children to be citizens tomorrow. But there's little point in extolling the virtues of citizenship

in the future, if the reality for our children is that they have little impact on the hierarchical, undemocratic institutions that are schools today. … Thought needs to be given to the kind of environment needed for the skills of teamwork, problem-solving and creative thinking to flourish. The concept of the *democratic classroom* is one that might provide the starting-point for such an environment. In essence, this is about the teacher and the class meeting together and deciding on ground-rules, addressing problems, agreeing on solutions and also devising sanctions if agreements aren't kept. A microcosm of society, in fact.

References

Brown, B. (1998), *Unlearning Discrimination in the Early Years*, Stoke on Trent: Trentham Books

Brown, R. (1995), *Prejudice – Its Social Psychology*, Oxford: Blackwell Publishers

CCEA (Council for Curriculum, Examinations and Assessment) (2002), *Curriculum Review: Detailed Proposals for the Revised Primary Curriculum and its Assessment Arrangements*, Belfast: CCEA

CCEA (Council for Curriculum, Examinations and Assessment) (2003a), *Pathways: Proposals for Curriculum and Assessment at Key Stage 3*, Belfast: CCEA

CCEA (Council for Curriculum, Examinations and Assessment) (2003b), *The Revised Northern Ireland Primary Curriculum, Key Stages 1 & 2* (draft issued December 2003), Belfast: CCEA

CCEA (Council for Curriculum, Examinations and Assessment) (2007), *The Northern Ireland Curriculum: Primary*, Belfast: CCEA

Claire, H. (ed.) (2004), *Teaching Citizenship in Primary Schools*, Exeter: Learning Matters

Connolly, P. (1999), *Community Relations Work with Preschool Children*, Belfast: Community Relations Council

Connolly, P. (2003), *Fair Play: talking to children about prejudice and discrimination*, Belfast: Save the Children and Barnardo's Northern Ireland

Connolly, P. and Keenan, M. (2000), *Racial Attitudes and Prejudice in Northern Ireland*, Belfast: Northern Ireland Statistics and Research Agency

Connolly, P. and Keenan, M. (2001), *The Hidden Truth: Racist Harassment in Northern Ireland*, Belfast: Northern Ireland Statistics and Research Agency

Connolly, P., Smith, A. and Kelly, B. (2002), *Too Young to Notice? The Cultural and Political Awareness of 3-6 Year Olds in Northern Ireland*, Belfast: Community Relations Council

DE (Department of Education for Northern Ireland) (1999), *Towards a Culture of Tolerance: Education for Diversity* (Report of the Working Group on the Strategic Promotion of Education for Mutual Understanding), Bangor: DE

DE (Department of Education for Northern Ireland) (2007a), *The Education (Minimum Curriculum Content) Order 2007*, Bangor: DE, available via http://www.opsi.gov.uk/sr/sr2007/nisr_20070046_en_1

DE (Department of Education for Northern Ireland) (2007b), *Core Syllabus for Religious Education*, Bangor: DE, available via http://www.deni.gov.uk/re_core_syllabus_pdf.pdf

Derman-Sparks, L., Higa, C.T. and Sparks, B. (no date), *Children, Race and Racism: How Race Awareness Develops*, accessed from the internet: http://www.rootsforchange.net/pdfs/F3C_Eng-ChildrenRaceAnd.pdf

Dutton, S.E., Singer, J.A. and Devlin, A.S. (1998), 'Racial identity of children in integrated, predominantly White, and Black schools', *The Journal of Social Psychology,* 138, 41-53

ETI/DE (Education and Training Inspectorate, Department of Education) (1999), *Report on the Educational Themes: Primary Inspections 1998-99*, Crown Copyright 1999, Bangor: ETI/DE

ETI/DE (Education and Training Inspectorate, Department of Education) (2000), *Report of a Survey of Provision for Education for Mutual Understanding (EMU) in Post-Primary Schools (Inspected: 1999/2000)*, Crown Copyright 2000, Bangor: ETI/DE

Glover and Smith, 1997: cited in Bernard, C.E. (1998), *Racial and Gender Awareness in Preschoolers*, New Orleans, Dept. of Psychology, Loyola University, accessed via the internet: http://clearinghouse.mwsc.edu/manuscripts/383.asp

Hall, E. (1999-2005), *Little Pathways* Programme (various titles), Belfast: Churches' Peace Education Programme

Hamill, M. and Edgar, K. (2007), *Living, Learning, Together – Personal Development and Mutual Understanding*, Belfast: CCEA [a series of packs to support PDMU, from Year 1 to Year 7]

Kenny, M. and McLaughlin, H. (2004), *Diversity in Early Years Education North and South*, Armagh: Centre for Cross-Border Studies

Milner, D. (1983), *Children and Race: 10 years on*, London: Ward Lock Educational

Montgomery, A. and Birthistle, U. (2001), *Primary Values – a literacy based resource to support the Personal Development Programme in the Primary School*, Belfast: CCEA

Naylor, Y. (2006), *Stepping Out – A Resource for Diversity and Inclusion*, Belfast: Irish School of Ecumenics, available for download via the Community Relations Education Northern Ireland [CRENI] website: http://www.creni.org/contents/resources/stepping_out/

NFER (National Foundation for Educational Research) (1999), *The Real Curriculum at the end of Key Stage 2 – N.I. Curriculum Cohort Study*, Slough: NFER (on behalf of the N.I. CCEA)

NIPPA/The Media Initiative for Children (2004): 'Media Initiative Builds Respect' (Press Release: 08/02/04), Belfast: NIPPA – the Early Years Organisation (see also website information on www.mifc-pii.org)

O'Connor, U., Hartop, B. and McCully, A. (2002), *A Review of the Schools Community Relations Programme 2002*, Bangor: Department of Education

OFM/DFM (Office of the First Minister and Deputy First Minister) (2005), *A Shared Future: Policy and Strategic Framework for Good Relations in Northern Ireland*, Belfast: OFM/DFM

PMB/CCEA (Partnership Management Board/ Council for Curriculum, Examinations and Assessment) (2007), *Personal Development and Mutual Understanding for Key Stages 1 and 2*, Belfast: PMB/CCEA

QCA (Qualifications and Curriculum Authority) (2000), *Personal, Social and Health Education and Citizenship at Key Stages 1 and 2: Initial Guidance for Schools*, London: QCA

Richardson, N. (2001), 'What's Right about Education for Mutual Understanding ... and what can we do to make it better?', in N. Richardson, (ed), *Transforming Conflict – the Role of Education*, Belfast: ENCORE (European Network for Conflict Resolution in Education)

Richardson, N. (2002), 'Schools as Bridges: Education for Living with Diversity', unpublished paper given at the Ninth Annual Conference on Education, Spirituality and the Whole Child – Education for Peace, University of Surrey at Roehampton

Richardson, N. (2003a), 'Religious Diversity in Northern Ireland: Questions and Challenges for Educators', paper presented at the Educational Studies Association of Ireland 2003 Annual Conference, Belfast

Richardson, N. (2003b), 'Curricular, Faith and Pastoral Issues for Minority Faith Children in Northern Ireland Schools: The Views of Their Parents', paper presented at the Diversity, World Faiths and Education Conference, Belfast

Richardson, N. (2005), *People Who Need People* (Updated Edition), Belfast: Churches' Peace Education Programme and Stranmillis University College

Richardson, N. (2006), 'Northern Ireland student teachers' choices and motivations in relation to R.E. as a main subject', unpublished paper given at the 2006 AULRE Conference, Belfast

Ruane, B. *et al* (2003), *Lift Off – Introducing Human Rights Education within the Primary Curriculum*, Cross-Border Primary Human Rights Education Initiative (plus recent additional titles: *The Right Start*, for Key Stage 1, and *You, Me, Everyone*, for upper Key Stage 2 – see also: www.liftoffschools.com)

Singh and Yancey (1974), cited in Bernard, C.E. (1998), *Racial and Gender Awareness in Preschoolers*, New Orleans: Dept. of Psychology, Loyola University, accessed via the internet: http://clearinghouse.mwsc.edu/manuscripts/383.asp

Siraj-Blatchford, I. and Clarke, P. (2000), *Supporting Identity, Diversity and Language in the Early Years*, Maidenhead: Open University Press

Smith, A. and Robinson, A. (1996), *Education for Mutual Understanding: The Initial Statutory Years*, Coleraine: University of Ulster Centre for the Study of Conflict

Tyrrell, J. (2002), *Peer Mediation – A Process for Primary Schools*, London: Souvenir Press

8

The influence of school and policy contexts on the implementation of CSPE

Jim Gleeson

This chapter locates the junior cycle Civic, Social and Personal Education (CSPE) programme in its historical, socio-cultural and policy contexts and considers key aspects of the implementation of the programme in the light of three research studies, particularly that conducted by Jarlath Munnelly, currently an elected member of Mayo County Council, in collaboration with the author (Gleeson and Munnelly, 2003). These findings are discussed from the perspectives of school leadership, classroom pedagogy and school culture.

CSPE in historical context

Various researchers have noted that curriculum reform has to be located in context if it is to be properly understood. As Cornbleth (1990:17) points out, when context is ignored, 'curriculum and its construction are ... seen as apolitical or neutral, apart from or above competing values and interests'. As explicated by Hyland (1993), citizenship education has been a sensitive topic since the foundation of the Irish state. While the Church of Ireland favoured its introduction, the Catholic Church did not want to see it become a separate subject on the school curriculum of the new republic because it feared that it would encroach on areas such as moral education and personal development, traditionally dealt with in religious education.

The raising of the school leaving age to fifteen and the introduction of 'free second-level education' coincided with the celebration of the fiftieth anniversary of the Easter Rising in 1966, a time of heightened nationalistic fervour, and Civics was introduced as a compulsory, non-examination, secondary school subject in 1967. It was born into a post-colonial Irish state that was conservative and respectful of authority (particularly ecclesiastical) and where politics remained hugely influenced by the war of independence. Remarking on the blandness of that Civics syllabus, Hyland (1993) acknowledged that 'one must face reality in relation to this more than other areas. Any unduly controversial syllabus would simply have floundered'.

From the beginning the Department of Education's approach to Civics was characterised by ambivalence. The focus of the 1967 syllabus was on training for citizenship and the accumulation of facts about public organisations. The primary aims included the inculcation of values such as civic responsibility, moral virtue, patriotism and adherence to the law, and there was little or no emphasis on teaching methodology. As the author can testify from personal experience, the prevailing practice was to treat Civics and Religious Education as one subject, taught by the same teacher. Indeed Civics was presented in *Rules and Programme for Teachers* (DoE, 1967) in language reminiscent of Kohlberg's conventional level of moral reasoning:

> teaching the young citizen to recognise and obey lawful authority, to help preserve law, order and discipline, to respect private and public right to property and to be ready to defend the national territory should the need arise.

On the other hand the Department of Education Inspector responsible for the *Notes on the Teaching of Civics* had a more enlightened view, one that saw the student not as the object of indoctrination but as an explorer of his or her social environment.

After some initial enthusiasm the new subject faced difficulties as reflected in Ireland's poor performance in the first International Study on Civic Education (Torney *et al*, 1975). The NCCA (1997:1) concluded that 'by the early 1970s it was clear that Civics was a dying subject' for a whole variety of reasons:

- 'one class period a week was not enough time'
- 'less important in comparison to other mandatory subjects'
- 'a lack of trained teachers for this subject'
- 'a lack of teaching and learning resources'
- 'the majority of principals did not take the subject seriously'
- 'examination competitiveness pushed it off the school curriculum'
- 'as no examination or assessment requirements existed for Civics the subject was quietly ignored'.

The establishment of the Interim Curriculum and Examinations Board (CEB) in 1983 was a watershed. Logan and O'Reilly (1985:475) saw the Board's introduction in democratic terms – 'to broaden the social base of decision-making so that the process of selecting knowledge, skill or experience for inclusion on the national curriculum will address the common good'. Drawing on Lawton's (1983) model of eight areas of experience, the Minister for Education, Gemma Hussey, stated her intention in 1984 to introduce 'Social and Political Studies' using an interdisciplinary, modular approach and asked the CEB to set up a syllabus committee. While there was increasing awareness regarding the importance of social and civic responsibility, the old sense of ambivalence resurfaced insofar as the Board in its famous 'wheel' appeared to regard moral education as an offshoot of religious education (CEB, 1984).

Gary Granville, who was Deputy CEO of the CEB during this period, noted in an interview with the author that Hussey's proposal was

> ... the cause of some grief at a political level ... This was a sensitive issue. An early draft of the programme was criticised as being CND [Campaign for Nuclear Disarmament] driven. I'd say the most contentious areas have been predictably enough civic, social, political which has an enormous tangle of ideological and other hang-ups and social, personal and health education ... in the past certain moral, ethical and cultural values were handled by religion and by the family and the schools didn't enter into that domain.

Hyland's (1993) recollections were similar:

> Following the cabinet reshuffle in 1986 there were indications that there might be difficulties in obtaining political approval for a syllabus entitled Social and Political Studies. Some lobbying had taken place by individuals and groups outside the educational area that objected to the introduction of such a subject. Leaflets were prepared and circulated to TDs and cabinet members.

Family Solidarity, a lay organisation established to uphold Catholic family values, took serious exception to the Hussey proposal and circulated a document during the 1987 election campaign, declaring that the CEB was subversive, anti-Catholic and anti-national. This provides a rare example of a curriculum issue being aired at election time in Ireland. The Board responded by including the word 'civic' in the programme title and they approved a draft syllabus for 'Civic and Political Studies' by a narrow majority at their final working meeting in June 1987. The ensuing General Election resulted in a change of government, and citizenship education moved down the list of priorities with the introduction of Junior Certificate taking centre stage. After the publication of the Education Green Paper post-primary curriculum debate was dominated by the proposed introduction of a new subject, 'Technology and Enterprise', with little reference to citizenship education.

Things rested so until the publication by the NCCA in 1993 of a Discussion Paper on Civic, Social and Political Education at Post-Primary level, followed by the introduction of a pilot project in fifty-seven schools in a context where 'in the vast majority of schools a civics programme does not exist and its time allocation has been given to areas such as health education, pastoral care, or to examination subjects in an overcrowded junior cycle curriculum' (NCCA, 1997).

The CSPE syllabus document (DES, 1996:1) presents education for citizenship in terms of active participation, the empowerment of young people and reflective citizenship 'based on human rights and social responsibility'. The inclusion of an Action Project with a 60 per cent credit weighting represented a commendable attempt to 'encourage active and co-operative learning' (ibid:2). However, this new subject was being bolted on to what was already a very overcrowded junior cycle curriculum. The manner of the establishment of CSPE as a mandatory junior cycle examination subject in 1997 locates it in the flawed category of top-down curriculum reform rather than ground-up curriculum change (Goodson, 2001; Gleeson, 2004). Its perceived status was arguably reflected in the recommended time allocation of one class period per week when the norm is between three to five periods per subject.

Implementation of CSPE

So would history repeat itself or has the reality of Irish citizenship education matched the rhetoric? While the current chapter focuses on the Gleeson and Munnelly (2003) study, these findings are considered in conjunction with those of Murphy (2003) and Redmond and Butler (2003).

Munnelly examined the implementation of CSPE in a random sample of twenty-one schools in the Dublin (twelve schools) and Mid-West (nine schools) regions during the school year 2001-2002. All school types were included and student respondents were evenly divided between Transition Year pupils and first year Established Leaving Certificate. Phase 1 of the study focused on the attitudes of participating pupils towards CSPE and their perceptions of the learning outcomes and of the status of the programme.

Taking school type and location into account, five of these schools were identified for follow-up case study involving two schools where students' attitudes to CSPE had been most positive (Green and Yellow), two schools where students' attitudes had been negative (Gold and White) and one where their attitudes were mixed (Blue). The focus of the case studies was on issues arising from Phase 1 of the research such as school organisational factors, the pedagogy of CSPE and the status of the subject in the schools. Structured interviews were conducted with CSPE teachers, coordinators and school principals while participating students engaged in 'group discussion'.

The case study schools are as follows:

- *Green* is a coeducational Community College with approximately 800 pupils, in a working class area of Dublin.
- *Yellow* is a coeducational Community School with approximately 700 pupils, serving a working class area of Dublin. This school participated in the CSPE pilot project from 1993-1996.
- *Blue* is a girls' secondary school under the ownership of a religious order. It is located in a provincial town, has approximately 700 pupils and has a mixture of urban and rural pupils.
- *Gold* is a boys' secondary school under the ownership of a religious order. It has approximately 400 pupils, is located in a provincial town and has a mixture of urban and rural pupils.
- *White* is a boys' secondary school in Dublin under the patronage of a religious order. It is a prestigious, fee-paying school for day pupils and has approximately 800 pupils.

Murphy (2003) conducted case studies in five schools, four privately owned secondary schools (two in disadvantaged areas, two with middle- and upper-middle class students) and one state-owned Community College (School C).

Redmond and Butler (2003) were commissioned by the NCCA to survey school principals and CSPE teachers in order to collect baseline information on the implementation of CSPE in schools. Their study was based on a postal survey to principals and CSPE teachers in a national sample of 300 schools, with 63 per cent of school principals and 33 per cent of CSPE teachers responding.

Student attitudes to CSPE

Responses from 732 senior cycle students (Gleeson and Munnelly, 2003) reflect positively on students' knowledge of civic affairs and on certain aspects of CSPE. For example, almost half of the respondents said they found CSPE enjoyable while more than half of them disagreed with the statement that 'CSPE has not made me more aware of what is happening in the world'. Almost three-quarters of respondents felt that CSPE had made them more aware of how government works, while four-fifths of respondents indicated that they would like to vote and almost three-quarters agreed that we should welcome immigrants to Ireland.

However, students' overall attitudes to CSPE as a school subject were not nearly as positive. Whereas 63 per cent of respondents rated their favourite subjects as being extremely or very enjoyable, only 17 per cent of respondents gave these ratings to CSPE while18 per cent rated it as 'not enjoyable'. When asked about the degree of importance afforded CSPE in their school compared to all the other Junior Certificate subjects, 13 per cent said it was rated as important/very important, 28 per cent responded that it was the same as every other subject, 34 per cent considered it unimportant and 25 per cent thought that CSPE was the least important subject in their school. Some respondents in the latter two categories made particularly critical and pejorative comments.

Students were particularly critical of teaching methodologies and teacher attitudes, e.g. 'this subject was not taught properly in this school, and anyway all you need to do is read the paper and watch the news'; 'CSPE was not taken very seriously by all teachers'. While 81 per cent of pupils indicated they had CSPE every week and 14 per cent had the subject twice weekly, 45 per cent of students reported that approximately once a month the CSPE period was used for another subject.

While Redmond and Butler did not include students in their study, Murphy (2003:173) concluded that 'overall, students both former and current, appear to be quite negative about various aspects of CSPE'. It is regrettable that the ESRI longitudinal study commissioned by the Department does not seem to include CSPE among the list of subjects when seeking student reactions to particular subjects (e.g. Smyth *et al*, 2006:146ff), probably on the grounds that it is not a 'full subject'.

Case study findings

The main findings are summarised in Figure 1 below under the headings of teacher selection, school organisational factors, pedagogy, leadership and teacher/student perceptions of CSPE. While between-school differences were to be expected in view of how the case study schools were selected, the marked differences between the responses from the state schools (Green and Yellow) and secondary schools were particularly striking. As discussed later, similar differences emerged from the work of Murphy (2003) where the most positive attitudes to CSPE were found in the only Community School in the study.

These differences serve to illuminate important aspects of the implementation of CSPE in schools and some of these issues are now discussed, namely leadership (incorporating programme coordination and teacher selection), pedagogy and the perceived status of CSPE.

Figure 1: *Summary of main case study findings*

	Green	Yellow	Blue	Gold	White
A	State owned, co-ed Community College, in disadvantaged working class community in a Dublin suburb.	State owned, co-ed Community School, serving a working-class community in a Dublin suburb.	Privately owned girls Convent school, located in provincial town; mixture of urban/rural students.	Privately owned boys Christian Brothers school located in provincial town; mixture of urban/rural students.	Privately owned, fee-paying boys day school located in Dublin; middle-, upper-middle class students.
B	General teacher willingness to become involved. Some teachers see it as an opportunity to expand on issues that come up in other subjects.	General teacher willingness to become involved. Teaching CSPE not considered onerous, although no one volunteering to teach it.	Form tutors required to teach CSPE. Some teachers involved against their will.	None teaching CSPE by choice. Teachers feel they lack the specialist skills required for CSPE teaching.	Form tutors required to teach CSPE. Teachers not involved by choice; some are doing it against their will.
C	CSPE Coordinator is a post holder. Frequent meetings of CSPE staff. In-service is welcomed.	CSPE coordinator is a post holder. CSPE staff meetings. Positive approach to in-service.	Subject coordinator is a post holder. Meetings of CSPE teachers infrequent. Poor structures for CSPE.	No CSPE coordinator or team meetings. Little uptake of in-service. Poor structures for CSPE.	CSPE Coordinator not a post holder. Annual meeting at the start of the year. Cautious in relation to in-service.
D	Teachers recognise that different teaching approaches are needed and try to implement them.	Teachers recognise that different teaching approaches are needed and they make use of such approaches, e.g. debates	Textbook-based. Teachers feel they lack qualities/skills required for this subject.	Textbook-based. Teachers feel unprepared to adopt new approaches.	More emphasis on RE and school ethos than CSPE.

Figure 1: *Summary of main case study findings (contd.)*

Green	Yellow	Blue	Gold	White
E Principal has a positive attitude towards subject. Sees that it makes a positive impact on the school.	Principal and senior teachers see CSPE as a vital component of the school & local community.	Principal has a positive attitude towards subject but sees all the practical obstacles.	Little evidence of leadership for CSPE.	Principal believes that school ethos and religious studies seen as primary means of catering for character/ personal development.
F Teachers feel that CSPE makes a positive difference to pupils and enables them to explore topics outside of academic subjects. Pupils see it as an enjoyable, useful subject.	Teachers regard CSPE as a positive subject for pupils and an important part of the school. Pupils are interested in the subject and are enthusiastic about it.	Teachers regard CSPE as a burden, although not a difficult subject to teach. Pupils not really interested; consider it as being 'easy' but not academically important.	Although teachers would consider it as necessary they are not interested in teaching CSPE. Pupils have no interest in it and consider it boring and irrelevant.	Teachers feel it does not have parity with academic subjects and regard it as a burden. Pupils see it as unnecessary and feel it taught them nothing they already did not know.

A – School type, gender, etc.   B – Teacher selection   C – Relevant organisational factors   D – Pedagogy of CSPE   E – Leadership and CSPE   F – Teacher and student perceptions of CSPE

School leadership issues

While the principals of the privately owned secondary schools expressed general support for CSPE, they did not give it priority when it came to allocating teachers and posts of responsibility or facilitating teacher participation in related in-service courses. The prevailing view in Schools Blue and White was that religious education and school ethos were sufficient to provide for citizenship education. CSPE teachers in these schools were required to teach the programme because they were Form Tutors, irrespective of their wishes or suitability, and none of the School

Gold teachers interviewed was teaching CSPE by choice. Some critical teacher comments included:

It was a decision made by management, nothing to do with me, (Gold)

I have met a lot of CSPE teachers who would prefer not to be teaching it. They probably feel that they are not adequately trained to teach it. (Gold)

The worst thing about CSPE is having to teach it, because I don't like the subject. (White)

CSPE appeared on my timetable ... I would think that teachers who are interested in it should teach it. I hate it really. (Blue)

Along similar lines, Murphy (2003:207) found that 'the majority of teachers (80 per cent) were conscripted to teach CSPE. The "conscripts" in this study were primarily negative about CSPE. These "conscripts" will do little to raise the status of the subject.'

On the other hand, CSPE teachers in Green and Yellow were generally interested in teaching CSPE and the principals recognised the importance of a strategic approach to teacher selection and timetabling. The existence of an effective programme coordinator was of great significance in these schools as reflected in the fact that both coordinators had posts of responsibility. The Green coordinator encourages teachers to attend relevant in-service and holds team meetings 'two or three times a term, as well as going around to them individually'. One teacher described the situation in Green as follows: 'We take pride with the action project reports; all the teachers meet together, get all the classes together, all the CSPE teachers are there, it's not just something that you take home and throw together.'

The coordinator in Yellow described her role in terms of: 'organising the nine CSPE staff members, looking after resources and information that comes from the Department, holding meetings, organising in-service for teachers... being available to discuss with the teachers issues that they mightn't be clear on with the course or the exam'.

On the other hand the CSPE coordinator in School White 'put teachers' guidelines and the syllabus into a folder and gave it out to all the teachers of CSPE and organised one meeting for all teachers of CSPE at the beginning of the year'. The School Blue coordinator said there were no team meetings in his school because 'it's a busy school' while School Gold did not have a CSPE coordinator.

Redmond and Butler (2003) reported that school principals experienced considerable difficulty in finding staff willing and/or suitably qualified to teach CSPE. Most of their teacher respondents said they were not teaching the subject by choice and the turnover rate of CSPE teachers was very high, with only 41 per cent of respondents having taken the same class group from first to third year. While many of these teachers were very positive about the beneficial effects of CSPE on their students, they depended mainly on informal peer support for their preparation to teach the programme. They identified some of the key organisational difficulties:

> The bulk of the comments made by principals relate to difficulties and frustration in organising or providing for CSPE planning meetings … As one principal explains, this is an endemic problem, not particular to CSPE (ibid: 13).

> A majority of teachers acknowledge that staff are not briefed on the work of CSPE in the school, that planning meetings are not facilitated, that CSPE is not timetabled to avoid poor time slots (ibid: 46).

The appointment of a CSPE coordinator was one of the measures identified by Murphy (2003:212) 'to help with the implementation of CSPE, select interested and enthusiastic CSPE teachers [and] make CSPE visible in the school'. She concluded that School C alone had a collaborative work culture, a key factor in the development of 'moving' (Stoll and Fink, 1996) or 'learning enriched' schools and identified the leadership of the school principal as a critically important factor in the success of CSPE in this school (ibid:215):

> [He] actively encouraged some of his teachers to obtain a professional qualification in CSPE and supported teachers by subsidising their fees. Consequently teachers became 'believers' and this belief manifested itself in the teachers' positive attitudes towards CSPE. In School C a great deal of restructuring and re-culturing has occurred and this has helped with the implementation process. In addition the 'right' teachers are being chosen to teach the subject which means that enthusiastic and interested teachers are implementing CSPE at classroom level. This enthusiasm is rubbing off on students. There is also a commitment to teacher support and development, which enables the teachers to understand the meaning of change. Consequently, the status of CSPE is high in this school.

On the other hand, the approach in Murphy's other schools was to 'let the teacher go it alone', resulting in high levels of teacher uncertainty about CSPE, teacher unwillingness to become involved and unsatisfactory programme implementation.

Pedagogy of CSPE

While Gleeson and Munnelly found a general consensus that one had to be a particular 'type' of teacher with particular skills to teach CSPE, it was teachers in the two state-owned schools (Green and Yellow) who displayed a willingness to experiment with pedagogy and embrace new teaching methodologies. Some typical comments included the following:

> *I saw it as an opportunity as an English teacher to broaden issues and discuss them with students.* (Yellow)

> *It's a huge change in teaching methods and I feel that teachers aren't being adequately trained to teach it … you are introducing a different way of doing things in the classroom. A lot of teachers would hate, say noise in the classroom, but you are going to have it teaching CSPE.* (Green)

> *You have to have more of a discussion [based] approach. It wouldn't work well within the rigours of a traditional classroom situation. Surprisingly, a structured approach to the class is not always best.* (Yellow)

> *It arouses their interest immediately… you can allow the class to turn into a discussion group.* (Yellow)

> *It requires lots of working on projects, and working in groups as opposed to teaching the whole class.* (Yellow)

While some teachers in the other case study schools showed awareness of what good CSPE teaching involved they remained dependent on traditional methodologies. Reliance on the textbook is very strong in Gold, a boys' secondary school. One teacher, who wanted to have 'the syllabus spelt out', felt he was 'not being fair to the youngsters because I am not interested in teaching it and I am ill prepared; [students see it as something] to be endured, like Religion'. A colleague acknowledged that 'it's a positive subject, just that kids aren't used to it. I don't know when they will be'. Some teachers in Schools Blue and White also expressed discomfort with the teaching methods required for CSPE, e.g.

... children should be more involved. I feel unprepared for using role-play, discussion groups ... you have to cover stuff for the exams too and you have to keep moving on. (Gold)

I can teach History, Geography no problem, just walk in to the class, but with CSPE, it's different. Sometimes you are unsure about what you are doing, whether it is relevant material, whether it fits in with the key concepts. (White)

Murphy (ibid:204ff) identified the reluctance of teachers to employ active learning methodologies as one of the obstacles to the implementation of CSPE in four of her case study schools where 'the majority of teachers surveyed indicated that their teaching is guided primarily by the textbook. This suggests that many teachers selected to teach CSPE are conservative'. Again, the Community School was an exception, with teachers passing on their commitment and enthusiasm to their students in contrast with the four secondary schools where teachers' 'lack of enthusiasm [was] passed on to students'. This reflects Lynch's (2000:10) observation that the enthusiasm, interest and engagement that comes from teaching a subject that really interests you 'becomes infectious, and encourages engagement and interest in the students'.

While Redmond and Butler (2003) also found a high level of dependency on the textbook, almost two-thirds of their teacher respondents felt that the action project should be the main focus of the programme. This needs to be seen, however, in the context of Wilson's (2003) finding that students in the same class normally submitted Action Projects on the same topic, which raises questions regarding the extent of the teacher input to the report. With over 25 per cent of all these Action Projects involving activities of a fundraising nature, and with one-off classroom visits from members of relevant agencies such as the legal profession and the police also very popular, Wilson's overall conclusion was that the Action Projects generally focused on 'safe' rather than controversial topics.

Perceived status of CSPE in schools

Principals in Schools Yellow and Green saw CSPE as an integral part of the school and felt that it made an important contribution to the personal development of students. This was particularly evident in School Yellow where the principal remarked: 'Students might say about some subjects, "that's just a free class". But they would never say that about CSPE ... A lot of them do get lots out of it. The status of CSPE is a lot better here than in most schools'. School Green teachers were also generally enthusiastic: 'I like teaching it. In this school we are very lucky because we have very good teachers teaching it … It has to take centre stage. We show that the subject is valued. You have to show the students that it is valued.'

However, there was considerable apathy in relation to the subject in other schools, with principals and staff less likely to devote resources to CSPE. For example, while the subject coordinator at School Blue felt that the status of CSPE had improved since it became an examination subject, others were less positive with one teacher remarking that 'it's way down the list. Actually this came up at a recent staff meeting, that CSPE isn't much of a subject.'

Religious education and school ethos were seen as the primary instruments in character formation in School White. While the coordinator seemed apologetic that 'CSPE looks like a bit of a joke', adding that 'there is more to the programme than meets the eye, negotiating on its behalf is the hardest thing', his colleagues' comments were not encouraging: 'I don't think its status is particularly high.' 'Very low. In general I wouldn't say it's thought much of, it's not up there with Maths and English as far as the pupils are concerned'.

When School Gold teachers were asked about the status of CSPE their responses were very negative: 'Not taken seriously'; 'Zero. It has the same status as religion'; 'I would say nil.' School Gold teachers were unanimous that the pupils are not interested in CSPE, e.g.

> *A lot of them wouldn't take it seriously; they see it as a 'doss'. To get the kids motivated is a big bogey. The second year class that I had this morning were very laid back about it … it's a weak class, and you're not going to get them interested in current affairs, reading the newspaper, even looking at the headlines.*

Based on the focus group discussions with students, it appears that students' perceptions of the value of CSPE were clearly related to their teachers' attitudes. Where teacher cynicism was at its most vociferous, this infected the pupils' views of CSPE. It also appears that teachers' perceptions of CSPE are influenced by the actions and attitudes of school management in relation to CSPE.

Murphy (2003:213) found that, with the exception of School C, the status of CSPE was low amongst both students and teachers in all her case study schools and she associated this with 'a lack of democracy manifested in the non-existence of truly active Students Councils. … In [three cases] the Student Councils in place appeared to be tokens'.

Redmond and Butler (2003:47) concluded that 'from the comments of many teachers it is apparent that CSPE may not have the status of other Junior Certificate subjects in school'. They report that some school principals saw the programme as a timetable 'filler' and found that the development of CSPE as a shorter course than all other subjects also diminishes its status. This low status affects the allocation of teachers to the subject and militates against the realisation of the subject's potential.

Some key emerging issues
Some of the main findings are now discussed from the perspectives of school leadership and type on the one hand and socio-cultural influences and policy developments on the other hand.

School leadership
The Report of the National Education Convention noted that instructional leadership 'is the most neglected aspect of the principal's work in the school … Pressure of time, with the urgent taking precedence over the important, and insufficient back-up support services, were cited as the main reasons for this neglect' (Coolahan (ed.), 1994:43). The findings of the three studies considered in this chapter reflect the plentiful inter-national research literature regarding the relationship between school leadership and curriculum change (Sergiovanni, 1996; Fullan, 1991; Hargreaves, 2003; Callan, 2006). At a local level they mirror the findings of Leader and Boldt (1994) regarding principals in Irish voluntary secondary schools where only 2 per cent of the respondents reported that they spent most time on curriculum development and planning and principals saw themselves as 'so involved with the immediate that they cannot fulfil their leadership and planning roles adequately … they involve themselves directly with low value tasks [many of which] are maintenance and janitorial in character' (ibid:95).

The particular leadership issues in the secondary sector should be understood in their historical context. This sector's independence comes at a price insofar as it is not as well resourced as the state sector (Sheehan *et al*, 1994) while that sector's traditional policy of promotion on the basis of seniority arguably militates against teacher empowerment and initiative.

School leadership plays a vital role in determining school culture and Kincheloe (1999:73) identifies the importance of democratic values and practices for education for democracy in terms of: '(1) teaching in a democratic workplace – teacher self-direction/empowerment; (2) the creation of democratic classrooms – developing student input into the nature of their own education; and (3) teaching for democratic citizenship – building a democratic society.'

This ideal scenario is in sharp contrast with the hierarchical nature of Irish post-primary schools. For example, the OECD (1991:55ff) commented critically on the 'formal, authority-based relationships between teacher and taught', adding that 'students as they mature should be shouldering more responsibility for their own learning and at every stage should be encouraged to display more initiative and independence of mind'. Lynch and Lodge (1999:224) found that 'the exercise of power and authority in school was the greatest single equality concern expressed by students in essays. A strong sense of social distance between teachers existed in certain schools.'

The senior cycle review instrument did not include questions about school culture in its original survey document. However, its subsequent proposals were predicated on the establishment of a different school culture that would afford students far more responsibility for their own lives. This resulted from the groundswell of opinion regarding the mismatch between school and youth cultures where participants 'often described schools as currently "keeping a lid on tensions" ascribed to the pace of social and economic change in the lives of students' (NCCA, 2004:24).

Significance of school type

Gleeson *et al* (2002) found that contextual variables such as school and teacher culture and school leadership play significant roles in the implementation of the Leaving Certificate Applied. The findings discussed in this chapter again highlight the importance of relating curriculum reform to school context and the need for greater attention to between-school differences at the implementation stage. Indeed the CSPE syllabus document (DES, 1996:3) recognises that:

> ... the ethos, organisation, extra-curricular activities and operational structures of schools also have a significant impact on the pupils' understanding of the civic, social and political dimensions of their lives. Through its 'hidden curriculum', a school provides aspects of CSPE even where this is not explicit.

It emerges from the Gleeson and Munnelly (2003) and Murphy (2003) studies that teachers and principals in the state-owned schools embraced CSPE more enthusiastically than their counterparts in privately owned schools. While the Redmond and Butler (2003) data do not lend themselves to analysis by school type, similar trends emerge in Geary and Mannix-McNamara's study in relation to SPHE (undated:36):

… comprehensive and community schools scored highest as the school type implementing SPHE and this decreases as the schools move into the voluntary secondary sector, mixed secondary schools scoring second lowest, and boys' secondary schools weakest of all with 57 per cent of them implementing SPHE.

The ambivalence towards citizenship education within the private school sector is consistent with the Catholic Church's historical antipathy to the subject. While the state increasingly dictates the ethos of schooling (Fuller, 2002), the residual influence of the Catholic Church on Irish secondary schools helps explain the emerging differences between the public and private sectors in relation to new curricular areas such as CSPE and SPHE.

Being generally less than thirty years old, it seems that Community Schools and Colleges have escaped the earlier apathy in relation to citizenship education along with the associated belief that religious education is the sole curricular vehicle for social, moral and personal development. Many of these newer schools have also developed stronger relations with their local communities than schools in the private secondary sector.

However, schools do not exist in a vacuum and are heavily influenced by their socio-cultural and policy environments.

Influence of broader socio-cultural environment

The influence of key contextual factors on Irish curriculum policy and practice is significant (Gleeson, 2004), and CSPE is no exception. Some of the relevant contextual factors include the conservative and consensualist nature of Irish politics (Bew *et al*, 1989); the subject-based Classical Humanist curriculum; the prevailing anti-intellectual bias; the prevalence of the rhetoric-reality dichotomy; the dominance of the technical rather than critical interest, reflected in the prevailing instrumentalist approach to schooling and the dominance of the economic imperative.

Within the confines of this chapter it is only possible to develop some of the more relevant themes from the above list, namely the rhetoric/reality dichotomy; the anti-intellectual bias; the emphasis on human rather than social capital and the prevalence of instrumentalism. The evidence presented earlier suggests that the impressive rhetoric of CSPE plays out very differently in different situations. This reflects what Lee (1989) calls the peculiarly Irish phenomenon of the 'say/do dichotomy' and his view that traditional Ireland is characterised 'by a capacity for self-deception on a heroic scale' (ibid:652). Lynch (1985:13) identifies 'the contradiction in Ireland between the rhetoric that we profess and the realities of our institutions. If you take Catholic teaching and the formal articulation of its policy, you find an emphasis on the education of the whole person. Yet the reality of that is very different'.

While the rhetoric of the CSPE syllabus document speaks the critical language of empowerment, the prevailing anti-intellectual bias provides ideal conditions for the technical paradigm to thrive (Dunne, 1995). This is reflected in the description by Baker *et al* (2004:156) of CSPE as 'relatively light-weight ... the closest the CSPE programme gets to the subject of class is through the analysis of poverty, which is by no means focused on either the causes or outcomes of social class inequalities and is in any case entirely optional' and in Garvin's (2004:7) remark that 'even in 2003, the Republic of Ireland has only a rather underdeveloped civic and political education programme for schools, unlike most advanced democracies'. On the positive side, the NCCA (2005:28) commitment to the introduction of a new senior cycle subject called Social and Political Studies appears to be on track.

The dominance of the Classical Humanist ideology has resulted in a strong emphasis on the transmission of subject knowledge and book-based learning (e.g. OECD, 1991; Callan, 1994) at the expense of cross-curricular outcomes such as active citizenship. This trend is reflected in a study by the National Economic and Social Forum (NESF, 2003:26) where the contribution expected of the formal education system to the development of social capital is minimal. The Forum looked instead to the service/community based learning aspects of the Leaving Certificate Applied, Transition Year and CSPE as well as out of school activities such as Comhairle na nÓg and Home-School-Community Liaison.

Irish post-primary education is characterised by instrumentalism (Hannan and Boyle, 1987; Lynch, 1989; Clancy, 1995) as reflected in the report of the Points Commission (Government of Ireland, 1998). There is an increasing emphasis on preparing young people for the labour market in a context where economic growth and development is the dominant political concern (O'Sullivan, 1992). One of the five goals of recent Department of Education and Science Strategy Statements (DES, 2002; DES, undated) has been to 'contribute to Ireland's economic prosperity, development and international competitiveness' in the context of the Lisbon Agenda, namely 'that Europe should become the most competitive and dynamic knowledge-based economy in the world, capable of sustaining economic growth with more and better jobs and greater social cohesion'.

The result is that 'knowledge is now construed as a commodity, education as a business, students and their parents as customers, and teachers as mere functionaries who must satisfy the demands of their managers and clients' (Dunne, 2002). Within this environment, school managers are experiencing a real tension 'because the school, as an agent of the State's educational provision, is required to legitimate and reinforce an excessively competitive and individualistic ethos' (Fuller, 2002:259). This makes it difficult for schools to promote empowerment, critical questioning of power relations (Lynch and Lodge, 2002) and education for important aspects of adult and working life such as CSPE and SPHE including the Relationships and Sexuality Programme (Hannan and Shortall, 1991; Smyth, 1999; Morgan, 2002).

Broader policy context

Ireland's membership of the EU is becoming increasingly significant for education policy and practice. The report of the EU Commission Study Group set up to consider future developments in European citizenship was called *Accomplishing Europe Through Education and Training*. This reveals a reconstructionist project with a clear political agenda. A more recent White Paper, *A New Emphasis for European Youth* (European Commission, 2002), promoted the key messages of active citizenship, developing autonomy among young people and recognition of the EU as a champion of values.

High-level goal 1 of recent DES Strategy Statements (DES, 2002; DES, undated) is to 'deliver an education that is relevant to individuals' personal, social, cultural and economic needs'. While this goal provides obvious scope for the treatment of citizenship education, there is no reference to citizenship in any of the objectives, related strategies, outputs or performance indicators of these statements. In fact the only reference to citizenship education occurs in an introduction: 'Quality learning outcomes are vital for the achievement of active citizenship, employment and social inclusion' (DES, undated:8). These strategy statements reflect the adoption of a contractual model of accountability at the expense of individual and institutional learning outcomes (Gleeson and Ó Donnabháin, 2006). This model will not serve to promote citizenship as envisaged by the authors of the CSPE syllabus document.

Alternative approaches to accountability must be pursued if the affective and democratic aspects of education are to be given the attention they deserve. Valuable signposts along the way include the Social Progress Index (SPI) developed for CORI (Clark and Kavanagh, 1996:77) now incorporated into *Measuring Ireland's Progress* and The Definition and Selection of Competencies (DeSeCo) Project (Rychen and Salganik, eds, 2003). While the SPI focused on social problems, a similar index might be developed focusing on active citizenship matters in the context of the Report of the Taskforce on Active Citizenship. The DeSeCo project identified key competences for an individually successful life, sustainable socio-economic and democratic development of society including interacting in socially heterogeneous groups and acting autonomously.

From a curriculum perspective, the importance attached by the NCCA (2004) to giving students more responsibility for managing their school experience has been noticeably watered down in the most recent set of proposals where the more traditional aspects of curriculum such as programmes of study, curriculum components, key skills and assessment and certification are prioritised (NCCA, 2005).

Conclusion

As Goodson (2001) points out, the sustainability of curriculum reform and change efforts can only be understood by reference to the conditions of change. This is particularly true of a developing area such as citizenship, which must be rooted in community life and civil society and where the schools themselves play such a key role. The significance of context has emerged very clearly in this chapter – historical background to the programme, the school contextual factors that impact on the implementation of the programme in schools, the influence of socio-cultural factors and policy developments at the macro level. Regrettably, many of the reasons identified by the NCCA (1997) for the weakness of Civics (see page 75 above) remain valid today, lending greater urgency to the concerns expressed by Dunne (2002: 86):

those of us concerned with such an education in Ireland – and that must be all of us concerned about the state of citizenship too – can be under no illusion about the scale of the challenge we now face.

References

Baker, J., Lynch, K., Cantillon, S., Walsh, J. (2004), *Equality From Theory to Action*, New York: Palgrave Macmillan

Bew, P., Hazelkorn, E. and Patterson, H. (1989), *The Dynamics of Irish Politics*, London: Lawrence and Wishart

Callan, J. (1994), *Schools for Active Learning. Final Report*, Maynooth: Education Department

Callan, J. (2006), *Developing Schools, Enriching Learning. The SCD experience*, Maynooth: Department of Education

CEB (Curriculum and Examinations Board), (1984). *Issues and Structures*, Dublin: CEB

Clancy, P. (1995), 'Education in the Republic of Ireland: the Project of Modernity?', in P. Clancy, S. Drudy, K. Lynch and L. O'Dowd (eds), *Irish Society: Sociological Perspectives*, Dublin: IPA

Clark, C.M.A. and Kavanagh, C. (1996), 'Progress, Values and Economic Indicators', in B. Reynolds and C. Healy (eds), *Progress, Values and Public Policy*, Dublin: Justice Commission, CORI

Coolahan, J. (ed) (1994), *Report on the National Education Convention*, Dublin: National Education Convention Secretariat

Cornbleth, C. (1990), *Curriculum in Context*, London: Falmer

DoE (Department of Education) (1967), *Rules and Programmes for Secondary Schools*, Dublin: Stationery Office

DES (Department of Education and Science) (2002), *Strategy Statement: 2003-2005*, Dublin: Stationery Office

DES (Department of Education and Science) (undated), *Strategy Statement: 2005-2007*, Dublin: DES

Dunne J. (1995), 'What's the Good of Education?', in P. Hogan (ed), *Partnership and the Benefits of Learning*, Dublin: ESRI

Dunne, J. (2002), 'Citizenship and Education: A Crisis of the Republic?', in P. Kirby, L. Gibbons and M. Cronin (eds), *Reinventing Ireland: Culture, Society and the Global Economy*, London: Pluto

European Commission (2002), *A New Impetus for European Youth: White Paper*, Luxembourg: Office for Official Publications of the European Communities

Fullan, M. (1991), *The New Meaning of Educational Change*, London: Cassell

Fuller, L. (2002), *Irish Catholicism since 1950: the Undoing of a Culture*, Dublin: Gill and Macmillan

Garvin, T. (2004), *Preventing the Future. Why was Ireland so poor for so long?* Dublin: Gill and Macmillan

Geary, T. and Mannix-McNamara, P. (undated), *Implementation of Social, Personal and Health Education at Junior Cycle*, available at SPHE website

Gleeson, J., Clifford, A., Collison, T., O'Driscoll, S., Rooney, M. and Tuohy, A. (2002), 'School Culture and Curriculum Change: The case of the Leaving Certificate Applied (LCA)', *Irish Educational Studies*, Vol.21, No.3, 21-44

Gleeson, J. and Munnelly, J. (2003), 'Developments in citizen education in Ireland: context, rhetoric, reality', paper presented at the International Civic Education Conference, New Orleans

Gleeson, J. (2004), 'Cultural and Political Contexts of Irish Post-Primary Curriculum: Influences, Interests and Issues', in C. Sugrue (ed), *Curriculum and Ideology*, Dublin: Liffey Press, pp101-140

Gleeson, J. and Ó Donnabháin, D. (2006), 'Accountability in Irish education: Strategy Statements and the adoption and use of performance indicators', unpublished paper read at AERA Annual Conference, San Francisco

Goodson, I. (2001), 'Social Histories of Educational Change', *The Journal of Educational Change*, Vol.2, No.1, 45-63

Government of Ireland (1998), *Commission on the Points System: Consultative Process – Background Document*, Dublin: Stationery Office

Hannan, D. and Shortall, S. (1991), *The Quality of Their Education, School Leavers' Views of Educational Objectives and Outcomes*. Dublin: ESRI

Hannan, D. and Boyle, M. (1987), 'Schooling Decisions: the Origins and Consequences of Selection and Streaming in Irish Post-Primary Schools', *ESRI Paper No.136*

Hargreaves, A. (2003), *Teaching in the Knowledge Society*, Maidenhead: Open University Press

Hyland, Á. (1993), 'Address to the first meeting of the teachers involved in the Pilot Scheme for the Introduction of Civic, Social and Political Education at Junior Cycle level', unpublished paper presented to DES/NCCA In-service course participants, Dublin Castle

Kincheloe, J. (1999), 'Critical Democracy and Education', in J.G. Henderson and K.R. Kesson (eds), *Understanding Democratic Curriculum Leadership*, New York: Teachers College Press

Lawton, D. (1983), *Curriculum Studies and Educational Planning*, London: Hodder and Stoughton

Leader, D. and Boldt, S. (1994), *Principals and Principalship. A Study of Principals in Voluntary Secondary Schools*, Dublin: Marino Institute of Education

Lee, J.J. (1989), *Ireland 1912-1985: Politics and Society*, Cambridge University Press

Logan, J. and O'Reilly, B. (1985) 'Educational Decision Making: the case of the Curriculum and Examinations Board', *Administration*, Vol.33, No.4, Dublin: IPA

Lynch, K. (1985), 'Ideology, Interests and Irish Education', *The Crane Bag*, Vol.9, No.2

Lynch, K. and Lodge, A. (1999), 'Essays on School', in K. Lynch, *Equality in Education*, Dublin: Gill and Macmillan

Lynch, K. and Lodge A. (2002), *Equality and Power in Schools: Redistribution, Recognition and Representation*, London: Routledge Falmer

Lynch, K. (1989), *The Hidden Curriculum: Reproduction in Education, An Appraisal*, London: Falmer

Lynch, K. (2000), 'Education for Citizenship: The Need for Major Intervention in Social and Political Education in Ireland', paper presented to the CSPE conference, Bunratty, Co. Clare, 29 September 2000

Morgan, M. (2002), *Evaluation of Relationships Programme*, Dublin: Stationery Office

Murphy, D.A. (2003), 'Civics Revisited? An Exploration of the Factors Affecting the Implementation of CSPE in Five Post-Primary Schools', unpublished dissertation submitted to the Education Department, National University of Ireland, Maynooth, in part fulfilment of the requirements for the Master of Education Degree

NCCA (National Council for Curriculum and Assessment) (1997), *The Development and Work of the CSPE Pilot Project 1993-1996*, Dublin: NCCA

NCCA (National Council for Curriculum and Assessment) (2004), *Proposals for the Future of Senior Cycle Education in Ireland*, Dublin: NCCA

NCCA (National Council for Curriculum and Assessment) (2005), *Proposals for the Future Development of Senior Cycle Education in Ireland*, Dublin: NCCA

NESF (National Economic and Social Forum) (2003), *The Policy Implications of Social Capital*, Dublin: NESF

O'Sullivan, D. (1992), 'Cultural Strangers and educational change: The OECD Report Investment in Education and Irish Educational Policy', *Journal of Education Policy*, 1992, Vol.7, No.5, 445-469

OECD (1991) *Reviews of National Policies for Education, Ireland*, Paris: OECD

Redmond, D. and Butler, P. (2003), 'Civic, Social and Political Education. Report on a Survey of Principals and Teachers', unpublished report submitted to the NCCA by NEXUS

Rychen, D.S. and Salganik, L.H. (2003), *Key Competencies for a successful life and a well-functioning society*, Gottingen: Hogrefe & Huber

Sergiovanni, T. (1996), *Leadership for the Schoolhouse*, San Francisco: Jossey-Bass

Sheehan, J., Durkan, J. and Thom, D.R. (1994*), Survey of School Unit Costs. Primary and Post-Primary Schools*, Dublin: Department of Education

Smyth, E. (1999), *Do Schools Differ?*, Dublin: Oak Tree Press

Smyth, E., Dunne, A., McCoy, S. and Darmody, M. (2006), *Pathways through the Junior Cycle*, Dublin: Liffey Press

Stoll, L. and Fink, D. (1996), *Changing our Schools*, Buckingham: Open Books

Torney, J., Oppenheim, A.N. and Farnen, R. (1975*), Civic Education in Ten Countries: An Empirical Study*: New York: Halstead Press of John Wiley

Wilson, M. (2003), 'A study of the CSPE Action Projects: 2001-2003', unpublished paper read at Conference of CSPE Network, Curriculum Development Unit, Dublin, November

9

Civics revisited? An exploration of the factors affecting the implementation of Civic, Social and Political Education (CSPE) in five post-primary schools

Deirdre A. Murphy

Since the 1991 OECD review of educational policy in Ireland, Irish education has developed exponentially. The 1990s, in particular, saw a clearer articulation of educational policy than in previous years and this led to proposals for educational change. These proposals found expression in the *Green Paper* (DoE, 1992), the National Education Convention in 1993 and its report in 1994 and the *White Paper* (DoE, 1995). The 1990s therefore marked a decade when 'ideas were on the move' (Coolahan, 1994:236). Proposals for educational change, at post-primary level, called for structural, curricular and pedagogic reform. In addition, subject syllabi were revised and new subjects were introduced at Junior Certificate level. Within these developments came the introduction of Civic, Social and Political Education (CSPE), a course which prepares students for active and participatory citizenship, and its introduction mirrored a renewed interest in civic education internationally. Introduced into the Junior Certificate curriculum on a mandatory basis, CSPE was to replace the old Civics course that was introduced into Irish post-primary schools in 1966. Unlike its predecessor, CSPE is formally assessed.

However, there is a growing awareness in the educational arena that reform efforts tend to fail more than they succeed (Eisner, 1998; Fullan, 1992, 2001; Sarason, 1990, 1996). Fullan (1992) articulated that educational change fails because of the complexity of implementing change, that is, putting theory into practice. CSPE, therefore, presents many challenges to the teacher, a key agent of change, who must deliver this relatively new innovation at classroom level. Effecting curricular change at classroom level can require a change in behaviour and a change in beliefs on the part of the teacher. Real change, Fullan argues, 'involves changes in conceptions and role behaviour, which is why it is so difficult to achieve' (Fullan, 2001:40).

The delivery of CSPE in schools therefore has behavioural and ideological implications. Behavioural change requires teachers to acquire new skills, partake in new activities or adopt new pedagogies and practices. This is true of CPSE, an innovation that requires teachers to introduce active learning methodologies into their teaching, methodologies that can signal a new departure for many teachers, particularly those who rely on the traditional methods of teaching and learning.

Implementing CSPE therefore requires teachers to abandon existing routines, norms and practices, all of which have provided their professional lives with certainty, security and stability. Curricular change threatens this stability and can fuel resistance on the part of the teacher. CSPE also requires a change in how teachers think about the subject. Effecting a change in teachers' beliefs is by far a more challenging undertaking. Hamilton (1975:179), found that 'a complex web of beliefs and ideologies about the nature of education' pervades school systems. Many of these beliefs are so institutionally rooted that any attempts at change come up against fierce resistance from those who operate within the school system.

This chapter presents research conducted in 2003 into the factors affecting the implementation of CSPE in five Irish post-primary schools (Murphy, 2003). The next two sections give a brief overview of the aims of, and the methodology employed in, this research.

Aims of the study

The main aims of this study were as follows:

- To identify and explicate any factors that may hinder the successful implementation of CSPE in schools
- To construct a social profile of CSPE teachers and to ascertain if some profiles are more successful than others *vis-à-vis* the delivery of CSPE in the classroom
- To record and explore teacher and student attitudes and views towards CSPE and to ascertain if these have a bearing on the implementation process.

Methodology

Bearing in mind the exploratory nature of this research and deciding what exactly the researcher wanted to find out, it was decided that the employment of both quantitative and qualitative research methods would ensure a thorough exploration of the factors affecting the implementation of CSPE. Access was negotiated into five schools in the Dublin region.

- *School A* An all-boys' voluntary secondary school in Dublin's inner city
- *School B* An all-girls' voluntary secondary school in West Dublin
- *School C* A mixed community college in West Dublin
- *School D* An all-boys' secondary school in South Dublin
- *School E* An all-boys' fee-paying school in South Dublin.

Three research instruments were employed to elicit information central to this study. Firstly, a questionnaire was distributed to five teachers in each of the research sites. The purpose of the questionnaire was to construct a CSPE teacher profile in each of the five schools and to get an overall 'feel' of where CSPE was 'at' in each of the respective schools. Secondly, a series of one-to-one semi-structured interviews with CSPE teachers in each of the research sites was conducted. Interview questions were partly formulated on the basis of the information obtained from the completed questionnaires. It was decided that three teachers from each of the research sites would be interviewed in order to give a reasonable representation of the overall CSPE teacher population in each of the schools. Thirdly, a series of focus group interviews was carried out with both current and former CSPE students in each of the schools. It was felt that the inclusion of both current and former CSPE students in the study would give the researcher a greater insight into the development of CSPE in each of the schools. In addition, the attitudes of both current and former students of CSPE could be compared.

The researcher feels that the main weakness of this study lies in the selection of schools. She feels that a greater cross-section of schools may have provided more quantitative indicators of factors affecting the implementation of CSPE. Despite this apparent weakness, however, the researcher was happy that the methodologies employed yielded valuable and crucial insights into the implementation of CSPE in schools from the perspectives of both teachers and pupils.

Research findings
This section presents the findings obtained from the three research instruments employed in this study.

CSPE teacher questionnaires
Questionnaires were employed in this study in order to collect data from which a profile of CSPE teachers could be formulated. They also enquired into the predominant teaching methodologies employed by teachers and the level of priority given to CSPE, as perceived by the teacher. The questionnaire sought to elicit opinions and attitudes *vis-à-vis* the status of CSPE as perceived by the teachers themselves, and their perception of

CSPE with regard to management and the students in their school. The accumulated findings are presented with the occasional reference to individual schools.

The research found that only 20 per cent of all teachers surveyed had volunteered to teach CSPE. Out of all schools surveyed, only School C had a majority of teachers who volunteered to teach CSPE. In addition, the majority of teachers had not been consulted about the fact that they would be teaching CSPE. This suggests that the majority of CSPE teachers are 'conscripted' to teach CSPE.

Most subject teachers are formally qualified to teach their subject. This is not the case with regard to CSPE. Only 24 per cent of those surveyed had a formal qualification in CSPE. Schools A, D and E have a cohort of teachers who have no formal CSPE qualification. This contrasts with School B which has 40 per cent of teachers qualified to teach CSPE and an overwhelming 80 per cent in School C. Overall, the fact that the majority of teachers have no qualification reinforces the concept that 'anybody' can teach CSPE.

However, opportunities for the professional development of CSPE teachers are provided by the CSPE Support Service, who facilitate a broad range of in-service activities for new and existing teachers of CSPE. Despite this, only 52 per cent of respondents had attended at least one CSPE in-service. This may suggest that teachers are not released from their teaching duties to attend the various in-services.

The questionnaire also enquired into the level of continuity with regard to the selection of CSPE teachers from year to year. The research found that, overall, low levels of continuity abounded. The majority of respondents had been teaching CSPE for only one year. A mere 4 per cent had been teaching CSPE since it was introduced into post-primary schools in 1996. These findings suggest that the majority of teachers do not have scope to develop or get to know the subject.

CSPE has a strong cross-curricular dimension in-built into the subject. To realise this inter-disciplinary dimension, it is necessary that the teacher teaches another subject to his/her CSPE class. However, only 20 per cent of respondents in Schools A, B and E and 40 per cent in School D teach another subject to their CSPE class, compared to 80 per cent in School C. This suggests that timetabling arrangements in School C take cognisance of the importance of forging links between CSPE and other subjects. The findings also reflect the fact that CSPE is not being accommodated or is not prioritised on school timetables.

Teachers were asked about the teaching methodologies they employ in the teaching of CSPE. The majority of respondents, 64 per cent, preferred using the textbook in their teaching of CSPE, despite the fact that 76 per cent felt that their students enjoyed active learning methods. These findings highlighted the disparity between what teachers 'do' and what students 'want'. School C had the highest proportion of teachers, 100 per cent, who liked using active learning techniques in their teaching of CSPE.

Teachers were asked if active learning was encouraged in their school. Overall, only 44 per cent of respondents responded positively. The majority of respondents in Schools A, D and E felt that active learning was not encouraged in their schools. In comparison, 60 per cent of teachers in School B and an overwhelming 100 per cent of respondents in School C felt that active learning was encouraged in their school. Findings suggest that most teachers tend to use the textbook a lot because they feel that active learning is not encouraged in their school.

Finally, teachers were asked to indicate if they felt that CSPE had a high status in their school. Only 32 per cent felt that the status of CSPE was high amongst school managers, just 26 per cent felt that the status of CSPE was high amongst other teachers and a mere 24 per cent felt that students conferred a high status on CSPE. Overall, CSPE was deemed to be a low status subject. Only respondents in School C felt that the status of CSPE was high in their school, with the majority of respondents agreeing that the status of CSPE was high amongst school management, other teachers and students.

CSPE teacher interviews

The interview method enabled the researcher to gain insights into the opinions, attitudes, perceptions and feelings of CSPE teachers on a number of issues pertinent to CSPE. This research instrument also enabled the researcher to put 'flesh on the bones of questionnaire responses' (Bell, 1993). A semi-structured mode of interview was employed and enabled the interviewer to probe when necessary. This section presents interview findings.

The questionnaire revealed that for the majority of teachers CSPE 'appeared' on their timetables. Teachers were asked how they felt about that.

> *Well I can't say I was over the moon about it … it's just typical of this school!* (Teacher, School A)

> *I wasn't happy at all … I felt a bit lost really.* (Teacher, School B)

> *The thing that bugged me most is that I was selected to teach CSPE, though I knew nothing whatsoever about the subject. I thought it was religion or something!* (Teacher, School D)

As the comments suggest, many teachers felt aggrieved that they had received no consultation about their teaching of CSPE. The comments of teachers also reveal that teachers felt very uncertain about the subject and some had little interest in the subject. The interviewer questioned the volunteers and those who had prior consultation from management about their teaching of CSPE.

> *I was more than happy to teach it. I'm big into that subject and the CSPE qualification gave me the confidence to teach it.* (Volunteer, School C)

> *I didn't mind being asked. I have a strong interest in politics … the principal knew this so I guess that's why he asked me.* (Consulted, School C)

The volunteers and consulted in School C seem to be more content and happy about their teaching of CSPE than their counterparts in the other four schools. A picture also emerges about the principal in School C who obviously put some thought into the selection of CSPE teachers and seems to be 'in tune' with his teachers.

Teachers were then asked to comment on the level of support, advice and assistance they received prior to their teaching of CSPE. With the exception of School C, the majority of teachers interviewed indicated they had received low levels of support prior to their teaching of CSPE.

> *No, I wasn't given any … sure I don't even know who's running the show here!* (Teacher, School D)

> *Support? In this school! You must be joking! You're told what to teach here, no bones about it!* (Teacher, School A)

> *I mean it's just typical of this school. The subject isn't really important but we still have to teach it, but how can we teach it if you know nothing about it? Teachers aren't exactly tripping over themselves to help you in this school.* (Teacher, School E)

A majority of teachers in Schools A, B, D and E indicated that they had received low levels of support prior to their teaching of CSPE. This would suggest the absence of a collaborative work culture in the school and a low level of collegiality amongst CSPE teachers. In contrast, teachers in School C indicated that they had received a lot of support. There was also evidence of a 'CSPE Team' whereby help and support was offered to teachers new to the subject.

I received a lot of support from my colleagues. We have a co-ordinator here who did a course in CSPE. She gave me a lot of materials like the syllabus, teachers' notes, videos and books when I first got started. She was really helpful. (Teacher, School C)

Teachers, in the course of the interview, were asked how important CSPE was in relation to other subjects on the curriculum. All the teachers in Schools A, B, D and E felt that it was not as important as other subjects on the curriculum. Most teachers felt this was due to its absence on the Leaving Certificate curriculum.

No, I wouldn't say it's as important. I don't think it's done to Leaving Cert. If you could get points for it, people would place more importance on it. In this school everything is points, points, points! (Teacher, School D)

Teachers in School C, however, felt that CSPE is as important as other subjects on the Junior Certificate curriculum.

The next series of questions asked respondents to discuss the type of teaching methodologies they employed in their teaching of CSPE. All the teachers in Schools A, D and E indicated that they tend to employ traditional methods of teaching CSPE. Many teachers felt that because CSPE is timetabled for just one period a week, this does not give them enough time to undertake active learning methodologies. In addition, some teachers suggested that the culture of the school often militates against them employing active learning methodologies.

In this school we're over-geared to discipline ... I use the book mainly but sometimes use discussion and debate although they can be a bit noisy. I think we expect a certain level of silence in this school. (Teacher, School A)

Teachers in School C and to a lesser extent, School B, commented that they employ active learning techniques in their teaching of CSPE.

Teachers were next asked to describe, in their own words, their attitudes and feelings about CSPE. Teachers, particularly in Schools A, D and E were quite negative about the subject.

A convenient timetable filler for management. (Teacher, School A)

I don't know what to think of it. It's ... it's like religion, I suppose. It's not taken seriously. It's religion without being 'Holy Mary'. (Teacher, School D)

I can't see many differences between CSPE and the old Civics ... well maybe it's examined ... but it's still a waste of time as far as I can see. (Teacher, School E)

On the whole, teachers in School B were slightly more positive. However, the most positive comments about CSPE and the healthiest dispositions toward the subject were evident in School C.

I feel really positive about this subject. It's one where the kids can do really well. The action projects are fantastic, you know; they give kids a certain degree of responsibility. They like that! (Teacher, School C)

The next series of interview questions asked the teachers to give their opinion and feelings on the mode of assessment utilised in CSPE. Teachers in Schools A, D and E and a minority of teachers in School B expressed their dissatisfaction with the assessment of CSPE, for various reasons.

No, I think there's something wrong there. The bad classes get the same assessment as the good classes. The fellas I have are just not able to read and when it comes to politics or democracy and proportional representation, sure they can't even get their tongues around the word, never mind understand them! (Teacher, School A)

The Action Project is a joke! I know for a fact that it tends to be teachers who do them and it's just not right! (Teacher, School A)

I think the whole area of assessment needs a re-think. Sixty per cent is probably too much for the Action Project. The kids get too much help from teachers. They practically write the reports for them! (Teacher, School B)

The majority of teachers in School B and all the teachers interviewed in School C were happy with the assessment of CSPE.

It's great to have a subject that doesn't depend on the completion of a terminal exam. The 60 per cent for Action Projects is good for all students, not just the clever ones. (Teacher, School C)

Finally, teachers were asked if they thought that CSPE, as it stands, has any disadvantages. All the teachers interviewed felt that the main disadvantage of CSPE lies in its timetable provision. Since most respondents were not timetabled to teach another subject to their CSPE class, many felt that there was 'no time' for CSPE. Consequently, many teachers were under pressure to cover the course, carry out action projects and experiment with active learning methodologies in their classrooms. A number of teachers also felt that the wrong teachers are being selected to teach the subject and one teacher commented that this phenomenon is 'killing the subject'.

Focus group interviews with current and former CSPE students

The focus group mode of research was employed to elicit from current and former CSPE students their opinions, attitudes and perceptions on various issues central to their study of CSPE. Two focus group interviews were conducted in each school. One group was comprised of current CSPE students and the other was comprised of former CSPE students. There were four students in each of the groups.

Students were firstly asked how they felt about CSPE. With the exception of students in School C, most students did not feel CSPE was as important as other subjects on the Junior Certificate curriculum, nor did they consider it a worthwhile subject. There was no difference in attitude between the current and former students of CSPE.

> *I don't think CSPE is important because … you know … you only do it once a week and it's just boring and I for one don't like it. You only learn about parliament and stuff … it's not that important.* (Current Student, School A)

> *It's a load of c..p! I mean what do you need it for?* (Former Student, School A)

> *No employer is going to ask if you have Civics in your Leaving Cert but they're definitely going to ask for Maths.* (Current Student, School B)

> *It's unimportant. It's boring. It's not worth a s...e!* (Former Student, School B)

> *It's a doss subject; you don't really need it.* (Current Student, School D)

> *It's a class to go asleep in.* (Current Student, School E)

As the above comments indicate, both current and former students in the aforementioned schools feel that CSPE is not an important subject. The status of the subject is also very low amongst these students. On the other hand, both current and former students in School C conferred a high status on the subject and many students interviewed felt that CSPE was indeed a worthwhile subject.

> *I like CSPE. It's important for when we get older and have to vote.* (Current Student, School C)

> *I thought it was really interesting. You need it because if someone asked you who the Minister of Finance was, you wouldn't have a clue only for CSPE. You should know about your country.* (Former Student, School C)

The researcher then asked each of the focus groups, in each of the research sites, to give their views on their CSPE teacher. Students in Schools A, D and E, in particular, were quite negative about their CSPE teachers.

> *I don't think he's into it, to tell you the truth. He can't come up with good things to learn. He keeps saying 'I'm not a CSPE teacher and I'm only doing this because no one else will.' He does the same thing over and over again.* (Current Student, School A)

> *The teacher I had couldn't care less about CSPE. He said he didn't like it.* (Former Student, School A)

> *It became obvious to me that my teacher just didn't care … he did Business with us instead.* (Former Student, School D)

> *My teacher hasn't got a clue.* (Current Student, School E)

In comparison, some of the students in School B and all of the students in School C had positive comments to make about their CSPE teachers.

> *She's a good teacher. Everyone says so. She respects us and lets us talk about things that interest us.* (Current Student, School C)

The interviewer then asked students to describe a typical CSPE class. Students in Schools A, B, D and E indicated that their teachers tend to read from the textbook. Students also commented that they rarely engage in discussion, debate and role-play even though they would prefer this type of teaching and learning. As a result many of the students interviewed felt that their CSPE classes were boring. Students in School C, however, indicated that active learning methodologies are utilised by their teachers on a regular basis. Consequently these students found CSPE a very interesting and enjoyable subject.

The focus of the interview then turned to the issue of assessment. As the former students of CSPE had already sat the exam, the interviewer asked them to give their views on the assessment of CSPE. All of the students interviewed found that it was an 'easy' exam. Many were quite cynical about the assessment of CSPE.

> *Everyone got an A or a B so it's no big deal.* (Former Student, School B)

> *Our teacher told us we had to do an action project five days before it was due to be handed up. We were supposed to do it in second year but none of us had it done. I had to make one up from something I did in Religion class. I just made it up and exaggerated it loads and the gas thing was I got an A!* (Former Student, School D)

> *It's just too easy!* (Former Student, School E)

The comments made by students indicate that they don't find the exam challenging enough. In addition, the comments made by the student in School D would suggest that the assessment of CSPE lacks rigour.

Finally, students were asked if they felt their voices were heard in the school, if they thought they belonged to a democratic school community. Students in Schools A, D and E, in particular, felt that their voices were not heard in the school.

> *We're never listened to in here!* (Student, School A)

Students in School C and to a lesser extent in School B felt that they were listened to in their respective schools. Both sets of students indicated that there was an active Student Council in operation in their schools.

Conclusions and recommendations

This study found that Schools A, D and E in particular are struggling with the implementation of CSPE. The main factors affecting the successful implementation of CSPE in these schools included the following:

1 Haphazard teacher selection

The selection of 'unenthusiastic' and 'disinterested' teachers of CSPE is proving to be a major impediment to the implementation of CSPE in the struggling schools. These teachers have a negative disposition towards CSPE and this negativity is transposed onto their students. In addition, many teachers indicated that CSPE had appeared on their timetables and this proved a bone of contention for many. A lot of the teachers in the struggling schools had been 'conscripted' into teaching CSPE and indicated that they had no genuine interest in the subject. This was picked up by their students. This contrasts with the situation in School C whereby teachers either volunteered to teach the subject or had been consulted. As a result those teachers in School C had a genuine interest in CSPE and had a genuine interest in the subject. This manifested itself in the students, who had a positive disposition towards CSPE. As a result the implementation of CSPE has been successful in this school.

2 Lack of teacher support and professional development

Many teachers in the study indicated that they had received little pre-service advice or support. This support is crucial. It is necessary for school management to support teachers as they grapple with the change process, a process that involves many cycles of trial and error. This support takes many forms. Firstly, the principal should ensure that all relevant literature and documentation about CSPE is distributed to all teachers. In addition, the principal must also promote the active learning dimension in CSPE. This is a challenging endeavour as it requires the principal to undertake the role of 'instructional leader' whereby the principal may invite teachers to observe him/her engaging with active learning techniques in the classroom. This style of leadership would empower, encourage and support teachers new to the subject. An active learning room would promote the adoption of active learning in the school, a place where teachers don't have to worry about the noise factor often associated with active learning.

The study also illuminated the fact that there were low levels of teacher development in the struggling schools. Teachers should be encouraged to obtain a professional qualification in the subject and to attend in-service. In addition, teachers should be given time for planning, meetings and problem solving, and this in turn would help to develop a collaborative work culture in the school.

3 Inadequate timetabling arrangements

The research found that inadequate timetabling can militate against the successful implementation of CSPE. Only 32 per cent of those surveyed taught another subject to their CSPE class. This had a number of implications. Firstly, the cross-curricular dimension of CSPE is not being realised. Secondly, there is the issue of time. Having contact with a class for just one forty-minute period a week meant that teachers were under pressure to cover the course, complete actions or engage in active learning.

Some teachers also indicated that the time factor meant they could not establish a relationship with their students because they only had contact with them once a week.

There is an onus on the principal, therefore, to restructure timetables so as to accommodate CSPE. There is also a need for policy makers to review the timetable provision of CPSE. Many teachers feel that forty minutes a week is an unrealistic time frame.

4 Assessment issues

Most students and teachers surveyed found the CSPE exam most unchallenging. Many students felt the exam was too easy and as a result assigned a low status on the subject. However, the most sinister revelation was that some students indicated that they had not carried out an action project but ended up getting an A grade. To counteract this, careful monitoring of action projects is required.

5 Low status of CSPE

The low status of CSPE was evident in the comments of both teachers and pupils. A number of measures could help raise the status of CSPE.

• Appointment of a CSPE coordinator
• Selecting interested and enthusiastic CSPE teachers
• Making CSPE 'visible' in the school
• Inclusion of CSPE in house examinations
• Inclusion of CSPE teacher on parent-teacher schedules.

6 Lack of effective leadership

All of the factors outlined above stem from poor leadership. Principals must take an active role if CSPE is to be successfully implemented in schools. Only School C seemed to have effective leadership in their school. The principal adhered to the CSPE guidelines and took cognisance of the recommendations outlined in Circular M12/01 (DES, 2001). As a result the 'right' teachers were selected to teach CSPE and teachers new to the subject were given high levels of support. Teachers were enthusiastic about the subject and this enthusiasm seems to have rubbed off on the students. The status of CSPE is high in this school. In addition, a Coordinator of CSPE is in place and teachers are encouraged to develop professionally. However, the other schools in this study lack effective leadership and as a result the status of CSPE is very low in these schools.

Conclusion

This chapter explored the factors affecting the implementation of CSPE in five post-primary schools. Is CSPE Civics in another guise? It would appear so for most of the schools in this study. This was evident in the perceptions, attitudes and opinions elicited in this study. School C was the only school that seems to have successfully implemented CSPE. It appears to be a 'lighthouse school' where there is a commitment to change and a focus on professional development. The remaining schools, however, have not observed best practice and this manifests itself in haphazard teacher selection, lack of teacher support and development and ineffective leadership.

Implementing CSPE presents many challenges, and failure to rise to them will invariably lead to another 'Civics'. Based on this study it is the opinion of the researcher that the implementation of CSPE, for the majority of schools, has proved unsuccessful.

References

Bell, J. (1993), *Doing your Research Project: A Guide for First-Time Researchers in Education and Social Science*, Buckingham: Open University Press

Coolahan, J. (ed.) (1994), *Report on the National Education Convention,* Dublin: Stationery Office

DoE (Department of Education) (1992), *Education for a Changing World – Green Paper on Education,* Dublin: Stationery Office

DoE (Department of Education) (1995), *Charting Our Education Future,* Dublin: Stationery Office

DES (Department of Education and Science) (2001), *Circular M12/01*

Eisner, E. (1998), *The Kind of Schools We Need: Personal Essays*, Portsmouth NH: Heinnman

Fullan, M. (1992), *Successful School Improvement,* Buckingham: Open University Press

Fullan, M. (2001), *The New Meaning of Educational Change: Third Edition,* London: Routledge Falmer

Hamilton, D. (1975), 'Handling Innovation in the Classroom: Two Scottish Examples', in W.A. Reid and D.F. Walker (1975), *Case Studies in Curriculum Change*, London: Routledge and Kogan Paul

Murphy, D.A. (2003), 'Civics Revisited? An Exploration of the Factors Affecting the Implementation of CSPE in Five Post-Primary Schools', unpublished dissertation submitted to the Education Department, National University of Ireland, Maynooth, in part fulfilment of the requirements for the Master of Education Degree

Sarason, S. (1990), *The Predicable Failure of Educational Reform*, San Francisco: Jossey Bass

Sarason, S. (1996), *Revisiting the Culture of the School and the Problem of Change,* New York: Teachers College Press

10

Changing practices within citizenship education classrooms

Conor Harrison

Introduction: *Hard Times* in the classroom

I'd like to begin by inviting you to travel back in time with me to Coketown, taking its name from the 'Coke', or treated coal, powering the factories and blackening the town's skies. It is modelled on Manchester, England, one of the most notoriously uninhabitable factory cities of the nineteenth century.

Dickens chooses to begin his novel *Hard Times* in the classroom, which he depicts as a microcosm of the inhuman world outside. However, this is not simply a literary device in which the author creates the world of the novel in miniature to foreshadow coming events. In Dickens' view, this classroom has been intentionally created as a factory whose express purpose is to manufacture future workers. Education in Coketown is a process by which innocence and imagination are rooted out of the children so that they will grow into soulless automatons expecting nothing other than the drudgery of industrial life. By depicting the potential evils of mass education in this very cynical light, Dickens adopts a position often espoused by radical theorists who state that the power structure uses society's supposedly benevolent institutions to perpetuate its own power and to subjugate those whom these institutions are supposed to help.

Dickens is a master at using overstatement to make a point, but the Coketown schoolroom is drawn more from fact than fantasy. It is based on a type of schooling referred to either as the Monitorial System or as the Lancasterian System after its originator, a London teacher named Joseph Lancaster. The system was employed both in England and the US in the early and mid-nineteenth century, especially in urban centres and especially with poor children. In a classic Monitorial classroom, a hundred or more students are taught by a single teacher. They are divided into a number of smaller groups presided over by older students, or monitors, who are in charge of general instruction and discipline. Dickens chose well when he used this factory-style method of mass education to begin his novel about the depersonalisation and dehumanisation caused by the excesses of the Industrial Revolution.

Hard Times opens as follows:

'NOW, what I want is, Facts. Teach these boys and girls nothing but Facts. Facts alone are wanted in life. Plant nothing else, and root out everything else. You can only form the minds of reasoning animals upon Facts: nothing else will ever be of any service to them. This is the principle on which I bring up my own children, and this is the principle on which I bring up these children. Stick to Facts, sir!' The scene was a plain, bare, monotonous vault of a school-room, and the speaker's square forefinger emphasised his observations by underscoring every sentence with a line on the schoolmaster's sleeve. The emphasis was helped by the speaker's square wall of a forehead, which had his eyebrows for its base, while his eyes found commodious cellarage in two dark caves, overshadowed by the wall. The emphasis was helped by the speaker's mouth, which was wide, thin, and hard set. The emphasis was helped by the speaker's voice, which was inflexible, dry, and dictatorial. The emphasis was helped by the speaker's hair, which bristled on the skirts of his bald head, a plantation of firs to keep the wind from its shining surface, all covered with knobs, like the crust of a plum pie, as if the head had scarcely warehouse-room for the hard facts stored inside. The speaker's obstinate carriage, square coat, square legs, square shoulders, – nay, his very neckcloth, trained to take him by the throat with an unaccommodating grasp, like a stubborn fact, as it was, – all helped the emphasis.

'In this life, we want nothing but Facts, sir; nothing but Facts!' The speaker, and the schoolmaster, and the third grown person present, all backed a little, and swept with their eyes the inclined plane of little vessels then and there arranged in order, ready to have imperial gallons of facts poured into them until they were full to the brim (Dickens, 1854:15-16).

Hard Times opens with a comic yet frightening lecture on the purpose of education. Significantly, the speech is not made by the schoolmaster, but by a businessman who underlines each point on the schoolmaster's sleeve, giving the impression that he is lecturing the instructor more than the students. It is appropriate that business interests dictate what the school should be doing, because the schoolmaster himself, we will find in the next chapter, is an insignificance, a worker whose job is to mould the students to the specifications of the industrialist in this factory-like school.

The image of the students as vessels to be filled makes it clear that they are expected to be passive receptacles of 'facts poured into them until they were full to the brim' rather than active learners. Note also the description of the room, which we will hear more of later. Dickens calls it a 'vault' – in other words, a safe in which a rich man locks up his possessions for use at a later time, as these children are being locked away until they are ready for employment in the factory. The vault is 'plain, bare, monontonous', much like the education offered the children.

When Civics was introduced to the curriculum in Ireland in 1966 things in the classroom were not a whole lot different. Yet it is interesting to read, almost forty years on, some *Notes on the Teaching of Civics* which were produced by the Department of Education to accompany the original syllabus in 1966. It stated:

> ... citizenship is not simply a matter of knowing about social and political institutions. It is also the willingness and the skill to participate actively and creatively in community affairs. The function of the civics teacher, therefore, is not merely to teach facts but also to foster civics virtue. Virtue implies action: so the teaching method we use must essentially be an *active* one. We must try to give our pupils, in their final years of compulsory schooling, some direct experience of the principal civic activities that we hope they will engage in during their adult life. We want them to become people who are well-informed and who keep themselves so, who are able to think clearly and constructively about social and political matters and who are ready at all times to serve the common good.

Classwork in civics therefore will consist of three related activities. They are:

- finding facts
- forming judgements
- engaging in practical social projects.

We shall be teaching civics properly if we can bring our pupils to do these things effectively for themselves (DoE, 1966:2-3).

These words were quite radical and visionary for the time and are as applicable today as they were then. Unfortunately, in the majority of cases classroom practice did not change very much. The reality was that Civics was frequently textbook bound where the focus was on the acquisition of unproblematic knowledge and the passive acceptance of social institutions. The subject failed to develop critical decision-making skills and was largely taught using traditional teaching methods. In short, as has been stated in *Education for a Changing World – Green Paper on Education,* '[The] experience with Civics has not been a successful one, and the topic has not always received the attention it deserves' (DoE, 1992:96).

By the early 1990s, when Civics had virtually ceased to be taught in the vast majority of schools, the original emphasis on active learning methods and student participation raised its head again in the NCCA Discussion Paper on Civic, Social and Political Education at Post-Primary level. This paper in many ways set the scene for the new revamped Citizenship Education course of Civic, Social and Political Education (CSPE) which became a mandatory subject as part of the Junior Certificate in 1997.

Active learning provides the most appropriate vehicle for the attainment of the types of objectives relevant to civic, social and political education, and for the consequent development of active citizens. Conversely, it is difficult to imagine students as active citizens if their experience of learning about citizenship has been predominantly passive. The NCCA proposes that all programmes or courses in civic, social and political education should subscribe to, and emphasise, guided active learning methods, as their primary method of teaching/learning (NCCA, 1993:16).

The CSPE syllabus also stresses this point:

> Civic, Social and Political Education seeks to be affective and to equip pupils with the skills and understanding of processes which enable them to see, decide, judge and act. Its employment of active and co-operatively structured learning methodologies enables and empowers the pupil to become an active and participative young person (DoE, 1996a:2).

So what about practices in citizenship education classrooms today? To those of us involved in the CSPE Support Team there are six key challenges which impact upon classroom practice in citizenship education classrooms in the Republic of Ireland. These challenges are outlined in the rest of this chapter.

Challenge 1: the seven concepts

The CSPE course, as it exists today, is constructed around seven core concepts: democracy, rights and responsibilities, human dignity, interdependence, development, law and stewardship. By taking up this course students should develop a broad understanding of these concepts and come to recognise how these concepts serve collectively though not exclusively to inform and clarify the concept of citizenship.

These concepts are presented in the form of concept descriptions rather than as a specific list of topics to be covered. By using this approach, the course committee set out clear directions and expectations for exploring the course concepts but left considerable scope for teachers to respond effectively to their students' needs and interests within the communities to which they theoretically belong.

This focus on concepts has presented many teachers with their first challenge. Post-primary schools in Ireland have traditionally focused on the acquisition of knowledge as the primary function of education. This has resulted from the heavy emphasis on didactic teaching in many schools because of the pressure of the examination system, even though as Handy puts it, 'Knowledge, for most people, has a very short sell-by date. Unless it is used very quickly it goes off' (Handy, 1998:217). Working in a system where the terminal examination in most other subject areas determines the course content, and where in many teachers' eyes the textbook is the course, basing a course on seven broad concepts causes some discomfort. Questions raised include: But where do I begin? What aspects of each concept should I cover? What can I leave out? What happens if something topical happens in my community?

CSPE begins, not with facts, as described in the opening lines of *Hard Times*, but with concepts. It does not deny the value of factual information, but gives priority to developing the sort of conceptual frameworks that help young people to make sense of it. Factual information is seen as something to be introduced at appropriate points on a 'need-to-know' basis, not as the be-all and end-all of the subject.

When teachers become comfortable with the CSPE syllabus and realise that this subject is different in its approach, many of them find it liberating that students are required only to develop a broad understanding of the seven concepts, but more importantly should be provided with opportunities which enable them to develop citizenship skills through active learning methods and action projects. It is also useful for them to focus on the percentages of marks allocated to the various modes of assessment. Why should any teacher spend 60-70 per cent of his/her class time cramming information into students' heads when only 40 per cent of the marks are allocated to the terminal written examination? Many teachers are now placing more and more emphasis on the methodology and action projects where students can develop skills and attitudes and also achieve 60 per cent of the marks.

Challenge 2: active learning methods

CSPE, while not denying a place for didactic education, places a greater emphasis on active and co-operatively structured learning situations within the classroom. Yet there is a contradiction which those of us engaged with and enthused by active and creative teaching and learning approaches associated with citizenship education must contend with on a regular basis. Looney commented on this struggle:

> Isn't there a sense deep down in all of us – educational professionals and those outside the schoolhouse – that the best classrooms are quiet, rows of heads bent over books, teacher pacing with authority, the hum of spellings in the next room and the prospect of a hard test on Fridays … no matter how hard we try, if we don't keep working at it we will succumb (Looney, 2001).

So if students are to become active participatory citizens, it is imperative that they are active participants in their own learning. 'There must be a means for students to apply their knowledge of democracy. Since students learn best by doing, the principles of democracy are best taught in such a way that they are practised' (Drisko, 1993:105). It is crucial that teachers are prepared to facilitate the provision of the real opportunities for involvement and participation. Each classroom of students has all (or most of) the characteristics of a pluralist society in miniature. It is made up of different individuals from different backgrounds, espousing different beliefs and values, all sharing membership of common institutions and having a common identity.

Students are not citizens-in-waiting; they are citizens in their own right. They have the same civil rights as people over eighteen years of age even though they may not be allowed to vote in elections. They have a legitimate interest in the future of the society as a whole, and are entitled to their say on the sort of direction it should take. For many students the classroom is the first sort of public forum they experience and provides the first opportunity they have to debate issues of public concern as citizens.

Quite often there can be a mismatch between the way in which students learn and the way in which they are taught. This mismatch can cause de-motivation, misbehaviour and under-achievement. It is critical then that all learners have multi-sensory learning experiences. The challenge is for the teacher to provide variety and choice in class to ensure that all learners will have frequent opportunities to work in their preferred learning style.

Howard Gardner's theory of multiple intelligences (Veneema *et al*, 1997:61) also provides a helpful and useful framework for thinking about, examining and extending one's practice in the CSPE classroom. The ways in which learning and teaching take place will influence significantly the skills that are developed, the attitudes and values that are fostered and the understanding that is acquired. A student must be able to do more than 'know about' what he or she is studying. Students understand and have a greater chance of remembering things in which they were actively involved in learning-by-doing. For this to occur, active group learning situations must take place. No wonder Naylor as part of his advocacy of active, participatory learning uses 'citizen' as a verb: 'If you want to learn to "citizen",' he says, 'you need to do more than read books and take courses' (Naylor, 1990:66). Civic, Social and Political Education seeks to employ a combination of participatory and experiential learning activities, co-operative learning techniques and cross-curricular/integrated exercises where possible.

Alongside acquiring some essential knowledge, CSPE also aims to help students to develop skills they already have and to acquire new skills, as mentioned above. The subject has as its focus that students learn how to access knowledge and information and to develop the skills necessary for active participation in society. Skills, therefore, take on special importance in the methodologies and in action projects. It is vitally important that the teacher helps students to name and explain the skills they use or acquire in the course of their CSPE experiences, as many of them may not be consciously aware of these skills at the time. Teachers are encouraged to hone in on this aspect with their students: 'What skills have you used today?' or 'Do you know what skill you are using now?'

Challenge 3: teaching controversial/sensitive issues

Within CSPE there are many opportunities to explore controversial issues – issues about which there is no fixed or universally held view. Such issues are those which most commonly divide society and for which significant groups offer conflicting explanations and solutions. There may, for example, be conflicting views on such matters as how a problem has arisen and who is to blame; over how a problem may be resolved; over what principles should guide the decisions that are taken, and so on.

Citizenship educators should not attempt to shelter students from the harsher controversies of adult life, but should prepare them to deal with such controversies knowledgeably, sensibly, tolerantly and morally. Teachers have to learn to adopt strategies that teach students how to recognise bias, how to evaluate evidence put before them and how to look at alternative viewpoints and above all to give good reasons for everything they say and do and to expect good reasons to be given by others.

Challenge 4: action projects

Action projects are at the very heart of Civic, Social and Political Education and students are encouraged to undertake at least two action projects over the duration of the course (DoE, 1996b). An action project is a project where the students are actively involved in developing an issue or topic that has arisen in class beyond the usual limits of textbooks and course materials. It is not the traditional style project, i.e. keeping a scrapbook or mounting a wall display. The students actually get involved in doing something about an issue.

> Often the school and its local community provide a perfect context for pupils to examine issues and events and to become involved in active, participatory activities and experiences where the emphasis is on learning through action. This can help pupils to make the connection between learning and acting locally to thinking globally (QCA, 1998).

For example, students might undertake a survey of attitudes amongst students in their class or school to a particular issue that may be important locally or nationally. Or they might research, organise and invite a guest speaker to talk to the class on a particular topic and thereby develop the skills of how to gain access to information and structures. Alternatively, they may run a referendum/election at the same time that this is happening nationally, thereby developing and practising the skills of participation in the democratic process. Teachers are encouraged to begin exploring action projects with their students in the first year of the course. Action projects can be undertaken at any stage of the CSPE course and at any stage during a unit or module of course-work.

Students may be studying a unit of work (6-8 classes) on rights and responsibilities with a particular focus on the rights of children. At some stage in this module it may be appropriate to invite a guest speaker from the Student Council to talk to the class about Article 12 of the UN Convention on the Rights of the Child – the right to have a voice in matters that affect young people. It is the children who should invite, welcome, interview and evaluate the visitor, having sought the prior permission of the teacher/school management. This is the action project component of their work. Traditionally the teacher organised and took charge of such a visit and in the process the students missed out on several learning situations which are important for developing active citizens.

Some teachers find this change in role quite difficult as it means handing over responsibility to the students. Many have commented on the sleepless night before the event spent worrying about what Student X might say and what Student Y might do. Most admit afterwards that the students behaved extremely well and took their responsibilities seriously. Once the teachers connect with the issue/topic the students are interested in and are prepared to hand over the responsibilities, the possibilities are endless. The following example illustrates just what can be achieved when students are enthused and motivated about their action project.

Bringing an ATM cash machine to 3,000 people
The residents of a Co. Sligo town have access to a cash machine thanks to a group of enterprising CSPE students.

A second year CSPE class in the Marist Secondary School in Tubbercurry, Co. Sligo, thought up the action project as a way of doing something for its community. Tubbercurry and its hinterland has a population of about 3,000 people and, up until now, there was no cash machine within 12 miles of the town.

The CSPE students set about finding out if the people of Tubbercurry wanted and would use an ATM machine. They researched the proposal, designed a survey, met bank officials and organised a petition.

The class of twenty students divided up into groups of three or four and took on different tasks. Some contacted the local banks and building societies to find out whether there was enough business to support a cash machine. They met bank officials and talked about the conditions necessary for the installation of an ATM. They learned that a machine needed 7,000–10,000 transactions per week to make it viable. They also discovered that the machine requires a 24-hour open telephone line. They were told that previous attempts had been made to bring in a machine.

Some students designed a survey to establish the demand for a cash machine. The survey form consisted of five simple questions including whether the person thought there was a need for an ATM machine, if he/she would use it and if so, how often.

Each student drew up a petition form during computer studies class and printed it out. They distributed the forms in the community and gathered more than 1,400 signatures.

Finally some students drew up a letter for the bank's head office and sent it off with their research and petition. The class received a response some weeks later and a few months later an ATM machine was installed in a new garage forecourt at the end of the town (Independent Newspapers, 1999).

As John F. Kennedy said, 'One person can make a difference and every person should try.' This action project achieved something that other people in the town failed to achieve!

Challenge 5: the role of the teacher

Harwood (1998:154ff) has identified eight alternative teacher roles relevant to democratic teaching (see Table below). He suggests that there is a rule-of-thumb hierarchy between these different roles. One of the most important, Harwood suggests, is that of the impartial facilitator who chairs discussion by organising and facilitating student contributions and by maintaining rules and limits. The impartial facilitator does not express a personal viewpoint and does not give positive or negative feedback after students' contributions. In contrast, the role of devil's advocate is one to be used particularly sparingly – only in situations when the class has overlooked a crucial argument or objection or is genuinely unable to generate any ideas about an issue.

Teacher roles relevant to democratic teaching

Role	Description
Participant	Is free to express ideas, opinions and feelings, just like any other member of the group
Devil's advocate	Tries to stimulate participation by deliberately taking oppositional stances
Impartial/neutral facilitator	Chairs the discussion by organising and facilitating students' contributions and by maintaining rules and limits; does not express personal viewpoint; does not give positive or negative feedback after students' contributions
Instructor	Explains and clarifies relevant information, concepts and ideas; asks task questions to assess understanding; gives positive or negative feedback after students' contributions
Committed instructor	Uses the instructor role, as above, in a sustained way, to propagate own viewpoint on controversial issues
Interviewer	Questions individuals to elicit their ideas, feelings and opinions
Observer	Observes the students during their discussions, but does not intervene
Absent leader	Withdraws from the group after the initial organisation of the work

(from Harwood, 1998)

Operating in many different roles within a forty-minute class period is new for many teachers. Opportunities to model and practise these different roles are necessary in order to develop confidence in the teachers. Students also need time to come to terms with their teacher in differing and varied roles.

One must not forget that the teacher him/herself is also a role model. It is important therefore that teachers try to model the skills of citizenship whenever they can – for example, by giving reasons for their views and expecting reasons to be given by others; evaluating an alternative course of action by reference to evidence and/or argument; and trying to see a situation from the viewpoints of all involved. Research by Wood (1988) suggests that where teachers use thoughtful, reflective reasoning, students are more likely to respond in kind.

Challenge 6: assessment

Action projects and the active learning methodologies used in their implementation are a central part of the assessment procedures that have been put in place for CSPE. To encourage and to reward action, 60 per cent of the final grade received by the student in the Junior Certificate examination in CSPE is allocated to this area. Action projects should be interesting and rewarding for students and it is only right that they are rewarded for doing them.

Assessment is carried out in two modes: a written terminal examination at the end of the third year of the course and the submission of either a report on an action project or a course-work assessment book. The weighting between the modes of assessment presented is 40 per cent for the written examination and 60 per cent for either the report on an action project or the course-work assessment book. For the purposes of assessment the action project itself is not submitted. Instead each student is asked to submit either a detailed report of the action project by completing what is titled a Report on an Action Project (RAP) or by submitting a less detailed description of the action project in the process of completing a Course-Work Assessment Book (CWAB) (DES and NCCA, 1998:39).

Assessment outside of the examination hall continues to challenge teachers of CSPE. Students are required to write their own individual report in their own words. This takes time and students need to be taught how to write a report. They also require guidance while working their way through the report writing. Very often this work may be left to the last term of Third Year and creates much angst. There is no reason why this work could not be undertaken during Second Year. It results in much less stress for students and teachers who complete this work in Second Year.

Of course while acknowledging that grades are important to all students, as Naylor puts it, 'the real test of any citizenship programme is what participants do in their lifetime office of citizen' (Naylor, 1990:33-36).

Conclusion: challenges for teacher educators/in-service support teams

Being a citizen is central to being a person. Similarly citizenship education is central to education. Even though there is specific subject provision, citizenship education does not fit neatly into a subject box – it inspires the whole school ethos. It is a subject of integrity, in that students learn democracy through experiencing democracy, they learn responsibility through being responsible, and they learn to participate through participating in methodologies and action projects.

Professor Bernard Crick highlighted just how important citizenship education is:

> We aim at no less than a change in the political culture of this country both nationally and locally … For people to think of themselves as active citizens … with critical capacities to weigh evidence before speaking and acting … and to make them individually confident in finding new forms of involvement and action among themselves (Crick, 1998).

If we are serious about the value of and need for citizenship education, the challenge is for all third-level teacher training institutions and all in-service training providers and support teams to grasp the opportunities offered by this dynamic subject.

- Teaching methods in some third-level institutions need to change. Pre-service teachers need to experience what it means to be in a democratic classroom not just in learning how to be a citizenship teacher but in learning the craft of teaching.
- Learning styles, personality types and multiple intelligences need to feature in teacher training courses.
- Active learning methods must feature so that trainee teachers can engage with and model the experiences before trying them out in their own classrooms with young people.
- Practising teachers should be invited to act as facilitators of pre-service training.
- Lessons can and should be learned from colleagues working in youth services, community development and adult education.

- Links with local communities must be made and maintained.
- Teachers should be trained in the art of critical thinking in order to become reflective practitioners.
- Teachers undertaking this kind of transformation require ongoing support and encouragement from in-service support teams and teacher educators.
- A climate of collegiality in schools needs to be nurtured to enable the sharing of best practice.
- Time and space should be provided on the school timetable for reflection and sharing.

References

Crick, B. (1998), *Education for Citizenship and the Teaching of Democracy in Schools. Final Report of the Advisory Group on Citizenship.* London: QCA

DES/NCCA (Department of Education and Science)/ (National Council for Curriculum and Assessment) (1998), *Guidelines for Teachers: Taking Action – A Guide to Action Projects and their Assessment*, Dublin: DES and NCCA

Dickens, C. (1854), *Hard Times*, London: Virtue and Company Limited

DoE (Department of Education) (1966), *Notes on the Teaching of Civics*, Dublin: Department of Education

DoE (Department of Education) (1992), *Education for a Changing World – Green Paper on Education*, Dublin: Stationery Office

DoE (Department of Education) (1996a), *The Junior Certificate Civic, Social and Political Education Syllabus*, Dublin: Department of Education

DoE (Department of Education) (1996b), *Guidelines for Schools: Civic, Social and Political Education*, Dublin: Department of Education

Drisko, J. (1993), 'The Responsibilities of Schools in Civic Education', *Journal of Education*, 175 (1)

Handy, C. (1998), *The Hungry Spirit*, London: Arrow Books Limited

Harwood, D. (1998), 'The Teacher's Role in Democratic Pedagogies', in C. Holden and N. Clough (eds), *Children as Citizens: Education for Participation*, London: Jessica Kingsley

Independent Newspapers (1999), *Tuition*, Vol.2, No.1, Dublin: Independent Newspapers

Looney, A. (2001), 'The Curriculum for Democratic Citizenship in the Republic of Ireland', paper presented to the International Conference on Citizenship Education, organised by the Centre for Cross-Border Studies, Monaghan/Armagh, 29-30 November 2001

Naylor, D. T. (1990), 'Education for Citizenship: LRE and the Social Studies', *Update on Law-Related Education,* 14 (2)

NCCA (National Council for Curriculum and Assessment) (1993), *Civic, Social and Political Education at Post-Primary Level*, Discussion Paper, Dublin: NCCA

QCA (Qualifications and Curriculum Authority, Great Britain) (1998), *Education for Citizenship and the Teaching of Democracy in Schools: Final Report of the Advisory Group on Citizenship Education*, London: Qualifications and Curriculum Authority

Veneema, S., Hetland, L. and Chaflen, K. (eds) (1997), *The Project Zero Classroom: New Approaches to Thinking and Understanding*, Boston: Harvard Graduate School of Education
Wood, D. (1998), *How Children Think and Learn*, Oxford: Blackwell

11

Frameworks for responding to diversity in schools

Mary Gannon

Introduction

How do we perceive cultural diversity in our schools? How do our perceptions and values influence our responses to it? Do human rights and responsibilities provide the best framework for educational responses to cultural diversity? What contribution can equality, cultural respect, and democratic citizenship make? Drawing on the findings of personal research as well as my work with the CDVEC Curriculum Development Unit Interculturalism and Equality projects, this chapter will explore these questions in relation to the responses to cultural diversity developing within Irish schools.

Since the late 1990s, Irish post-primary schools have experienced a rapid growth in the levels of cultural and religious diversity represented in their student bodies, reflecting the general growth in levels of diversity in Irish society, alongside increased transfer rates of Traveller students from primary to post-primary level. Accurate statistics are difficult to obtain due to the absence of ethnic monitoring in schools, but it is now common for students from minority ethnic or religious groups to form 15 to 25 per cent of the student body in urban post-primary schools. These figures include Traveller students, Irish students of dual heritage, and students from families who have recently arrived in Ireland as migrant workers or as refugees/asylum seekers; and students encompassing a wide range of religious and secular beliefs.

Levels of ethnic, cultural and religious diversity in schools continue to rise, with diversity fast becoming the norm, rather than the exception, for the majority of schools. This growth is occurring within an educational system that is still relatively homogeneous in terms of structures and staffing. Students from minority ethnic and religious groups find themselves in a largely denominational schooling system, with teachers who come almost exclusively from settled Irish, middle-class backgrounds. It is within these contexts that the following reflections on educators' responses to cultural and religious diversity are offered.

124

The reflections arise from a two sources: findings from research that I carried out among post-primary principals and teachers for a PhD thesis *Framing Diversity: Responding to Cultural Diversity in Irish Post-Primary Schools* (Gannon, 2004); and findings[1] from two CDVEC Curriculum Development Unit projects – Interculturalism and Equality (2002-2003 and 2004-2006) – which supported teachers, students and parents in a total of twelve schools in developing a whole-school approach to interculturalism and equality, and for which I was respectively project advisor/ research team member, and project co-ordinator/ research team member.

In reflecting on some of the frameworks that teachers and schools use in developing responses to cultural diversity, I am particularly interested in four areas:

- *Perceptual frameworks:* what are educators' perceptions of culture and diversity, and how do these perceptions influence their attitudes to cultural diversity among their students?
- *Educational/ideological frameworks:* what are their preferred educational approaches to students from minority ethnic and religious backgrounds and to the relationships between majority and minority students?
- *Value frameworks:* what values do they believe schools should promote and practise in relation to cultural diversity?
- *Implications:* what are the implications of these frameworks for citizenship education?

Perceptual frameworks

All of us 'frame' our reality in certain ways, viewing it from varying perspectives which are influenced by our life experience, values, social status, gender, and a great number of other factors. In examining the perceptual frameworks that educators use in responding to cultural diversity, those found to be most relevant were related to culture itself, e.g. perceptions of culture and racism; and those related to ethnocentrism, e.g. perceptions of diversity and difference.

Culture

The attitudes of Irish teachers and principals towards cultural diversity are greatly influenced by their own understandings and perceptions of culture, both Irish culture and culture in general. The majority of teachers and

---

[1] The CDU research findings referred to in this chapter are those from the research carried out in the three schools that participated in the first project 2002-2003 (CDU, 2003) and the nine schools that participated in the second project 2004-2006 (Gannon and Kenny, 2006).

principals whom I interviewed demonstrated an understanding of culture as being composed of its more visible elements such as music, song, dance and language, and this view continues to be replicated by a large percentage of the teachers I encounter through in-service or school-based support activities. These visible elements do indeed form an important part of cultural identity and expression among all cultures. However, limiting culture to its visible elements ignores its deeper, and what some would see as its primary elements, such as the meanings, values, beliefs and symbols shared by a group, which shape their view of themselves and the world (see Geertz, 1973; Chryssochoou, 2004).

Viewing culture within a narrow perceptual framework has a number of drawbacks in a situation of cultural diversity. Where culture is viewed as something static, as product rather than process, it is generally accompanied by a fear that the majority culture can potentially be threatened by increasing levels of cultural diversity, and by demands from minority ethnic and religious groups for recognition of their identity. My findings showed that educators who saw Irish culture in traditional terms are often wary of Irish culture 'losing out' (Principal, Girls' Secondary) in the face of the arrival of immigrant students. While many welcome and want some acknowledgement, understanding or celebration of immigrant students' cultures, they saw the most appropriate vehicle for this as being in the form of cultural events, days or weeks, a method that would not threaten the dominant position of majority Irish culture within mainstream school life.

In contrast, a small number of educators saw culture in much broader terms, recognising that Irish culture continues to change and that culture is a fluid process. These teachers, whether in schools with visible cultural diversity or not, believed there was a need to include multiple perspectives in the curriculum, and to develop all students' abilities to relate to people from varying cultural backgrounds. This position is central to the NCCA guidelines on intercultural education (NCCA, 2006).

Ethnocentrism

The examples above provide a reminder of the need to examine our assumptions and perceptions regarding culture and religion in the light of current social realities. Ethnocentrism is a natural consequence of socialisation in any culture, but providers of education within a multicultural society, such as Ireland has become, need to be aware of the effects of ethnocentrism on both minority and majority ethnic students. Amongst principals and teachers who viewed culture within a narrow perceptual framework, ethnocentrism was noticeably present (Gannon, 2004). Irish culture was very much seen as the norm, and minority ethnic students were described in terms of their deviance from it, or of how well they 'fitted in' with it. In schools with visibly diverse student bodies, ethnocentrism manifested itself in relation to two issues – language, and the reflection of students' cultural identities in the curriculum. In more homogenous schools, it manifested itself in relation to the perceptual frameworks teachers used in the classroom.

Ethnocentrism and language

Ethnocentric positions in relation to language manifest themselves among teachers in the frequency with which bilingual students are described in terms of how well they speak English, rather than in terms of their language ability (CDU, 2003; Gannon, 2004; Gannon and Kenny, 2006). Reflecting negative official descriptions by the Department of Education and Science of bilingual students as 'non-English speaking non-national students' (DES, 2001), this perception has been found to be common among teachers who are faced with the difficult challenge of teaching within multilingual classrooms with little support and/or training. 'English language fluency was a key and pervasive concern for teachers', who were so conscious of this issue that they were 'silent about the richness and diversity of students' linguistic skills' (CDU, 2003:61). The project found that there was little or no acknowledgement of the fact that out of the thirty-seven minority ethnic students surveyed, twenty-two spoke more than two languages other than English or Irish, or of the possibilities for enrichment of the school which these abilities offered.

Practically all education in Ireland is delivered through the medium of English and therefore it is essential that students within the system learn English to an adequate academic standard in order to ensure equal levels of achievement with English language speakers. However, in a world with 6,912 living languages, 516 in Nigeria alone (Gordon, 2005), a broader perspective on the function and status of language, and a more inclusive approach to language within the classroom are needed. Were schools and the system as a whole to actively recognise, value and support bilingual students' first languages, this would not only benefit the bilingual students' academic progress but would also provide an environment where all students could more easily learn to value diversity, broaden their understanding of language itself, and develop a more inclusive worldview.

Perceptions and worldviews in the curriculum

Teachers' concerns about English language abilities are often accompanied by a marked lack of consciousness of the ethnocentrism within the taught curriculum. This manifests itself in an additive as opposed to transformative approach to the recognition of minority ethnic students' cultural identities. Such an approach is most commonly expressed through the addition of 'intercultural events' or specific cultural celebrations, while the mainstream curriculum is left unchanged. My research found that while teachers and schools were very anxious to provide for the needs, and appreciate the culture, of minority ethnic students, this was primarily seen as a question of adding on specific cultural elements to the curriculum or extra-curricular activities. There appeared to be a widespread lack of awareness among teachers and principals of the need to reflect diverse cultural and religious identities within the mainstream curriculum or of the effect its absence can have on students (Gannon, 2004). A Traveller parent interviewee described the experience of attending a primary school where his identity was not recognised as entering an environment that 'was totally alien to us', where the settled and Traveller worlds did not connect. He later described the joy of his son on bringing home a book which included material on Travellers.

> He's been in school now six years and this was the first school publication or document that showed Travellers. And he was absolutely over the moon about it, very excited by it. And that one incident brought it home to me what could happen if it happened more often and what it would mean to young Traveller pupils in the school (Traveller Parent).

The majority of teachers had not consciously considered the perceptual frameworks within which they taught the curriculum in relation to cultural diversity in their classrooms (Gannon, 2004). In making the transition from a relatively homogenous society to an intercultural one, this finding suggests a need for educators to examine the assumptions and worldviews which frame our teaching, and of which we are all too often unaware. The maps in Figure 1[2] illustrate how we often fail to realise or question the view of the world and our place in it that we have received through our own socialisation and education.

When I use these maps with teachers, the reactions to them usually range from negative to uncomfortable. This politically correct map of Ireland challenges us to question unconscious assumptions or images of Ireland and its two political jurisdictions. 'Upside-down' and Pacific-centred maps of the world[3] challenge us to re-look at our perceptions of Ireland's and Europe's positions in the world and the power relations

---

[2] From Gannon (2002), *Changing Perspective. Cultural Values, Diversity and Equality in Ireland and the Wider World*, Dublin: Curriculum Development Unit and National Consultative Committee on Racism and Interculturalism.

[3] There are a number of these world maps available to download or buy. Up-to-date sources can be found through searching for Upside Down World Maps on www.google.ie.

Figure 1: *Maps of Ireland and the World, Gannon (2002)*

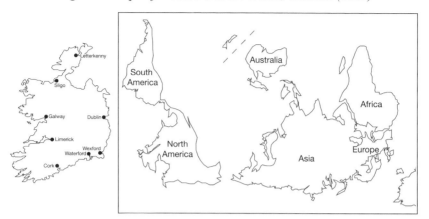

between North and South. Many teachers initially describe this world map as being 'wrong', but then come to the conclusion that it is only wrong or upside down if we see it from a European perspective. The maps are a reminder that our teaching needs to be framed in such a way as to acknowledge and accommodate multiple perspectives in order to include all students in diverse classrooms, and to help our students do likewise.

Racism

Racism does not sit comfortably with the image of 'Ireland of the welcomes'. It is rarely discussed in the media and would appear to be a topic that schools shy away from. Where it is discussed or acknowledged, this is principally in relation to racist incidents as opposed to institutional racism. Additionally, staff and majority ethnic students can be unaware of the level at which these occur[4] or the level of hurt and exclusion that results from them. The CDU student surveys carried out in 2003 and 2004 showed that majority ethnic students were either unaware of racist name-calling occurring in the school, or where they were aware of it, generally felt it did not concern them. However, the evidence from the minority ethnic students showed that there was a general experience of racism in the form of name-calling, and they strongly expressed the hurt and exclusion they suffered.[5]

---

[4] There are more recent indications, however, that teachers are now more aware of tensions between majority and minority ethnic students, and a number of schools are concerned enough that they have requested support or in-service on this issue (personal communication with schools 2006-7).

[5] This was also a finding in research carried out by Keogh and Whyte (2003).

The two principals quoted below illustrate both an understanding of racism as incident and the perception of an absence of any real problem in their schools in relation to racism (Gannon, 2004):

We have been very fortunate. Even though it's a vocational school, I have not had to my knowledge, not one complaint from the twenty-five odd non-nationals here regarding racist remarks or anything like that, which in the case is amazing. (Principal, VEC school)

We've had two [incidents]. That's all I can think of I'm glad to say. (Principal, Secondary Girls' school)

Regardless of their perceptions of levels of racism in the form of racist incidents or comments within their schools, teachers and principals did not appear to be aware that schools, whether intentionally or unintentionally, could be institutionally racist[6] through their policy, practice or curriculum. This finding has considerable significance for schools in relation to areas such as admission policies, curriculum content and methodologies, and the overall educational approach they take to diversity. While dealing with racist incidents or comments may be an immediate concern for schools, the level of occurrence of such racist incidents is greatly influenced by the overall school climate and ethos (Epstein and Sealey, 1990). It is therefore of long-term importance for schools that they review their policy, practice, and school climate – their 'institutional body language' (Richardson and Wood, 1999:vii) – to ensure that they are inclusive and do not, however unwittingly, discriminate against students from minority ethnic, cultural or religious backgrounds.

Perceptions of diversity as otherness
A common human reaction to difference and diversity is to define ourselves in opposition to the 'Other', 'Us' as opposed to 'Them', and to seek reassurance that the 'Other' does not threaten us, our identity, our security, the *status quo* to which we subscribe. Teachers' attitudes to cultural diversity were strongly influenced by the ethnocentrism and conceptualisation of culture already described but, additionally, underlying much of their discussion was a conceptualisation of diversity as

[6] The generally accepted definition of institutional racism is that of the Stephen Lawrence Inquiry, which defined it as 'The collective failure of an organisation to provide an appropriate and professional service to people because of their colour, culture, or ethnic origin. It can be seen or detected in processes, attitudes and behaviour which amount to discrimination through unwitting prejudice, ignorance, thoughtlessness and racist stereotyping which disadvantage minority ethnic people' (Macpherson Report, 1999: section 6.34).

'Otherness' and of minority ethnic students as 'Them' as opposed to 'Us'. Phrases such as 'Our own students,' or 'Our own', as frequently used by teachers and principals (Gannon, 2004), evoke a powerful image of the separation or distinction between Irish students – the ethnic majority – and those from minority ethnic or religious groups. For example one principal in discussing the need to treat all students the same stated *(emphasis added)*: 'They don't get anything *our own students* don't get, they're not deprived of anything *our own* get' (Principal, VEC school).

The descriptor of minority ethnic students as 'Them' was applied not only to immigrant or foreign national students but also to Traveller students. Seen in juxtaposition to settled students, Traveller students were also seen as the 'Other', with similar concerns expressed about both groups in relation to growing numbers, and the threat that the presence of a high percentage of minority ethnic students might pose to the *status quo* (Gannon, 2004).

Teachers' attitudes to immigrant students could best be described as a qualified welcome. Their welcome was 'almost drowned in a plethora of concerns' (CDU, 2003) regarding language issues, cultural difference and concerns that they would fit in. While there was some concern that numbers of immigrant students would grow too big to be absorbed into the school, this was a much greater concern in relation to Traveller students, with two principals expressing their reluctance to take any more Traveller students, while at the same time feeling duty bound to do so because of their admissions policy or mission statement (Gannon, 2004).

Preferred educational approaches

Both sets of research findings show that, with very few exceptions, teachers were concerned with doing their best for the students in their care. However, the ethnocentric framework already described meant that their vision of students 'fitting in', or of integration, was largely (Gannon, 2004) or partly (CDU, 2003) that of absorption or assimilation, rather than inclusion on the basis of equality. The following quotes from two female teachers in one of the CDU schools illustrate the difference between these two positions (CDU, 2003).

> *The ethos to remain unchanged. Integrate and have parents understand that our function is to teach the majority and give assistance to the minority as needed. Do not take in too many minority students.*
> (Teacher, Girls' Secondary)

> *We have been white, Irish and Catholic. We need the wider view.*
> (Teacher, Girls' Secondary)

Other approaches that were advocated included diversity blindness, or a response based on a charity/welfare model. Both of these approaches spring from a deficit model of diversity, a model that concentrates on what minority ethnic students lack rather than what they have. This model often places them within a poverty framework, where they are seen, as two principals described them to me, as 'the new poor' whom schools have a duty to help (Gannon, 2004).

It is inevitable that changes such as increasing levels of diversity among students with the new questions and new challenges they pose for schools will result initially in a variety of *ad hoc* responses, with some confusion and/or conflicting ideas about how to respond to the new situation. Lessons from other countries that have experienced high levels of immigration show clearly that society as a whole, and the education system which reflects the values of society, must decide on the underlying approach it wishes to adopt in relation to cultural diversity.

In the Irish context, schools operate under relevant legislation and government policy. The official government position towards immigrants is that of integration, although this is defined in quite a minimalist way as 'the ability to participate to the extent that a person needs and wishes in all of the major components of society, without having to relinquish his or her own cultural identity' (DoJELR, 1999:9). In relation to a vision of participative citizenship, this definition is quite weak and lacks any real image of an actively inclusive society. A much stronger basis for inclusion, equality and protection of cultural rights is provided by the Convention on the Rights of the Child (UN, 1989), The Equal Status Acts 2000, 2004, and the National Children's Strategy (2004), as will be discussed later.

Value frameworks

As schools continue to develop responses to cultural diversity, a helpful starting point would be, firstly, to examine their own understandings and perceptions of diversity and secondly to analyse their basic approach to diversity in light of equality and human rights legislation and policy. Thirdly, clarifying the core values they believe are important for culturally diverse schools, and how these values translate into practice on a daily basis, would help resolve some of the issues that are currently perceived as problematic. I asked thirty-six educators which values they would like their schools to practise and promote in relation to cultural diversity. The seventeen values they identified are shown in the table below, ranked according to frequency of choice (several mentioned more than one value).

Values identified by principals, teachers, co-ordinators and union representatives

Respect	20
Tolerance	11
Openness	10
Human rights	5
Acceptance	5
Equality	3
Valuing self	3
Sharing	2
Christian values	2
High expectations of minority ethnic students	2
Anti-racism (countering prejudice)	2
Fairness	2
Visibility	2
Democracy	1
Inclusion	1
Appreciation/co-operation	1

Respect was clearly the value most interviewees wanted to promote and practise. Yet when this statement was compared to how respect was actually implemented in their schools, some contradictions became apparent. Where respect was a central value of the school, it was visible in that teachers listened to students; different viewpoints were tolerated and respected; and there was a concern with developing students' self-esteem, in order to support them in respect for self and others. However, there were other examples where schools had not thought through the full implications of respecting students' identities in a situation of cultural diversity, for example the reluctance to reflect the cultural identity of students in the curriculum, and the absorptionist or diversity blindness of educational approaches already mentioned.

The table of values indicates a basic desire to promote what could be described as human rights values – values such as respect, tolerance, acceptance, equality, and fairness. The ambiguities and inconsistencies associated with their practice point to a need for the development of a holistic response to cultural diversity that integrates values and practice in a clear and consistent manner across all aspects of school life and relationships.

A viable framework for developing respect in a consistent manner could be provided by the twin pillars of cultural respect and human equality which, taken together, ensure respect for diverse identities within an environment where equality is promoted. Cultural respect is concerned with our diversity, and with ensuring that cultural diversity is understood and that different cultural identities are valued and respected. Human equality is concerned with recognising our common humanity and ensuring that relationships between majority and minority are based on equality in its fullest meaning (as discussed below). Blum (2000) and Parekh (2000) encapsulate the need for both of these principles.

> We are the same as others in some ways that warrant valuing, and different from others, in other ways, some of which warrant valuing (Blum, 2000:12).[7]

> Human beings are at once both natural and cultural beings, sharing common human identity but in a culturally mediated manner. They are similar and different; their similarities and differences do not passively coexist but interpenetrate, and neither is ontologically prior or morally more important. ... Since human beings are at once similar and different, they should be treated equally because of both (Parekh, 2000:239-240).

Education, therefore, if it is to reflect and respect the many possible ways of being human, should necessarily develop an approach that includes both cultural respect and human equality.

Many of the current policy and academic debates around education and cultural diversity centre on a cluster of themes related to human rights and responsibilities, equality and democratic citizenship. These are seen as key elements in the promotion of inclusion and the fight against racism (Osler and Starkey, 2000; Council of Europe, 2003), and all three necessitate the practice of both cultural respect and human equality. However, my research found that at school level this debate is only at a very early stage and there are a number of issues which need to be faced. Some of these are discussed in the following sections.

Human rights
Reflecting the general lack of awareness of human rights or promotion of a rights-based approach to minority groups in Irish society, none of the teachers or principals I interviewed located diversity within a human rights framework, not even those who were CSPE teachers or who taught about social justice issues in other subject areas. In fact, when explicitly asked about the relationship between diversity and human rights, two principals expressed their concerns about placing diversity within this framework.

---

[7] Blum's reference to 'some of which' is a reminder that cultural practices or values contrary to human rights are not to be valued or accommodated.

The first believed that while human rights could be helpful in some respects, they were often demanded without a corresponding acknowledgement of responsibilities. She was reluctant to place too much importance on human rights, as cultural diversity was often not about rights but 'just about difference or interesting things'.

The second principal was concerned that stating the rights of immigrants would be seen as singling them out as having human rights that conflicted in some way with the rights of the majority, and encourage the view that 'their human rights are different from our human rights'. This concern reinforced her belief that all students should be treated identically.

These examples point to the need for a clearer understanding in schools and society generally of human rights and responsibilities, and of the obligations of schools under the Convention on the Rights of the Child (UN, 1989), the National Children's Strategy (2004) and the Equal Status Act (2000, 2004).

Equality

Awareness of equality and equality issues is slowly becoming more prevalent in Irish society and within the education sector. However, teachers and students often find it difficult to distinguish between treating students identically and treating them equally, particularly in a context of cultural, religious and other kinds of diversity. The following quote encapsulates some of the difficulties teachers have. When asked whether his school had developed any new policy to accommodate the cultural diversity in the school, this teacher's reply was to ask:

> *Do you mean is there favouritism shown? ... You have to try and introduce an idea that everyone is equal in the school, so there can't be any favouritism – no group can be singled out.* (Teacher, Community School) (Gannon, 2004)

Fear of differentiation, exemplified in the assimilation or diversity blindness approaches, combined with a fear of Irish culture or 'our way of doing things' being threatened, can prevent schools from affording equal recognition and respect to the identities of all their students, and thus unwittingly contribute to inequality. The main inequality experienced by minority ethnic students is often unequal recognition of and respect for their identity (Lodge and Lynch, 2004). Redressing this inequality requires a level of differentiation in order to meet students' needs in an equal manner (Eagleton, 2000). One of the very practical challenges facing schools is to determine when equality demands that all students are treated in an identical manner, and when respect for their cultural identity demands that they receive differentiated treatment. There is also a need to work with students so that they too understand the difference between identical and fair treatment, and thus avoid students feeling aggrieved that some are treated more favourably than others, a concern which emerged quite strongly from students in the CDU research carried out in 2004.

One of the factors which have the potential to support schools in developing a culture of inclusion and genuine equality for all members of the school community is the growing awareness of equality engendered by the Equal Status Acts 2000, 2004. While schools may initially be more concerned with avoiding complaints being made against them under the legislation, the holistic interpretation of equality promoted by the Equality Authority (Equality Authority and DES, 2003) offers a positive vision of inclusion and equality. Here the inclusive school is described as one which:

- prevents and combats discrimination
- respects, values and accommodates diversity
- creates positive experiences and a sense of belonging for all students
- ensures outcomes for all students
- teaches students about diverse identities and equality issues
- ensures that the school ethos promotes equality and respect.

For Lodge and Lynch (2004) and Baker *et al* (2004), equality is not merely about equality of access, opportunity and outcomes, but also requires schools to look at the issue in relation to respect for all identities, participation by all, and the types of relationships that exist within the total school community.

Situating cultural diversity within an equality framework has a number of benefits. It ensures that the focus remains on the whole school community, rather than on a particular minority. It counteracts the assimilationist, diversity blindness or charity approaches discussed earlier. It is actively supported by equality legislation. More importantly, it stems from human rights and, in its holistic interpretation, provides a very practical framework for implementing human rights values. In its emphasis on participation, representation and relationships, it is also very closely tied into the concept and practice of democratic citizenship.

Democratic citizenship
Democratic citizenship, democracy in schools, human rights, equality, and diversity, are related in a number of ways. Democratic, as opposed to authoritarian school structures are much more likely to ensure that 'the diversity of children's experiences, cultures and lifestyles [is] recognised and given expression' (Government of Ireland, 2000:10); that all the

students, as well as staff and parents, are consulted about and involved in decisions that affect them (UNHCR, 2001); that difficult issues and conflict are dealt with; and that all students achieve educational outcomes appropriate to their ability levels.

From a curriculum perspective, the concept of citizenship as both local and global allows relationships in Irish classrooms, communities and society as a whole to be placed in a global context. Teaching methodologies and strategies that promote the development of skills and attitudes central to citizenship education, such as critical thinking, identification of multiple perspectives, active listening, respect for differing viewpoints, and others, contribute to the inclusion and integration of students on an equal basis and support teachers and students in dealing with racism and controversial issues related to diversity. The development of democratic classroom practices, the training of students in conflict resolution strategies and the development of a student peer mediation service all contribute to the development of active citizenship within a diverse society.

At an institutional level, the development of structures that enable students and parents to participate with staff in decision-making is a key factor in determining successful outcomes for students, as well as their inclusion on the basis of equality. Blair and Bourne (1998), in their large-scale research into the characteristics of effective multi-ethnic schools in Britain, identified 'the listening school' and effective leadership as the two most important characteristics. In an Irish context, the development of Student Councils, and the support for this provided through the Office of the Minister for Children and the Second-Level Support Service, offer schools the opportunity to foster democracy and participation among their students, provided that the council has a real partnership role in decision-making in school life as appropriate to the relative roles and responsibilities of students and teachers. Ensuring that minority ethnic students are actively encouraged to engage with, and be represented, on Student Councils can support the normalisation of diversity and promote genuine inclusion.

The involvement of parents as active partners in education (Government of Ireland, 1998) is often difficult to achieve at school level. For minority ethnic parents, language and cultural barriers add to these difficulties and it requires perseverance and creativity on the part of schools to overcome them. One of the areas where parental involvement is crucial is that of whole-school planning. The schools involved in the CDU interculturalism project managed with varying degrees of ease to establish intercultural planning committees which included parents from both minority and majority ethnic backgrounds, as well as teachers, students, administrative staff and management (Gannon and Kenny, 2006). There is also anecdotal evidence that participation by minority ethnic parents in Parent Councils and other activities within schools is increasing.

Implications for citizenship education

Cultural diversity offers schools opportunities and challenges on two levels – the individual level, whether teacher, student or parent; and the institutional or whole-school level. It also presents challenges and opportunities to the system itself in terms of responding effectively to the new social realities.

On an individual level, teachers and school staff will benefit from reflection on their perceptual and ideological frameworks and from the development of inclusive, democratic strategies for teaching in diverse classrooms, which include global as well as local perspectives. At an institutional level, schools can develop ways to nurture cultural respect and human equality through reflection on their institutional values and their translation into practice. These will best be supported by the conscious development of democratic structures for listening, democratic dialogue, conflict resolution and mediation.

At system level, the development of Politics and Society as a full subject at Senior Cycle offers an opportunity to raise the profile of democratic citizenship within schools and challenges them to develop the structures referred to above. Additionally, at system level there is an obvious need for the inclusion of consideration of cultural diversity and citizenship at all levels of teacher development, both pre-service and in-service. At pre-service level, this is currently only provided in either a fairly minimalist way or as an elective. DES continuing professional development provision does not currently include the area of cultural diversity and this situation needs to change, particularly in light of the distribution to all teachers of the NCCA intercultural guidelines (NCCA, 2006).

Conclusion

This chapter began with asking questions about the appropriateness of human rights, equality and democratic citizenship as potential frameworks for responding to cultural diversity in schools. One could argue that any one of them should be the dominant framework, but perhaps the reality is more complex. All three comprise concepts, values and practices which are constantly being refined and re-evaluated in the light of changing social and political realities. In an Irish context we are only just beginning to move towards the notion of a rights-based approach to diversity, and our understanding of equality and of active citizenship is still developing. All three are closely interlinked and, while each has its own emphasis, they share a common value basis.

Education for a culturally diverse society encompasses a much broader arena than what is strictly considered citizenship education. Likewise, citizenship education involves much more than just a consideration of cultural diversity. However, citizenship education, with its basis in human rights and responsibilities, equality and participation, if reflected in all aspects of school life, can provide a very helpful framework for schools seeking to respond positively and effectively to cultural diversity, and seeking to help students develop into adult citizens of a truly intercultural society.

References

Baker, J., Lynch, K., Cantillon, S. and Walsh, J. (2004), 'Equality in Education', in *Equality: from Theory to Action*. Basingstoke: Pallgrave Macmillan

Blair, M. and Bourne, J. (1998), *Making the Difference: Teaching and Learning Strategies in Successful Multi-Ethnic Schools*, Sudbury: DfEE

Blum, L.A. (2000), 'Values, Underpinnings of Antiracist and Multicultural Education', in Modgil and Modgil (eds), Leicester (ed.), *Systems of Education: Theories, Policies and Implicit Values*, Vol.1, London: Falmer Press

Chryssochoou, X. (2004), *Cultural Diversity. Its Social Psychology*, Maldon and Oxford: Blackwell

Council of Europe (2003), 'Declaration by the European Ministers of Education on Intercultural Education in the New European Context', paper presented at the Standing Conference of European Ministers of Education 21st session, 'Intercultural education: managing diversity, strengthening democracy', Athens

CDU (Curriculum Development Unit) (2003), 'A Whole School Approach to Interculturalism and Inclusion', Dublin: CDVEC Curriculum Development Unit (unpublished)

DES (Department of Education and Science) (2001), *Information Booklet for Schools on Asylum Seekers*, Dublin: Stationery Office

DoJELR (Department of Justice, Equality and Law Reform) (1999), *Integration – A Two Way Process*, Dublin: Stationery Office

Eagleton, T. (2000), *The Idea of Culture*, Oxford: Blackwell Publishers

Epstein, D. and Sealey, A. (1990), *Where It Really Matters. Developing Anti-Racist Education in Predominantly White Primary Schools*. Birmingham: Development Education Centre

Equality Authority and DES (Department of Education and Science) (2003), *Schools and the Equal Status Act*, Dublin: Equality Authority and Department of Education and Science

Gannon, M. (2004), *Framing Diversity: Responding to Cultural Diversity in Irish Post-Primary Schools*, Dublin: Trinity College

Gannon, M. (2002), *Changing Perspectives. Cultural Values and Equality in Ireland and the Wider World*, Dublin: CDVEC CDU and NCCRI

Gannon, M. and Kenny, M. (2006), 'A Whole School Approach to Interculturalism and Equality. A Report on an Action Research Project of the CDVEC Curriculum Development Unit', Dublin: CDVEC CDU

Geertz, C. (1973), *The Interpretation of Cultures*, London: Hutchinson

Government of Ireland (1998), *Education Act.* Dublin: Stationery Office

Government of Ireland (2000), *The National Children's Strategy, Our Children – Their Lives*, Dublin: Stationery Office

Gordon, R.G. Jr (ed.) 2005, *Ethnologue: Languages of the World,* 15th edition, Dallas, Texas: SIL International. Online version: http://www.ethnologue.com

Keogh, A.F. and Whyte. J. (2003), *Getting On. The Experiences and Aspirations of Immigrant Students in Second Level Schools Linked to the Trinity Access Programme*, Dublin: Children's Research Centre, Trinity College

Lodge, A. and Lynch, K. (2004), 'Young People's Equality Concerns: The Invisibility of Diversity', in M. Shevlin amd R. Rose (eds), *Encouraging Voices: Respecting the Insights of Young People Who Have Been Marginalised*, Dublin: National Disability Authority

Macpherson, Sir William (1999), *The Stephen Lawrence Inquiry*, London: Stationery Office

NCCA (National Council for Curriculum and Assessment) (2006), *Intercultural Education and the Post-Primary School: Guidelines*, Dublin: NCCA

Osler, A. and Starkey, H. (2000), 'Citizenship, Human Rights and Cultural Diversity', in A. Osler (ed.), *Citizenship and Democracy in Schools: Diversity, Identity, Equality*, Stoke on Trent: Trentham Books

Parekh, B. (2000), *Rethinking Multiculturalism. Cultural Diversity and Political Theory*, Basingstoke: Macmillan Press Ltd

Richardson, R. and Wood, A. (1999), *Inclusive Schools, Inclusive Society: Race and Identity on the Agenda*, Stoke-on-Trent: Trentham Books

UN (1989), Convention on the Rights of the Child

UNCHR (2001), *The Aims of Education: 17/04/2001. Crc/Gc/2001/1, CRC General Comment 1*, Geneva: Office of the United Nations High Commissioner for Human Rights

12

New migrant communities and equity in education: approaches to strategic policy, a Northern Ireland case study

Daniel Holder

The Dungannon South Tyrone local government district is the area of Northern Ireland that has proportionately most benefited from inward migration in the new millennium. Migrant workers, mostly citizens of Portugal,[1] Lithuania and Poland, have brought major social and economic benefits to the mainly rural borough. The downside has been the poor way some migrant workers and their families have been treated. Many have had positive work, home and service experiences, but others have suffered abuse, discrimination and degrees of hostility and racism.

The best available official data would indicate that the migrant population of the area has risen from just over 1 per cent of the population at the time of the 2001 census to an estimated 9.5 per cent of the population in 2007. The migrant population has 77 per cent of working age and 19 per cent children. 2006 official data indicate 16 per cent of local births to migrant mothers. This constitutes a major opportunity for education and the sustainability of education in the rural area. Falling enrolments threaten the sustainability of rural schools; a new young population can ensure their sustainability and survival.

All of this is dependent on everyone involved in the planning and delivery of education 'getting their act together'. Resourcing *should* not be an issue. Additional tax revenues brought in by migrant workers actually currently outstrip the corresponding resources needed to provide services. However, this is dependent on government providing new resources on the ground where they are needed. Education is also unlike any other 'public service' in the sense that it is an investment in the future; it is also a legal requirement.

---

[1] There is considerable ethnic diversity within the migrant worker population who are Portuguese citizens, including a sizable Tetum-speaking Timorese population.

To state the obvious, this is not just an issue of population change but rather the context of children from different linguistic, cultural and national backgrounds. This is an issue not just of planning but of accessibility. Teaching in a diverse environment requires specific skills for interaction both with 'newcomer' children from a migrant background and with host population pupils. The skills and knowledge needed and the overarching approach to be taken is the subject of this chapter. The case study is a critique of a draft policy proposed by the Northern Ireland Department of Education in 2007.

Migration and the right to education

Beyond the numbers lie people, namely families and children with a right to education. The onus is on the state to ensure education is delivered in a way that is accessible to all. The human right to education covers all children, and is a right to education in a non-discriminatory manner. The European Convention on Human Rights (ECHR) is legally binding on both governments, north and south, and is enshrined in domestic legislation. Article 2, Protocol 1 of the ECHR covers the Right to Education, stating that no one will be denied this right. This can be read with Article 14 of the ECHR which states that the rights in the convention are to be secured without discrimination on any ground.[2] There is anti-discrimination and equality legislation in both jurisdictions. There is also a pragmatic welfare rights approach, namely that education is paid for in the north through taxation, which migrants also pay.

Whilst this information seems obvious it is relevant since it is often misconstrued. Some UK political and media discourse has effectively blamed migration (and at times migrants) for 'pressure' on public services, rather than indicating that this is an issue of poor planning. It is tantamount to stating that if a service to which you are unequivocally entitled (and as a secondary issue you are paying for) is not accessible to you, it is your fault. Such discourse can reach the classroom. Anti-racism and explaining migration are key challenges for education both for the citizenship curriculum and beyond.

The role of Councils

Local Government in Northern Ireland has a legal duty to tackle racism and promote racial equality within its District. Dungannon and South Tyrone Borough Council has engaged in a number of initiatives in this

---

[2] Those listed include 'race, colour, language, religion and national or social origin'.

regard including the three year (2004-7) 'Animate' inter-agency migrant worker equality project, run jointly with the South Tyrone Empowerment Programme (STEP), a community-based NGO. At the time of writing the Council employs both an Anti-Racism Officer and a Racial Equality Policy and Research Officer. The role of the latter includes engagement with other public services as regards promotion of racial equality, and it is in this context that the Council engaged with the Department of Education regarding its approach to education policy and minority ethnic children.

The Council's assessment of the situation at the time of this engagement was two-fold. Firstly it concluded that, albeit within the constraints of limited resources, there was good practice on the ground locally. This had been developed by individual schools and in the Southern Education and Library Boards' Ethnic Minority Achievement Service. Secondly, however, it concluded that this was being undertaken in the absence of a strategic direction and policy from the Department, raising serious questions about sustainability and equality of provision as to how best practice was to be rolled out. It was in this context that the Council welcomed the opportunity to comment on a draft policy released in the spring of 2007.

The Department of Education draft policy and critique

The consultation document released by the Department of Education under the then direct rule administration was entitled *Draft Policy on Supporting Ethnic-Minority Children and Young People who have English as an Additional Language* and presented a particular model of support for minority ethnic children. Dungannon and South Tyrone Council sent in a detailed submission which was drafted through the all-party Equality and Good Relations Subcommittee. It was prepared in consultation with local educationalists and STEP as well as the participation of elected members.

The submission effectively critiqued what it saw as weaknesses in the draft policy whilst making practical suggestions on alternatives. The submission also raised issues regarding process and structure; however, these are not matters of interest to this chapter. There has been a number of encouraging developments since the return of the devolved Northern Ireland Assembly which will also not be referenced, to allow focus on a contrast between overall approaches.

A welcomed aspect of the Department's approach was a move to mainstreaming in which there was specialist support to develop skills across the education sector. This moved away from a peripatetic or floating support model, and towards a recognition that education in an ethnically diverse environment is now the norm rather than the exception.

Concerns with the overall approach

A major area of concern was the effective reduction of ethnic minority achievement within the draft policy to English language acquisition. There was an absence of a whole-child approach. The starting point of the policy appeared to be not the child but rather what was pejoratively referred to as the child having difficulties with English that needed to be resolved. Suggestions included schools 'considering' some extra English classes out of school.

Though learning English is one important area, the concern was that other essential areas including the ethos of schools, racial equality, anti-racism, prejudice and attitudinal matters, intercultural education, mother tongue acquisition and development or other issues were not considered. In fact at no point in the document were the words 'racism' or 'inclusion' actually mentioned.

The proposed service was termed 'Ethnic Minority Achievement Service' (EMAS), yet the policy focused only on pupils requiring English as an Additional Language (EAL), overlooking English-speaking minority ethnic pupils whether migrant or part of the broader minority ethnic population – including locally the Chinese and Traveller communities. Even for EAL pupils there was only focus on one aspect of support, learning English, to the detriment of other areas that are crucial to promoting minority ethnic achievement in schools.

The Equality Impact Assessment within the draft policy document stated: 'this policy does not deal with issues like cultural differences or school ethos'. The submission argued that such matters are absolutely crucial and that if they are omitted the policy will not achieve its own stated objectives. It argued that as the policy clearly makes the case that there is a need for expert specialised support to schools regarding English language acquisition, surely the same argument counts regarding the other well-researched specific needs of minority ethnic pupils. The submission outlined a number of key areas of omission in the role of the service, as follows:

• **Anti-racism and attitudinal work**: We have serious concerns regarding the level of racism in classrooms. This is echoed in research including that of the Northern Ireland Commissioner for Children and Young People. Yet there is no indication that racism will be dealt with at all. The word is not mentioned in the policy. Rather this whole area is seen as something left to the citizenship curriculum. In practice this will be a key area of expertise that the staff working in any EMAS will need. Why would the EMAS not input into the citizenship curriculum and provide specific support in this area?

- **Mother tongue education**: There is no reference to mother tongue language acquisition. This will place migrant and other minority ethnic children, and the language skills base in general, at a serious disadvantage.
- **Intercultural learning**: There is no reference to intercultural learning despite research indicating that this is a crucial area for classroom cohesion and minority ethnic achievement.
- **School ethos and inclusion**: Clearly the school ethos of inclusion or otherwise, and the pastoral care it provides, will make or break the education of minority ethnic children. It is astonishing that this area is specifically excluded from the role of the service.
- **Revised curriculum**: There appears to be no reference to the principles underpinning the revised curriculum and how the EMAS will relate to them.
- **Education sector language skills strategy**: There does not appear to be a strategy for mother tongue awareness or for language skills.
- **English-speaking minority ethnic pupils**: The policy does not contemplate addressing barriers and issues faced by members of minority ethnic communities who speak English, including Travellers.

In general the draft policy did not indicate which good practice model the service was to adopt in relation to its remit. There was no apparent philosophical basis for the approach taken (e.g. child-centred learning, constructivist theories). The policy only indicated that there were 'different options'. What these different approaches were, and their merits, were not referenced. It also did not appear to build on the ongoing existing pockets of good practice on the ground in Northern Ireland but regarded this as a subject for future research. The submission urged that the policy and service should build on existing good practice and also should recognise that the education of the whole child (pastoral, social and curricular) is paramount and that language development is a significant part of that. It should also recognise that language is learned in a context and is not a prerequisite for accessing learning.

A further concern regarding the overall approach was that, whilst there was a section on 'relevant laws', there was no reference to international instruments to which the UK is a signatory that would be relevant to the policy. For example, the Department is bound by obligations under the UN Convention on the Rights of the Child in terms of compliance with the principle of non-discrimination in Article 2 and Article 29, which states that:

> States Parties agree that the education of the child shall be directed to
> ... [t]he development of respect for the child's parents, his or her own
> cultural identity, language and values, for the national values of the
> country in which the child is living, the country from which he or she
> may originate, and for civilisations different from his or her own.

There was also no cross-reference to the then relevant high-level policy
instruments in Northern Ireland, in particular the Government's *Racial
Equality Strategy* or *A Shared Future Strategy*. Such instruments and
documents would have indicated the need for a broader overall approach.

Mother tongue education

A further area of omission within the draft policy was lack of consideration
of the importance of mother tongue education. In the section on relevant
laws the draft policy asserted that there was no right to mother tongue
education, making reference to the ECHR. The submission pointed out,
however, that there were other human rights instruments that indicate this
right. For example, Article 14 of the Council of Europe's Framework
Convention for the Protection of National Minorities, which is binding on
the UK, states:

1   The Parties undertake to recognise that every person belonging to a
national minority has the right to learn his or her minority language.

2   In areas inhabited by persons belonging to national minorities
traditionally or in substantial numbers, if there is sufficient demand,
the parties should endeavour to ensure, as far as possible and within
the framework of their educational systems, that persons belonging
to those minorities have adequate opportunities for being taught the
minority language or for receiving instruction in this language.

3   Paragraph 2 of this article shall be implemented without prejudice
to the learning of the official language or the teaching of this
language.[3]

Moreover, the submission argued that there is a strong equality,
pedagogical and business case for mother tongue provision within English-
/Irish-medium education, which likewise were not referenced in the draft
policy. The submission outlined the following:

---

[3] See also Article 5 on duties re maintaining and developing minority languages and culture;
Article 6 duties re intercultural dialogue in education; Article 12 teacher training and others

- [Mother tongue development] is an important element of minority ethnic achievement and the socio-cultural development of children.
- There is a strong methodological case for mother tongue being concomitant with [learning English], building on cognitive development, etc.
- There is a need to develop language skills to broaden Northern Ireland's currently poor language skills base.
- English language acquisition is beneficial but so is a level of mother tongue development, including the offering of exams. For example, if GCSE-age children return to, say, Poland without a Polish GCSE they will be at a considerable disadvantage. Schools should also offer this option – indeed we are aware that this route has already been taken in local good practice.

Scope of policy

The scope of the policy was also a subject raised in the submission. Notably, the draft made no reference to and may well have excluded early years, post-16, further education and life-long learning.

The consultation document indicates that support for Irish-medium education is not dealt with by the policy. Clearly there will be minority ethnic pupils availing, and who wish to avail, of Irish-medium education. The submission urged that this sector needed to be included in the policy.

The draft policy was ambiguous regarding admissions policies. The submission referenced ongoing concerns about *de facto* racial discrimination for entrants in post-primary schools. Secondary education in Northern Ireland is divided into Grammar and Secondary schools. There are concerns that in South Tyrone virtually no child arriving in the country aged over 11 has entered a Grammar school. Admissions and preventing *de facto* racial segregation at any level of the schooling system are clearly an important area. This is not just at secondary level but in general where some schools are geared up and accessible to newcomer children and others are not, leading inevitably to patterns of *de facto* racial segregation.

Conclusion

The new context of greater ethnic diversity has the potential not only to make rural schools more sustainable but also to prompt a greater mainstreaming approach to developing the skills of intercultural education across the teaching profession. This has the potential to improve equality of access and attainment to newcomer pupils as well as to long-standing ethnic minorities.

There are different methodological models of support. A holistic model encompasses anti-racism and attitudinal work, mother tongue education, intercultural learning, school ethos and inclusion, English language learning and other areas. An approach advocated but unlikely to achieve objectives is that built exclusively around English language learning. English language acquisition, though an important component, is not the whole.

The prize of getting this right is apparent. The price of getting this wrong may well be effectively a two-tier educational attainment (on top of all existing tiers) between the majority and minority ethnic pupils, and a legacy of racial inequality.

13

Citizenship and diversity: special educational needs

Una O'Connor

Introduction

This chapter will focus on some issues relating to pupils with learning difficulties that have emerged as an inherent feature and by-product of the citizenship curriculum. In particular, it will consider current debate around the introduction and delivery of a citizenship curriculum to pupils with learning difficulties; differentiation; and the (potential) impact on pupil empowerment. This is by no means a definitive list; rather it represents a preliminary overview of issues that merit some consideration within the overall implementation framework for citizenship.

From the 1980s onwards, national legislation and reform has increasingly sought to make specific provision for children with special educational needs (SEN) a component feature of inclusive educational policy. Associated policy definitions have been articulated in inclusive terminology that is characterised by cross-references with equality, anti-discrimination and human rights language (DfEE, 1998, 2001; DENI, 1998, 2005a, 2005b; Scottish Executive, 2002, 2004; DfES, 2001, 2002, 2004). For schools in Northern Ireland, the most significant policy developments have been the new statutory arrangements for special education and the revision of the terms and conditions to identify and deal with disability discrimination (DENI, 2005a, 2005b; Equality Commission, 2006).

Overall, the fundamental philosophy of policy reform has been, generally, that of social inclusion and, specifically, that of proper and equitable access to education for all pupils with learning difficulties and disabilities (Ainscow, 1999; Avramidis and Norwich, 2002). However, some reservations persist that ambiguous and rhetorical inclusive strategies, coupled with limitations in individual and institutional capacity to respond to diversity, have instead prevailed to limit the participative experiences of children and young people with SEN in the mainstream environment (Giangreco *et al*, 1998; Hornby, 1999; Croll and Moses, 2000a, 2000b; Slee, 2001; Avramidis and Norwich, 2002; EDA, 2003).

Background

Over the past five years, the number of children with a statement of special educational needs (SEN) in primary, post-primary and special schools has risen by just over 25 per cent.[1] At the same time, a large proportion of children have been identified as having additional learning need(s) that require supplementary support and intervention, but without a statutory statement.[2] Corresponding statistics indicate that the numbers of these children in primary and post-primary schools is approximately 4-5 times higher than their statemented peers.[3] The incremental rise in the numbers of pupils with learning difficulties has occurred alongside a contrasting decline in the overall pupil population. Figures across school sectors reveal a drop of between 2 and 6 per cent; in addition, the projected drop of 9 per cent at post-primary level by 2010 may impact significantly on the composition and constitution of schools, as well as on the generic profile of the pupil population. It is a situation that, while underlining SEN as an integral yet distinct aspect of education, also queries educational standards, in particular the nature and quality of provision (Norwich, 2002).

It is acknowledged that pupils with learning difficulties are not a homogeneous group (Lawson *et al*, 2001). Although there may be some commonality in learning needs, pupils will often have particular requirements, behaviours and approaches to learning – even pupils with the same learning difficulty (Norwich, 2002). It is also acknowledged, however, that young people have a greater fundamental connection through their *sameness* than through their *difference* (Gross, 2002).

Education is an evolving, organic process that is inextricably linked to, and reflective of, cultural, social and political reform. Undeniably, changes in provision for children with SEN have been introduced at a time of significant change within the education system in Northern Ireland. The next decade will certainly see significant shifts in the composition and function of schools as well as in where, what and how pupils learn. The introduction of a common curriculum framework from September 2007 is intended to be strongly pupil-centred, with the needs of the individual child at its core (DfES, 2004). The revised curriculum will confer fixed expectations and accountability measures for the way in which schools fulfil their institutional responsibility to all pupils through their school development plans and self-evaluation strategies, as well as through individual education plans (EPs) and pupil profiles (CCEA, 2007).

[1] DE Statistics and Research, 2007
[2] DE Statistics and Research, 2007
[3] DE Statistics and Research, 2007

Embedded within the arrangements for the revised curriculum is the stipulation that pupils with SEN should have access to the same range of learning pathways available to other pupils (DfES, 2004). The premise of equitable provision has been underpinned by a fundamental principle that the interests of the child should be at the heart of all decision-making and should be based upon informed choice by both pupils and their parents. It is inevitable that the collective changes within the education system will have short- and long-term implications for all pupils, not least those with SEN. Clearly then, the meaningful inclusion and education of children with SEN has become a common issue for many teachers, in particular appropriate access to a full curriculum and opportunities to develop their knowledge, aptitudes and skills (build on their strengths).

The citizenship curriculum

In September 2007, education for Local and Global Citizenship was introduced as a core statutory element of the revised Northern Ireland curriculum. In the primary sector, citizenship features within the learning area Personal Development and Mutual Understanding; in the post-primary sector, it features within the learning area Learning for Life and Work. In the post-primary sector, Local and Global Citizenship is addressed through four key concepts: diversity and inclusion; equality and social justice; democracy and active participation; and human rights and social responsibility.

The overall aim of the revised curriculum is 'to empower young people to achieve their potential, and to make informed and responsible decisions throughout their lives' (CCEA, 2003). The three inter-related curriculum objectives are intended to provide learning opportunities 'to help young people develop as individuals; as contributors to society; and as contributors to the economy and environment' (CCEA, 2003). The aim and objectives are intended to promote and encourage a variety of learning experiences, through active and participatory pedagogies – including enquiry-based and values-based approaches – that nurture informed and inquisitive pupils rather than passive learners.

Generically, the remit of citizenship curricula has been defined as part of a broader social agenda that 'promotes social cohesion whilst at the same time, recognising diversity' (Pavey, 2003:58). This includes the function of education as a social tool to prepare young people to manage their own lives, relationships and lifestyles through offering pupils sustained opportunities for personal development, including autonomy, independence, decision-making, participation and self-efficacy.

In Northern Ireland the relationship between the revised curriculum and social cohesion and diversity lies in the extent to which young people are empowered with the knowledge, skills and aptitudes to navigate their future educational, employment, social and political prospects, and take their place as informed and participatory citizens. Concurrently, the introduction of Local and Global Citizenship has underlined the importance attributed to developing young people's understanding of how their lives are governed and how they can participate to improve the quality of their own lives and that of others through democratic processes (CCEA, 2007).

Regular or special citizenship?

It is acknowledged that while there is a utilitarian element to some models of education, any discussion of its fundamental purpose reveals its values-based, humanistic background (Garner and Gains, 2000; Gilmore *et al*, 2003; Pavey, 2003). A key consideration in the development of any curriculum (citizenship included) is its relationship to and compatibility with a generic framework of entitlement, commonality and differentiation (Norwich, 2002). Given the increasing ability range of the pupil population in many mainstream schools, the potential dilemma of access to a *regular* or *special* version of the citizenship curriculum has generated some speculation on the inextricable connections between the learning outcomes of citizenship lessons, the quality of provision in relation to SEN and the relationship with the values of education.

It is argued that the concept of educational need should be modelled on both the commonality and individuality of needs, and that associated provision should seek to ... 'accommodate the greatest diversity without high visibility identification' (Norwich, 2002:499). A recurrent concern in the implementation of a programme for citizenship has been the concern that not all pupils would be able to access the content in a meaningful way, particularly the more abstract and/or conceptual elements of the curriculum (Pavey, 2003). In Northern Ireland, an alternative resource has been developed for the special school sector. An experienced team was established to examine the statutory requirements and minimum entitlements of Learning for Life and Work (including Local and Global Citizenship), with the remit to refine and connect these into thematic units (with appropriate resources). Although the resource was developed in the first instance for the special school sector, given the diversity of the pupil population in post-primary schools (particularly secondary schools) there is a sound argument for its universal availability to all schools.

Citizenship and efficacy

The expectations of citizenship and of what it means to be a citizen carry equal weight for children, most notably in legislation, where their equal access to protection, provision and participation has reinforced their status as citizens (Verhellen, 2000). A key challenge in the implementation of a differentiated citizenship curriculum to pupils with learning difficulties is that '... in assuming complexity of conceptualisation of some issues, does this deny pupils' rights and opportunities for empowerment and, unintentionally, shelter and protect rather than enable?' (Lawson, 2003:118). Such commentary is a customary reaction to the application of reductionist connotations that can perpetuate expectations of what a child with SEN can achieve (Croll and Moses, 2000b; Pollock-Prezant and Marshak, 2006; Haller *et al*, 2006). With regard to citizenship education, it is an apposite and potentially far-reaching argument, particularly where '... there is a danger of disenabling some pupils by not considering some more complex or abstract issues as possibilities and thus foreshortening expectations' (Lawson, 2003:118).

However, with the prominence of the inclusion agenda alongside a greater emphasis on a rights-based approach within both citizenship and inclusion, it is contended that standardised pre-conceptions of how much (or little) understanding pupils with learning difficulties will have of the conceptual aspects of the citizenship curriculum is inaccurate and outdated. Instead, it is argued that a rights-based agenda (whether in relation to citizenship or to inclusion) offers greater awareness of entitlement for teachers and pupils alike, while the associated powers of advocacy, efficacy and empowerment are integral outcomes of a successful citizenship curriculum.

For these reasons, educators have a responsibility to use their skills to find ways of making the conceptual framework accessible, so that young people with learning difficulties are not denied access to those aspects of regular adult life, and are empowered to take more control of their lives (Pavey, 2003:59). In consequence, an alternative position is articulated around the fundamental philosophy that teachers should nurture '... high expectations for all young people and should provide suitably challenging opportunities for each young person to take part fully and effectively in lessons, to experience success in learning and to achieve as high a standard as possible' (CCEA, 2007).

Differentiating for citizenship

Within the revised Northern Ireland Curriculum, it is stipulated that, to ensure pupils with additional learning needs are not denied appropriate learning experiences, curriculum planning and assessment for pupils with special educational needs must take account of the nature, extent and duration of the difficulty experienced by the pupil. The revised Northern Ireland Curriculum contains an access statement that outlines how learning opportunities can be adapted or modified to provide all young people with relevant and challenging work appropriate to their needs. Importantly, it is stressed that in many cases necessary action for curriculum access can be met through greater differentiation of tasks and school-based interventions as set out in the SEN Code of Practice (DENI, 1998).

Access to learning, by necessity, requires teachers to be active participants (Wenger, 1998; Bourke *et al*, 2004). The challenge for teachers in diverse classrooms is to engage all students in high-quality learning activities (Johnson, 1999; Murphy *et al*, 2005). Teachers' attitudes and motivation towards pupils with learning difficulties and their willingness to respond to difference often correlate with lack of knowledge, confidence and skills, and with the type and severity of learning difficulty (Scruggs and Mastropieri, 1996; Ainscow *et al*, 2003). As a result, their understanding of, and reaction to, diversity is often reflected in the nature of instruction that takes place in classrooms (Johnson, 1999).

At the same time, consideration of differentiated approaches to teaching citizenship, by necessity, requires some reflection of what defines the essence of citizenship (Lawson, 2003). The key characteristics of the Local and Global Citizenship curriculum as enquiry-based and experiential represent a move away from prescriptive approaches to education that tended to stifle rather than empower. The intention to nurture active and inquisitive learners is a pivotal aspiration, particularly since behavioural patterns of exploring issues, questioning established orders, and defending one's own viewpoints are integral components of autonomy and self-efficacy. It is particularly important that these initial experiences take place in a safe and managed environment, particularly for those pupils who have had little (or no) opportunity to engage in open and honest discussion on issues that affect their lives. For this reason, the guiding principle in any differentiation is that the curriculum (whether citizenship or other subject areas) is sufficiently flexible to be adaptable to pupils' needs, without compromising learning (Lawson *et al*, 2001).

The provision of opportunities for all pupils to experience success is vital in order for them to enjoy learning and develop their self-esteem (EDA, 2003). For pupils to acquire knowledge, and to develop skills and understanding that best suits their abilities, the application of a range of strategies is advocated. Generically, this can include the identification of teaching techniques (e.g. multi-level instruction; activity-based experiential learning; student-directed learning; co-operative learning; peer collaboration and heterogeneous grouping); teaching approaches (e.g. adaptation of age-appropriate materials that continue to challenge knowledge, skills and aptitudes); the learning environment (e.g. suitable time to complete tasks); and resources (e.g. access to ICT and other technology).

What should not be overlooked in the differentiation process is that the strategies employed for teaching children with learning difficulties commonly benefit *all* children, regardless of ability (Johnson, 1999; Frederickson and Cline, 2002; Gross, 2002). It is a valuable reminder that diversity is a reciprocal process, since a child with SEN is potentially a teacher to his/her peers, teacher, school and community.

The challenge of heterogeneity

Acceptance of difference implies non-discrimination. It is the manifestation of a physical, social, emotional and cultural base that empowers children with learning difficulties to grow to their full potential and to confidently enter the adult world (McDougall *et al*, 2004). The fundamental benefits of diversity, articulated in social, political and educational policy, essentially reiterate the philosophical values base that characterises inclusion (Gilmore *et al,* 2003). The development of positive or negative responses to difference is not a simplistic process; often it is a composite assimilation of learned influences, acquired through direct and indirect interactions with other people and events (Scheepstra *et al*, 1999).

The ratification of greater equality and inclusion legislation within education policy has meant that the pupil profile in mainstream classrooms is more heterogeneous than ever before. Although diversity can exist in terms of religion, gender and ethnicity, the presence of children with learning difficulties constitutes one of the largest groups. At the same time, it should be acknowledged that children with learning difficulties may also represent one or more of the other forms of diversity. Dealing with difference is one of the most recurrent challenges for many teachers. Comparative studies on inclusion have recurrently found that teachers were generally dissatisfied with preparatory arrangements for an inclusive classroom and felt insufficiently skilled to respond to a diverse pupil population; this was most apparent amongst teachers in post-primary schools, where the more rigorous demands of curriculum and assessment often assumed priority (Bennet *et al*, 1998; EDA, 2003).

It is a prospect, then, that can become more complex in the teaching of diversity. The key theme of Diversity and Inclusion contains specific reference to disability and difference. Although the broad thematic area of disability has been a popular option for many teachers, it is one that has increasingly challenged some citizenship practice, particularly when diversity is manifest in the classroom population. What is important, then, is the confidence to address the generic framework of diversity through universal concepts of respect, acceptance and acknowledgement of individuality. This is an important consideration, particularly since research has identified implicit and explicit exemplars that, just as many children with learning difficulties know they are 'different', so too do other children.

Conclusion

This chapter has attempted to demonstrate the duality of the citizenship curriculum, in that it is both challenged by, yet can offer opportunities, to young people with learning difficulties. The diversity of learners is now a fundamental characteristic of all classroom environments. It is a potentially rich and rewarding climate in which to fully and meaningfully engage with the diversity of citizenship. This requires citizenship educators to respond confidently and imaginatively to the diversity in their midst.

References

Ainscow, M., Howes, A., Farrell, P. and Frankham, J. (2003), 'Making sense of the development of inclusive practices', *European Journal of Special Needs Education*, 18(2), 227-242

Ainscow, M. (1999), *Understanding the development of inclusive schools*, London: Falmer Press

Avramidis, E. and Norwich, B. (2002), 'Teachers' attitudes towards integration/inclusion: a review of the literature', *European Journal of Special Needs Education*, 17(2), 129-147

Bennet, J., Gash, H. and O'Reilly, M. (1998), 'Ireland: integration as appropriate, segregation where necessary', in T. Booth and M. Ainscow, *From them to us: an international study of inclusion in education*, London: Routledge, pp 149-163

Bourke, R., Kearney, A. and Bevan-Brown, J. (2004), 'Stepping out of the classroom: involving teachers in the evaluation of national special education policy', *British Journal of Special Education*, 31(3), 150-156

CCEA (Council for Curriculum, Examinations and Assessment) (2003), *Proposals for the curriculum and assessment at key stage 3, part 1: Background rationale and detail*, Belfast: CCEA

CCEA (Council for Curriculum, Examinations and Assessment) (2007), *The statutory curriculum at key stage 3, part 1: Rationale and detail*, Belfast: CCEA

Croll, P. and Moses, D. (2000a), 'Ideologies and utopias: education professionals' views of inclusion', *European Journal of Special Needs Education*, 15(1), 1-13

Croll, P. and Moses, D. (2000b), *Special Needs in the primary school*, London: Cassell

DENI (Department of Education for Northern Ireland) (1998), *Code of Practice on the Identification and Assessment of Special Educational Needs*, Bangor: DENI

DENI (Department of Education for Northern Ireland) (2005a), *The Special Educational Needs and Disability (Northern Ireland) Order 2005*, Bangor: DENI

DENI (Department of Education for Northern Ireland) (2005b), *Draft supplementary guidance to support the impact of SENDO on the Code of Practice on the identification and assessment of special educational needs*, Bangor: DENI

DfEE (Department for Education and Employment) (1998*)*, *Meeting special educational needs: a programme of action*, London: DfEE

DfEE (Department for Education and Employment) (2001), *Special Education and Disability Act*, London: DfEE

DfES (Department for Education and Skills) (2001), *Special educational needs code of practice*, London: DfES

DfES (Department for Education and Skills) (2002), *Special Educational Needs and Disability Act*, London: DfES

DfES (Department for Education and Skills) (2004), *Removing barriers to achievement: the government's strategy for SEN*, London: DfES

EDA (European Development Agency – European Agency for Development in Special Needs Education) (2003), *Inclusive education and classroom practices*, Brussels: EDA

Equality Commission (2006), Commission response to OFM/DFM. *Consultation paper: a single equality bill for Northern Ireland.* Belfast: Equality Commission

Frederickson, N. and Cline, T. (2002), *Special Educational Needs, Inclusion and Diversity*, Buckingham: Open University Press

Garner, P. and Gains, C. (2000), 'The debate that never happened', *Special!* Autumn, pp 8-10

Giangreco, M.R., Cloninger, C.J. and Iverson, V.S. (1998), *Choosing outcomes and accommodations for children: a guide to educational planning for students with disabilities,* second ed., Baltimore, MD: Paul H Brookes

Gilmore, L., Campbell, J. and Cuskelly, M. (2003), 'Developmental expectations, personality stereotypes and attitudes towards inclusive education: community and teacher views of Down syndrome', *International Journal of Disability, Development and Education*, 50(1), 65-76

Gross, J. (2002), *Special educational needs in the primary school: a practical guide,* Maidenhead: Open University Press

Haller, B., Dorries, B. and Rahn, J. (2006), 'Media labelling versus the US disability community identity: a study of shifting cultural language', *Disability and Society*, 21(1), 61-75

Hornby, G. (1999), 'Inclusion or delusion: can one size fit all?', *Support for Learning*, 14(4), 152-157.

Johnson, G.M. (1999), 'Inclusive education: fundamental instructional strategies and considerations', *Preventing School Failure*, 43(2), 72-78

Lawson, H. (2003), 'Citizenship education for pupils with learning difficulties: towards participation?', *Support for Learning*, 18(3), 117-122

Lawson, H., Waite, S. and Robertson, C. (2005), 'Distinctiveness of curriculum provision at 14 to 16 for students with learning difficulties', *British Journal of Special Education*, 32(1), 12-20

McDougall, J., DeWit, D.J., King, G., Miller, L.T. and Killip, S. (2004), 'High school-aged youths' attitudes toward their peers with disabilities: the role of school and student interpersonal factors', *International Journal of Disability, Development and Education*, 51(3), 287-313

Murphy, E., Grey, I.M. and Honan, R. (2005), 'Co-operative learning for students with difficulties in learning: a description of models and guidelines for implementation', *British Journal of Special Education*, 32(3), 157-164

Norwich, B. (2002), 'Education, inclusion and individual differences: recognising and resolving dilemmas', *British Journal of Educational Studies*, 50(4), 482-502

Pavey, B. (2003), 'Citizenship and special educational needs: what are you going to do about teaching them to vote?', *Support for Learning*, 18(2), 58-64

Pollock-Prezant, F. and Marshak, L. (2006), 'Helpful actions seen through the eyes of parents of children with disabilities', *Disability and Society*, 21(1), 31-45

Scheepstra, A., Nakken, H. and Pijl, S.J. (1999), 'Contacts with classmates: the social position of pupils with Down syndrome in Dutch mainstream education', *European Journal of Special Needs Education*, 14, 212-220

Scottish Executive (2002), *Improving our schools: SEN the programme of action*, Edinburgh: Scottish Executive

Scottish Executive (2004), *Additional Support for Learning (Scotland) Act*, 2004, Edinburgh: Scottish Executive

Scruggs, T.E. and Mastropieri, M.A. (1996), 'Teacher perceptions of mainstreaming/inclusion, 1958-1995: a research synthesis', *Exceptional Children*, 63, 59-74.

Slee, R. (2001), *The inclusive school*, London: Falmer

Verhellen, E. (2000), 'Children's rights and education', in A. Osler (ed.), *Citizenship and democracy in schools: Diversity, Identity, Equality*, Stoke-on-Trent: Trentham

Wenger, E. (1998), *Communities of practice: learning, meaning and identity*, Cambridge: Cambridge University Press

14

Young people with disabilities: citizenship real or imaginary?

Michael Shevlin

Introduction

> Children with disabilities have been (and still are) particularly susceptible to benevolent, but often misguided, attempts to plan for them. … But in an education system that aspires to be inclusive, it is important that discourse does not exclude the perspectives and interpretations of children, particularly the perspectives of those children with disabilities. If planning is informed by stereotypical images of disability or outdated models of childhood the risk is that marginalisation and exclusion will continue (Thomas *et al*, 1998:17).

People with disabilities and in particular children and young people with disabilities have experienced many forms of exclusion and marginalisation within society. Their right to be fully included participants in society has often been questioned at the very least and in many cases participation, if not rejected outright, has been heavily conditional. Within this context it is evident that enabling young people with disabilities to become active citizens is highly problematic for our society. As Middleton (1996) observed, there is a real risk that unless society actively encourages and supports participation by young people with disabilities their lives will be characterised by dependence and a form of second-class citizenship:

> A disabled adult is viewed as less than a full citizen, as dependent: in fact, as occupying a permanent childlike status. The preparation of a disabled child for full adulthood is therefore overridden by their preparation for life as a permanent child. As such, a disabled child is likely to experience neither a normal childhood, nor adolescence, and is conditioned into an adulthood of dependency (Middleton, 1996:53).

Facilitating an active form of citizenship will involve a concerted effort to recognise existing limitations and challenge current preconceptions about the capacity of young people with disabilities to become dynamic participants in our society. The conditional nature of much of the existing participation that has evolved needs to be actively exposed and challenged for real progress to occur. The first step in this process involves understanding how society has been traditionally organised so that people with disabilities have been marginalised, and the impact of this historical legacy on their current status within society. From this acknowledgement we need to energetically engage with young people with disabilities, seek out their voices and ensure that as a starting point they are involved in all the decision-making processes that affect their lives (Lewis and Porter, 2007).

Within this chapter young people with disabilities speak to critical issues that affect their participation in society; the lack of knowledge and awareness; coping with how difference is construed and attributed; developing autonomy in school life and peer relationships; the representation of their views and concerns. From this informed perspective we can begin the process of developing structures that encourage and facilitate the societal participation of young people with disabilities on an equal basis alongside their non-disabled peers.

Context

In order to understand the factors that affect people with disabilities in their interactions with society we need to acknowledge their historical experiences. 'Across the range of human behaviour, there is some point at which different societies and cultures make a judgement as to whether an individual is normal or abnormal. Those considered abnormal are variously labelled exceptional, different, disabled, or deviant' (Winzer, 2007:21).

Historically, people with disabilities have been labelled as abnormal and have struggled to survive on the margins of society. Beliefs about the causes of disability have moved through various phases including the supernatural and the demonological. In the Early Modern Period attempts were made to cure various disabilities and this represented a significant shift from the dominant supernatural understanding of the causes of disability. The Industrial Revolution heralded a rapid expansion of institutional provision, some of which was motivated by humane factors (education/health), though there was evidence of less benign impulses.

These less benign forces were manifested most clearly in the Eugenics movement which had a powerful impact on societal attitudes towards and treatment of people with disabilities from the end of the nineteenth century until well into the twentieth century. The Eugenics movement was initiated by a combination of medical professionals, scientists, politicians and writers. They asserted that people with general learning disabilities, in particular, were a social menace and a serious threat to the purity of the gene pool. One solution consisted of placing these people in segregated institutions. Another involved the refusal of doctors to treat infants born with disabilities, and life-saving treatments were routinely withdrawn.

By the middle of the twentieth century significant changes in societal perceptions of people with disabilities had begun to emerge. Many institutions were closed and the emphasis shifted towards more inclusive provision. Enabling legislation was enacted to sustain this initiative. The Americans with Disabilities Act (1990) marked a significant shift in official thinking:

> This law recognised that discrimination against people with disabilities in the form of purposeful unequal treatment and historical patterns of segregation and isolation was the major problem facing people with disabilities and not their individual impairments. The ADA also stated that people with disabilities have been relegated to powerless positions based on stereotypical assumptions about their disability (Braddock and Parish, 2001:50).

Children and young people with disabilities

Children with disabilities are a heterogeneous group comprising those who have physical or sensory impairments, those who have a range of identified general learning disabilities and others who have mental health difficulties or hidden/invisible disabilities. Traditionally education for children with disabilities was according to a disability category (physical, sensory, general learning disabilities, emotional and behavioural difficulties) and took place separately from their peers. Recently there have been concerted efforts to promote more inclusive school provision, though this process is far from complete and has been quite controversial.

Barriers to participation

There are a number of barriers both implicit and explicit that can limit and curtail the participation of young people with disabilities in society and more particularly within our schools. We will begin to explore these barriers and the implications for developing more inclusive provision.

Lack of knowledge and awareness

We can easily acknowledge that we lack detailed knowledge about fundamental aspects of the lives of children with disabilities. As Baldwin and Carlisle (1994) observed: 'We lack children's accounts of pain, discomfort, dependence on others for feeding, bathing and toileting. We do not know how they feel about the way doctors, social workers, therapists and other children treat them' (p.35). One way to overcome this lack of knowledge is to listen to the voices of young people with disabilities as they describe their interactions with society.

Lack of basic knowledge about disabling conditions and their impact on daily functioning constituted a serious problem according to the young disabled participants in the *Hidden Voices* study (Kenny *et al*, 2000). For one young person with a physical disability a lack of awareness was evident in ordinary communication: 'It can come across in the way they speak to you – they might speak slower which is really annoying' (p. 45). Another young person had experienced a life-threatening illness and as a result had impaired mobility, so in a sense she had experience of both the non-disabled and disabled worlds. She discovered that her peers lacked basic knowledge of her condition: 'A lad in my class said, "Being sick wouldn't have anything to do with your brain," and I said I think it might. He didn't realise what is wrong with me, which is hard to cope with in some ways. I feel I have to put it out in the open when I see people' (p.40).

Private needs often become public property. The young person believed that her able-bodied friends would have great difficulty in a disability-specific environment: 'If one of my [able-bodied] friends walked in here they would be frightened to talk to someone and that is horrible to say, I think ... They would be frightened of the unknown, really, like I was when I first got sick' (p.38). This lack of awareness could often lead to cruelty: 'It was unreal, the slagging, and it can be at disabled people. They're just doing it for a joke; they don't know what the person feels' (p.40).

Concept of difference

While recognising certain differences between them and their peers, young people with disabilities often experienced socially created and reinforced interpretations of difference and normality. In the *Life as a Disabled Child* project (1999) Watson and his co-researchers commented that within the research settings:

> ... adults often began to label the children for us, promoting the idea that disabled children were both distinct from themselves and from other children. We were regularly told how different these children were from other children, how they did not understand things in the way other

children could, how they were dependent on adults, and how it was only through adults that they were able to interact (p.13).

This approach, not surprisingly, reinforced the view that disabled children were innately passive and helpless.

Young people with disabilities reported similar experiences of a well-meaning adult world informed by over-protectiveness, as teachers 'treated them like "Babies", giving them work which was too easy and not expecting enough of them. This was particularly true for students with speech and language difficulties, or who used wheelchairs' (Wilson and Jade, 1999:5). In the *Educable* study (2000) young people with disabilities became researchers and interviewed other young people with disabilities about their school experiences. One young woman commented that in the special school she attended: 'they couldn't let you do that [talk about having sex] because the cotton wool would be broken. The cotton wool that they wrap you up in the day you start. Then by the time you leave, the cotton wool has pretty much smothered you' (p.17).

Toolan (2003) reflected on how his experiences of growing up with a physical disability had reinforced his status as different to his peers: 'Perhaps it should not, but having a physical impairment in a culture that is (at a minimum) passively uncomfortable with perceived difference, I have grown up constantly seeing my experiences as having been different or going to be different' (p.92). In effect, he was engaged with two distinct worlds – the disabled and the non-disabled: 'Because of my experience of disability and how society engaged with that experience, I occupied at least two distinct worlds from birth up to my teenage years' (p.92).

In addition, he was forced to undergo a rehabilitative regime whose purpose was to render him normal: 'Spending time in a clinical, institutional space away from family and community was difficult, as was the rehabilitative process I was going through and what it was telling me about myself and my identity. I was spending time in these environments not only engaging in tests to determine why my muscles did not allow me to walk, but also painfully learning to walk at other people's bidding. ... As a child in these environments, the first question I was asked and learned to ask other children was, "What's wrong with you?"' (p.93). Middleton (1996) supported this view of rehabilitation and its impact on the child's self-identity: 'All these efforts to make a child normal by stimulating brain waves, hanging them upside down, pushing, pulling and cajoling, mean that the child receives the very clear message that there is something about them that nobody likes' (p.37). This sense of being different was reinforced on a daily basis in Toolan's interactions with the non-disabled world: 'I grew to expect from an early age that people would stare at me and talk about me as if I was not there' (p.95).

Fostering independence

Young people with disabilities in schools are often subject to high levels of adult surveillance compared to their peers. Educators can assume that offering help is undeniably a 'good thing' and unproblematic for young people with disabilities. However, in a number of studies (Skar and Tamm, 2001; Wilson and Jade, 1999), young people expressed serious reservations about these 'helping' relationships. The relationship with the special needs assistant can be complex and ambivalent – the young people felt very vulnerable as they had to communicate the most intimate needs sometimes to a person of the opposite sex. As a result, the young people experienced a lack of privacy and often felt they had little control over their lives.

They preferred that the special needs assistant be available to help rather than taking over control of academic work or social interactions with peers. There is obviously a fine balance required to ensure that the young people with disabilities receive the appropriate support without compromising their need to develop autonomy. Actively involving these young people in the decision-making processes will be a positive first step in this direction.

Watson *et al* (1999) reported that interaction between children with and without disability was often hindered by the existence of physical barriers and attitudinal issues. Interactions appeared to be dominated by a discourse of need and care and as a result 'the non-disabled children behaved not as equals, but as guides or helpers' (p.17). Difficulties with physical access could complicate social interactions with peers as highlighted in the *Hidden Voices* study (Kenny *et al*, 2000): 'It was kind of difficult just to get around. And asking for help, I found that difficult. I didn't like asking the same person all the time. ... Some people would make a fuss over me and others wouldn't think – it was a mixture of reactions' (p.25).

Struggling with fundamental access issues and relying on peers for help often resulted in fatalistic acceptance of the *status quo*: 'There were glass fire doors. I couldn't open them. I went to the Principal. I went to everyone and they did nothing. ... If I wanted to go to the bathroom during class, or if I was carrying something for art, it was a long way. There were really steep ramps and twice I fell. I'd have to wait for someone to help me. But you get used to it after a while' (p.24). This sense of helplessness was echoed in the experiences of another participant: 'It was a very old school and our parish priest got a ramp put in. If I wanted to go to the toilet, the cubicles were very small; I had to go to the teachers' room. They knew and I had someone outside the door just in case they'd come. It wasn't too bad' (p.23).

Achieving a measure of equality in social interactions was extremely difficult for young people with disabilities as they relied on their peers for basic access: 'If a class was downstairs, no problem. But stairs, there'd be a problem. Prefabs were a big problem, big steps into them. I had to be lifted. If my friends weren't around I wouldn't get there. I wouldn't go to the class' (p.24).

Representation

The young disabled participants in the *Hidden Voices* study offered some insights into how they would wish disability to be understood and represented:

> With genetics there seems to be this idea we want perfection. There are people with different disabilities; it doesn't need to be hidden. We all have capabilities and non-capabilities; there is nobody in this room that hasn't and we should be able to accept people for who they are (p.45).
>
> They want us like machines but we are human. Being human is everybody having a different mind; people are different. And there might be hope for all this hatred against people with disability if we accept who we are. Then we can accept everything else that comes along with it. … If we can narrow it down to whatever disability people have (p.45).

In the following extended discussion the participants developed these ideas in greater depth as they examined and critiqued many of the preconceptions informing disability-related practice:

Student 1: I never liked the word handicapped. I prefer disability. Handicap is something you have in golf. Disability is like you're disabled; everyone has a disability. For instance learning [I'm ok] but bowls I'm disabled, I can't. So that'd be my disability. It's not your physical appearance, it's what's inside.

Student 2: Some people's disability can be shrouded in different ways. In today's world if you can't see it they assume 'he'll be able to do this', and you might not be able to.

Student 3: It should be recognised more publicly, not only in education.

Student 2: In the whole of society.

Student 3: People don't understand, and you can't really expect them to either because there is nothing out there to tell them about this.

Student 1: My county council is fully accessible and even has one member of staff in a wheelchair.

Student 2: I think that's marvellous.

Student 3: That shouldn't be looked on as 'that's brilliant'. This should be an everyday thing and it should be ongoing as well (pp 46-7).

The disabled participants argued very forcefully that representation of their views and concerns about inclusion required sustained and systematic societal commitment. Within schools they were sceptical about the effectiveness of representation on and through a student council: 'I don't know. We had something like that before and it hadn't really done anything' (p.50). Representation by another student was considered to be equally problematic: 'I don't think another student, I think a professional should be there. Somebody connected but detached a little. To know the facts, have the information to back up what you're saying, explain the situation' (p.50).

There was consensus that informed professional input was essential for real progress: 'It definitely shouldn't be a student. It's the teachers themselves, a matter of getting maybe a law passed stating a minimum amount of attention to be paid to people with disabilities, and making sure people are aware of it' (p.50). 'A mentor, their job to see if you were okay ... part of their job as well as teaching' (p.50).

Another participant explored the concept of representation at a systemic level within society:

He could be the spokesperson for people with disabilities, because some disabled people would be afraid to admit openly that they've a problem. ... People assume 'Oh God love him', and pity him. I think if someone was on a council ... designated ... they would say 'Listen, if he's on the government, he's bright' and then naturally from the top it would go down very slowly to everywhere, and everyone would be offered jobs, disabled and able bodies working together in the same place and Ireland would become a better place to live in ...' (p.50).

Conclusion

While for these young people becoming active Irish citizens will involve in some ways a similar process to their non-disabled peers there will be crucial differences both in substance and emphasis. As a society and as educators we have to create the conditions that will enable young people with disabilities to contribute to their communities through challenging the preconceptions that usually surround these young people. We do not yet know what citizenship for young people with disabilities will look like.

However, if active participation of young people with disabilities is to become the norm we can be certain that it will not be achieved by endless cycles of training courses with no discernible follow-up, it will not be through grouping, labelling, categorising and stereotyping through spurious assessment procedures, and it will certainly not be through organisations that speak for instead of to and with young people with disabilities. What is required is a new construction of society that welcomes diversity and ensures that these young people have opportunities to succeed in school and employment. Otherwise we will continue to have a tokenistic approach to equality and citizenship.

References

Baldwin, S. and Carlisle, J. (1994), *Social Support for Disabled Children and their Families: A Review of the Literature,* London: HMSO

Braddock, D. and Parish, S. (2001), 'An Institutional History of Disability', in G. Albrecht, K. Seelman and M. Bury (eds), *Handbook of Disability Studies*, London: Sage Publications, pp 11-68.

Educable (2000), *No Choice: No Chance. The educational experiences of young people with disabilities*, Belfast: Save the Children/Disability Action

Kenny, M., Mc Neela, E., Shevlin, M. and Daly, T. (2000), *Hidden Voices: Young People with Disabilities Speak about their Second Level Schooling*, Cork: South West Regional Authority

Lewis, A. and Porter, J. (2007), 'Research and Pupil Voice', in L. Florian (ed.), *The SAGE Handbook of Special Education*, London: Sage Publications, pp 222-232.

Middleton, L. (1996), *Making a Difference: Social Work with Disabled Children*, Birmingham: Venture Press

Skar, L. and Tam, M. (2001), 'My Assistant and I: disabled children's and adolescents' roles and relationships to their assistants', *Disability & Society*, 16 (7), 917-931

Thomas, G., Walker, D. and Webb, J. (1998), *The Making of the Inclusive School*, London and New York: Routledge

Toolan, D. (2003), 'Shaped Identities', in M. Shevlin and R. Rose (eds), *Encouraging Voices: respecting the insights of young people who have been marginalised*, Dublin: National Disability Authority, pp 91-99

Watson, N., Shakespere, T., Cunningham-Burley, S., Barnes, C., Corker, M., Davis, J. and Priestley, M. (1999), *Final Report: Life as a disabled child: a qualitative study of young people's experiences and perspectives*, London: Economic and Social Research Council

Wilson, C. and Jade, R. (1999), *Whose voice is it anyway? Talking to Disabled Young People at School*, London: The Alliance for Inclusive Education

Winzer, M. (2007), 'Confronting difference: an excursion through the history of special education', in L. Florian (ed.), *The SAGE Handbook of Special Education*, London: Sage Publications, pp 21-33

15

Public achievement and active citizenship – an informal education model[1]

Paul J. Smyth

I have devised my own test, which I am immodest enough to believe is pretty fool-proof. I invite you to try it yourself. Ready?

Deep breath in ... and out ... In ... and out.

If you can keep that up for twelve to fifteen times a minute, sixty minutes an hour, twenty-four hours a day, you are a fully functioning citizen and anyone you encounter from the moment you cross your front door step who is doing that is a fully-functioning citizen too. No ifs, no buts, no matter that their skin colour is not quite a match for your own, or that their accent, or even language is not the one you hear from your own mouth, or that they spend their Sundays – or Saturdays – or Fridays – praying somewhere other than where you pray, if you pray at all, if they pray at all.

(Glenn Patterson, Writer in Residence, Queen's University, Belfast, at the 'Talking Citizenship' Conference, Derry, October 2004)

Patterson's 'citizenship test' is refreshing in a number of ways. In Northern Ireland, citizenship is contested. In spite of the availability of dual British and Irish citizenship, citizens most choose one and deny or even despise the other. The UK has recently introduced a citizenship 'test' for new immigrants, akin to those of the USA. Young people are often referred to as 'tomorrow's citizens' (see Hallgarten and Pearce, 1999), citizens in preparation. Definitions of citizenship become increasingly politicised, narrow and exclusive at the very time when educators attempt to make it a more universal, inclusive and enriching experience for young people.

[1] This chapter and the work it describes was made possible through the support of a range of funders, including the European Programme for Peace and Reconciliation (Peace II).

The introduction of the theme of citizenship onto the curriculum of schools in Northern Ireland poses additional challenges to those facing educators in other European societies – not least the legacy of over 30 years of violent conflict and the realities of a political system constructed around the ethnic divisions that gave birth to and fed the conflict for so long.

Northern Ireland has the characteristics of what Butenschøn (2001) refers to as an 'Ethnocracy'.

> Ethnocracy is a political regime which, in contrast to democracy, is instituted on the basis of *qualified rights to citizenship*, and with *ethnic affiliation* (defined in terms of race, descent, religion, or language) as the distinguishing principle. The *raison d'être* of the ethnocracy is to secure that the most important instruments of state power are controlled by a specific ethnic collectivity. All other considerations concerning the distribution of power are ultimately subordinated to this basic intention *(original emphases)*.

Butenschøn suggests that there are '... democratic as well as non-democratic aspects of ethnocracies'. Whilst Northern Ireland has left behind the Unionist domination and the accompanying discrimination of the first 70 years of its existence, what has been created by the Good Friday Agreement might be described as 'benign apartheid' (O'Connor, 1995), where communities live separate lives in a state of mutual tolerance. A fundamental issue facing the Northern Irish populous is whether we become what you might call a 'dual benign ethnocracy' based on 'tolerance' and 'co-existence', or develop a truly innovative pluralist democracy of interdependent communities. The signs are that the former option is the one preferred by the new devolved administration at Stormont, as the *Shared Future* policy of the previous direct-rule administration has been sidelined, and Sinn Féin and the Democratic Unionist Party carve up the resources between them to keep their respective constituencies loyal.

The challenge for civic educators in Northern Ireland is how to move citizens young and older to envision a different type of society, based on more equitable arrangements of governance and administration of justice, a deeper understanding of and appreciation for diversity and more democratic relationships based on the interdependence of people and communties (Eyben *et al*, 1997).

> For years I would not let the dark gods of politics and religion possess me. Unlike many of my age and background, I had made that mythic

leap and crossed the Jordan. My Protestant working-class background and all its shibboleths would not contain me. I chose to ask questions and not accept ready-made answers. We discover our own answers if we have the will to do so; and if we are not afraid of the confrontation with ourselves that such a journey might entail.

... Those who 'cross the Jordan' and seek out truth through a different experience from the one they are born to, ... theirs is the greatest struggle. To move from one cultural ethos into another, as I did, and emerge embracing them both demands more of a man than any armed struggle. For here is the real conflict by which we move into manhood and maturity. For unless we know how to embrace the other we are not men and our nationhood is wilful and adolescent. Those who struggle through turbulent Jordan waters have gone beyond the glib definitions of politics or religion. The rest remain standing on either bank firing guns at one another. I had had enough of gun-fire, the rhetoric of hate and redundant ideologies (Keenan, 1993:16).

Two ceasefires, an Agreement, and a visit to the USA

On 10 April 1998, after protracted and often acrimonious haggling and negotiation,[2] a political agreement was hatched in Belfast, brokered between the factions, the British and Irish Governments and with the skilful facilitation of US Senator George Mitchell and the accompanying support and pressure from the Clinton administration. Within weeks I was in Washington and Minnesota on a US Government-sponsored visit for civic educators from Northern Ireland, looking at models of practice in the US.

It was a peculiar moment. Our delegation – very diverse in terms of backgrounds and political aspirations – were all very excited about the Agreement and a little anxious about the referendum to come because the outcome was difficult to predict. So we looked at a range of practice, hosted by the Washington DC based 'Streetlaw'[3] organisation. Our programme took us to Minnesota (which I had to look up on the map) where we were introduced to, amongst other things, a programme called

[2] This came at the end of years of secret talks and negotiations between the protagonists in the conflict, the public face of which were the 'Hume/Adams Initiative' and subsequent inter-governmental and multi-party talks and joint statements from the two governments. The momentum of this process was greatly assisted by the instigation of ceasefires by the IRA and the combined Loyalist paramilitaries in 1995. There was also a very significant and largely secret initiative involving an order of Catholic priests on the Falls Road who were intermediaries, mediators and peace builders, particularly between the IRA and the British and Irish Governments.

[3] Streetlaw addresses citizenship education through the medium of human rights and has major programmes in the US and around the world. www.streetlaw.org

'Public Achievement'. In general the work we saw in the US was of a good standard, though not particularly better than much of the work going on at home. One major difference was in terms of marketing – American organisations were significantly better at packaging and marketing their work.

However, the one exception on the trip was Public Achievement (PA). We visited the Hubert H. Humphrey Centre at the University of Minnesota where the initiative is based, and then St Bernard's School, which was the first practice base. It was the visit to the school that made a lasting impression on our group.

At the school we heard about the work of PA, and were then invited to talk to a series of small 'teams' of children who had been working on projects. What made an immediate impact was the obvious enthusiasm of the young people involved, the natural way they spoke about their work and the lessons they had learned, as well as the ways in which adults worked with but did not attempt to speak for the young people involved.

> Public Achievement, developed by the University of Minnesota's Centre for Democracy and Citizenship, is an experiential civic education initiative based on the concept of 'public work'. Public work embodies the idea that an important component of democracy is the 'work of the people' and an important component of citizenship is being a co-creator of our public world (in contrast to being a consumer, client or volunteer) (Hildreth, 2000).

Central to this praxis was the creation of what Boyte and Kari (1996) call 'free spaces'. Elsewhere (Boyte, 1999) argues: '… creating a vibrant public culture requires public spaces for deliberation, for intellectual life, for discussion of ideas, for self-naming, and for the exchange of power.'

Challenges of implementation

What struck our delegation was that these ways of working, combined with existing models developed through various community relations and 'Education for Mutual Understanding' programmes (Smith and Robinson, 1996) at home, could potentially make a qualitative difference and respond to the changing political environment by providing the civic dimension so often missing in earlier models (Richardson et al, 1995).

So, on our return to Northern Ireland we set about attempting to pilot this initiative, adapting it to our local culture and needs. This was no easy task. We encountered a range of challenges and problems in terms of attracting funding, matching what we wanted to do to the needs and requirements of funders, staffing problems, organisational and structural problems and the challenges of adapting an American model to a very different political situation (McCully and Green, 2001, 2003).

There were also other challenges. Within a few days of our return, a referendum was held in both parts of Ireland, and in Northern Ireland a resounding 71.12 per cent of the population voted in favour of the Agreement in the biggest electoral turnout (81 per cent) in many years. I remember it as the first (and so far the only) time in my life when I could vote with enthusiasm for something I believed in. Just over a month later, we elected 108 members to the local Assembly. However, it was more than 18 months before the new Assembly sat, and in the intervening period there were several killings – the most gruesome being of 3 young boys from the Quinn family in a sectarian petrol-bombing of their Ballymoney home in July, followed in August by the devastation of the centre of Omagh and the killing of 30 people by the splinter group calling itself the 'Real IRA'.

The context of the work in the two settings was clearly very different – as illustrated in Table 1 below. The lives and experiences of young people and the educational responses to their needs were and continue to be shaped by local realities.

In order to adapt PA to meet the needs of young people, neighbourhoods and society in Northern Ireland, we needed to take account of these important differences as well as the absence of any significant discourse on what it is to be a citizen of this dysfunctional and changing place.

Developing the local model

Since 2003 the organisation has worked in a wide range of settings in Northern Ireland, including a variety of communities, schools and museums. We have also explored the possibility of working with the Fire Service in local fire stations. This work is rooted in our 'Democratic Civic Practice' model, and revolves around the relationship between a volunteer 'coach' and a team of young people who identify an issue they want to work on and then design, implement, evaluate, make public and celebrate an action project that addresses that issue. Through this 'action project cycle' participants learn key concepts of citizenship and democracy and how to practically apply these in their local context.

There are four important principles in our work, which it is useful to articulate here:

• Young people are citizens **now** (not future citizens or citizens in preparation). This is not just a rhetorical device, but a philosophical orientation to young people and their role in society.

Table 1: *Key contextual differences, USA and Northern Ireland*

Feature	USA	Northern Ireland
Democratic stability	A long-established democracy with widely agreed systems and safeguards[4]	A society that was a failed 'ethnocracy'[5] moving from a situation of 'Direct Rule' to a devolved local administration – in a situation of flux, but also of stop-start politics
Schools system	A diverse and broadly accepted school system that plays an important role in preserving and promoting the values of the state	An education system trying to make sense of the emerging new context that had in large part been a product and preserver of the ethnocracy and sectarian division
Youth work	Little in the way of organised youth work practice and no overall 'Youth Service' structure – though several good examples of youth programmes including those with an emphasis on citizenship	A structured 'Youth Service', with hundreds of youth work programmes, but without a clear overall vision of its role. Again to some extent a product and preserver of the *status quo* with a good deal of 'segregated' or denominationally organised provision
Youth	A multi-ethnic society with at least a superficial sense of common commitment to agreed notions of citizenship. An established commitment to the teaching of citizenship within the federal curriculum	A deeply divided populous with young people as both the victims and perpetrators of sectarian and political violence. Little experience of significant political or citizenship education within schools

- Young people in Northern Ireland are citizens of a **divided and contested society**. In our work we must acknowledge that, ensure that coaches, young people and others don't avoid the controversial issues related to this reality and work in ways that build democracy, equity and stronger interdependent relationships.
- The process of working with young people is a **co-creative process involving young people and adults**. In a place where most adults have more experience of being 'subjects' rather than citizens, we have as

---

[4] Albeit with growing apathy and discontent
[5] See Butenschøn, 2001

Figure 1: *Public Achievement Action Project Cycle*

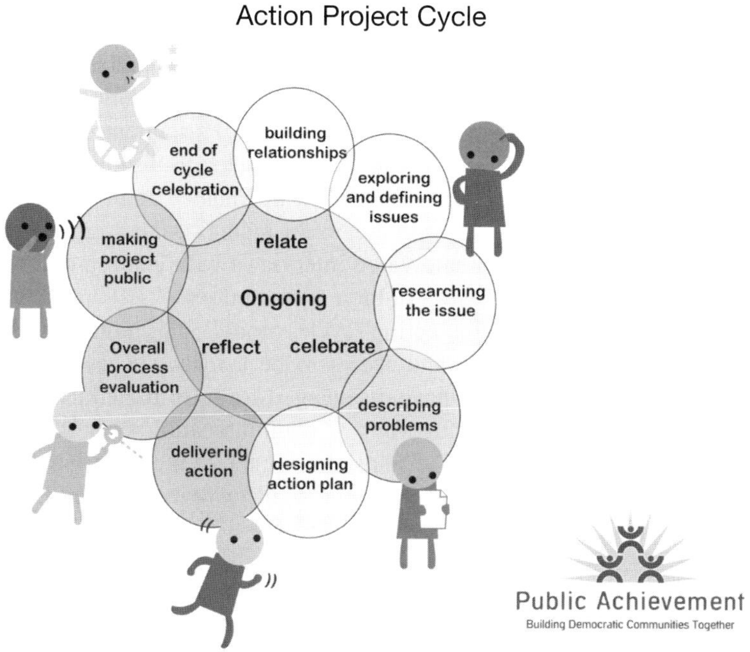

Action Project Cycle

Public Achievement
Building Democratic Communities Together

much to learn about how to be productive citizens as do the young people we work with.

- It is important to go **beyond traditional notions of volunteering** to look at civic responsibility and the need to create new ways of doing politics, not as a service to society but as one's responsibility as a member of that society.

In training coaches we have teamed up with the George Williams YMCA College in London who have a very strong record in youth work training and are allowing us to adapt their training to fit with our model of working with young people.[6] This is important not only in helping some of the coaches (teachers, museum staff, fire-fighters, etc) to gain recognised and important new skills, but also to the young people who coach, many of whom will have no other formal educational qualification. In the past year, Public Achievement has had four short courses accredited through Queen's University in Belfast, and it is planned to increase the number and level of courses over the next few years.

---

[6] Visit www.infed.org for more information on their training and for the work of Mark Smith and others.

In 2004 the organisation received funding for a new project that sought to increase the civic engagement between young people and politicians. A group of young people devised the name WIMPS (Where Is My Public Servant?) and, working with a local design company, created a website that allowed young people to identify and email their representatives at local Council, Assembly, Westminster and European Parliament levels about issues they feel are important. In 2006, thanks to funding from the Electoral Commission and the Department of Finance and Personnel, the site was re-launched to incorporate multi-media technology. This has enabled young people to create video interviews with leading politicians, and to create films about issues in their communities.

The combination of the action cycle model and multi-media has produced interesting results and seems to be a more successful way of engaging young people who have disengaged from formal education. The films they create are powerful ways of communicating their issues to a wider audience. Also, since the re-establishment of the Northern Ireland Assembly in May 2006, there has been a significant increase in the direct engagement between young people and local politicians. In the next phase of the project the model will be internationalised. This is an exciting development in terms of its potential both to broaden the horizons of young people and to create an international network of socially active youth. It also offers exciting opportunities for the future resourcing of this work.

This opportunity arose through the international network that Public Achievement has built with youth workers and youth organisations in contested societies through a project called 'Youth Work in Contested Spaces'. This project links youth workers, young people, researchers and youth policy-makers in a range of conflict regions including the Middle East, the Balkan States, the Basque Country (Euskadi) and South Africa with their counterparts in Northern Ireland and with a core interest in youth citizenship in contested societies.[7]

Our most recent project is called 'Away from Violence'. Based on evidence from the evaluation of our projects (VeLure Roholt, 2005), we decided to focus more explicitly on the larger issue of violence and the ways in which it impacts on the daily lives of young people. The project will employ local workers who will be trained through an apprenticeship model to support local teams of young people across a range of communities. Young people will name the forms of violence they experience, select a specific problem they want to address and develop

---

[7] Visit www.publicachievement.com to find out more about the 'Youth Work in Contested Spaces' project led by Public Achievement in partnership with local and international organisations.

alternatives to violence and avoidance as ways of dealing with or responding to conflict.

The legacy of violence is all-pervasive and poisonous. If we can give meaning to what it is to be a citizen of a post-conflict democracy, and can find new ways of doing politics that move us away from ethnic spectra, Northern Ireland might just provide the 'beacon of hope' in a world in crisis referred to by former US President Bill Clinton on one of his visits to Ireland. If we can take the brutality out of young people's worlds and put the fire back into all our bellies, then this will have been a mighty experiment!

References

Boyte, H. and Kari, N. (1996), *Building America, the Democratic Promise of Public Work*, Philadelphia: Temple University Press

Boyte, H. (1999), 'Education for Democracy', in *Creating the Commonwealth*, Kettering Foundation

Butenschøn, N.A. (2001), Adaptation of paper for National Conference of Political Science, Geilo, Norway 1993, available on www.statvitenskap.uio.no/ansatte/serie/notat/fulltekst/1093/index.html

Eyben, K., Morrow, D. and Wilson, D. (1997), *A Worthwhile Venture? – Practically Investing in Equity, Diversity and Interdependence*, Coleraine: University of Ulster

Hallgarten J. and Pearce, N. (1999), *Tomorrow's Citizens*, London: Institute for Public Policy Research

Hildreth, R.W. (2000), 'Theorizing Citizenship and Evaluating Public Achievement', *Political Science and Politics*, September 2000

Keenan, B. (1993), *An Evil Cradling*, London: Vintage

McCully, A. and Green, R. (2001), *Interim Evaluation of Public Achievement*, Coleraine: UNESCO Centre, University of Ulster

McCully, A. and Green, R. (2003), *Evaluation of Public Achievement, Northern Ireland*, Coleraine: UNESCO Centre, University of Ulster

O'Connor, F. (1993), *In Search of a State – Catholics in Northern Ireland*, Belfast: Blackstaff Press

Richardson, C. *et al* (1995), *Community Relations Project*, Belfast: Youth Council for Northern Ireland

Smith, A. and Robinson, A. (1996), *Education for Mutual Understanding: The Initial Statutory Years*, Coleraine: University of Ulster

VeLure Roholt, R. (2005), *Public Achievement, Internal Evaluation Report, 2004/2005*, available on www.publicachievement.com

16

The Action Project as a teaching/learning tool[1]

Máirín Wilson

Introduction

Civic, Social and Political Education (CSPE) is a course in citizenship based on human rights and social responsibility. The course reflects many of the aims of its predecessor, the old Civics course, but the under-pinning philosophy and pedagogical emphasis has changed from '... the common practice being to teach about civic responsibility and citizenship rather than to educate for and through citizenship' (NCCA, 1993). Right from the outset the syllabus for CSPE sets out the aim of the course, namely 'to prepare students for active participatory citizenship'. It aims to 'encourage and develop the practical skills which enable pupils to engage in active, participatory social interaction ...'

The syllabus goes on to define an action project as follows: 'An Action Project is one where the pupils are actively involved in developing an issue or topic which has arisen in class ...' (1.3.5). It states that the aim of CSPE is to 'encourage and develop the practical skills which enable pupils to engage in active, participatory social interaction ...' (2.1) and it highlights the skills component of the subject when it says, 'Pupils should be skilled in the ability to act, to apply the results of experience, analysis, reflection and communication in a practical way to a chosen situation or issue' (2.2.3). The first statement under the heading of the Attitudes and Values that the subject aims to foster is 'a personal commitment to active, constructive, participative citizenship' (2.2.4).

The subject is clearly founded on the principle of active participation and takes a responsible stance in relation to rekindling young people's sense of engagement in the societies in which they live, which is described by the Council of Europe (2000) as 'an urgent task'.

[1] The substantial information upon which this chapter is based emerges from research undertaken by the author 2001-2004 during the State Examinations. I wish to acknowledge the support of the SEC for this work and for the opportunity to publish some findings under my own name.

The principle of participation is essential for the empowerment of the citizen and to our understanding of democracy. Gone are the days when acquiring knowledge and information on citizenship was sufficient. There is universal recognition of the fact that if people are to become active citizens, the process of participation must go hand-in-hand with the learning. Active learning for active citizens is the cornerstone of the teaching methodology for CSPE and the Action Project is central to engaging students around real issues in society. In effect it is about 'educating learners to contribute to society rather than simply to receive its services; to fulfil their civic duties with generosity rather than just the legal minimum' (Groome, 1997).

The Action Project is the culmination of the active learning process in CSPE. Rooted in one of the seven core concepts[2] upon which the course is based, it is a means of ensuring that the classroom becomes the focus of community-based learning, connecting schools with the outside world. It plays a vital role in fostering critical thinking, confidence, skill development and a sense of belonging. It encourages attitudes of respect and tolerance; it broadens awareness; it empowers students to act.

Issues

Some issues have arisen in relation to Action Projects. For example, the nature and extent of the action undertaken is often dictated by the fact that there is just one period a week allocated to CSPE. Time is a big factor. There are challenges for teachers too, as undertaking Action Projects calls for new and different approaches to teaching methodologies. The turnover of CSPE teachers and the subsequent training needs of the newcomers are real issues.

Some express concern regarding the demands of the subject and the student in need of learning support or the student with special educational needs. However, there is clear evidence that students of all ability levels are capable of engaging successfully in Action Projects. In fact, assumptions are sometimes made that students who have literacy difficulties also have difficulties taking action. These assumptions are mistaken.

There is also the question of assessing a subject that is so patently based on action. There is a risk that, because there is a terminal written exam, the focus of the exam becomes dominant and the subject becomes exam-led.

The question has been asked: Can one assess citizenship education with a terminal written examination? The fact is that the CSPE examination

---

[2] Human Dignity, Rights and Responsibilities, Stewardship, Democracy, Development, Law, and Interdependence

aims to complement the subject. A new model of assessment, unlike any other subject in the Junior Cycle, has been designed for this purpose.

Assessment in CSPE

'The critically innovative aspect of Civic, Social and Political Education is that active learning is recognised and rewarded in the Junior Certificate Examination' (Waddell and Wilson, 1999). CSPE is a core subject within the Junior Cycle, it is mandatory and is the only subject within the Junior Certificate that is assessed at a common level. There are two components to the CSPE examination, a written paper which carries 40 per cent of the total mark and a Report on an Action Project (RAP) or a Course-Work Assessment Booklet (CWAB) which carries 60 per cent of the marks. Currently approximately 56,000 students take the RAP option while approximately 2,000 opt for the CWAB. Students submit either an RAP or CWAB in May of Third Year and sit the written paper as part of the Junior Certificate in June.

The exam structure supports the emphasis on participation. The weighting of the marks – 60 per cent for the action component – is evidence of this. So too is the acceptance of a 'failed' action – where perhaps in spite of best efforts an Anti-Litter Day fails to produce the desired results or a speaker fails to show! The written paper has a large focus on action, with many questions asking students to identify or describe actions that could be taken in a given situation.

To help standardise the reporting process and to support students and teachers in the reporting of their Actions Projects, pro-forma booklets have been designed by the Department of Education and Science/ State Examinations Commission. The structure of these booklets furthers the aims of the subject as set out in the syllabus.

To understand the value of the Action Project as a valuable teaching tool it is important to identify the component part of the Report. The focus of an Action Project Report is as follows:

• A core concept upon which the action is based
• A rationale for undertaking the particular Action Project
• An outline of the complete action undertaken
• A description of a specialised individual task
• An explanation of the skills acquired/developed
• A statement of the knowledge acquired
• A reflection on the whole learning experience.

The Course-Work Assessment Booklet contains a similar emphasis and differs from the Report in that the particular action undertaken is set within the context of a module of work and students include a report on three classes within the module identified.

Research on Action Projects

During 2001-2004 the titles of Action Projects were gathered. This information helps to provide evidence of the success of the Action Project, of the breadth of work undertaken and the experiences of young people in our schools.

From 2001 to 2004, 170 (approx.) Assistant Examiners each year recorded the titles of a random sample of twenty Action Projects and this has given the SEC an opportunity to analyse the exact areas in which students are engaged in action. Since in the region of 55,000 to 58,000 students sit the Junior Certificate Examination in CSPE each year, this has allowed for a substantial body of information to emerge.

The total number of titles recorded in the years 2001-2004 are as follows:

2001: 3,302 Action Project titles were generated.
2002: 2,952 Action Project titles were generated.
2003: 2,972 Action Project titles were generated.
2004: 3,308 Action Project titles were generated.

The purpose of this investigation has been to identify the range of Action Projects being undertaken by CSPE students and to gather real evidence of what is happening in Irish schools. It is also hoped that this may become a basis for further research into young people engaging in 'active citizenship' and being participative in society.

All the titles have been categorised based on the seven core concepts, with the additional necessary heading of 'Community', to classify community-based Action Projects. Two other categories have also been identified, one to represent titles that were impossible to classify because of the vagueness of the title itself, and a second to represent those that were outside the scope of the syllabus.

The titles have been counted and analysed. The following results were noted and are listed below in order of popularity:

Category	2001	2002	2003	2004
Rights and responsibilities	1,001	808	849	990
Stewardship	778	580	558	561
Democracy	476	478	575	601
Law	439	322	330	392
Development	159	204	63	49

Community	110	79	82	120
Interdependence	107	83	115	117
Outside the syllabus	100	93	81	110
Human dignity	72	89	198	227
Impossible to quantify	60	116	121	81

In percentage terms this is as follows:

Category	*2001*	*2002*	*2003*	*2004*
Rights and responsibilities	30.31	28.33	28.56	29.92
Stewardship	23.56	20.34	18.78	16.95
Democracy	14.41	16.76	19.34	19.98
Law	13.29	11.29	11.10	11.85
Development	4.89	7.15	2.12	1.48
Community	3.33	2.77	2.76	3.62
Interdependence	3.24	2.91	3.83	3.53
Outside the syllabus	3.05	3.26	2.75	3.32
Human dignity	2.18	3.12	6.68	6.86
Impossible to quantify	1.82	4.07	4.08	2.24

Rights and responsibilities

This has been the most popular of the concepts undertaken, giving rise to many Action Projects. The types of action undertaken have been fundraising, doing surveys, raising awareness and inviting in guest speakers. Common topics broached under the umbrella of this concept are racism, homelessness, bullying, refugees, Chernobyl, Travellers, the elderly, sites of Third World famine, children's rights, destruction and war. Organisations most frequently mentioned include Trócaire, Concern, Amnesty, Simon, St Vincent de Paul, ISPCC, Bóthar and Focus Point.

Stewardship

This has also been a very popular concept to date. Typical Action Projects would include the tidying up of areas such as the school, local community or a specified amenity. Anti-litter days feature prominently here, alongside action to restore some area or plant some trees. Recycling in many forms attracts a large number of actions, and surveys on many aspects of responsible environmental living have been reported upon each year.

A significant number of Action Projects have been presented around the rights, welfare and protection of animals under this concept.

Democracy

Students have been clearly exploring many aspects of developing political literacy and awareness. Action Projects recorded focus on a broad range of topics such as visits to the Dáil and to local authorities. Each year large numbers of visits from individuals in the political arena have been noted. Reports based on visiting TDs, Councillors, Ministers, representatives from Áras an Uachtaráin, political parties, the Taoiseach, the European Union and mock elections have been very popular.

Often students undertake surveys to find out levels of political knowledge in their school or locality. Other awareness-raising activities have also been reported.

Law

This concept has been characterised predominantly by visits to the school from the Gardaí, Junior Liaison Officers, a Judge, a Barrister, a solicitor and the like. Some students have organised visits to such places as the Four Courts, local courts and prisons. Road Safety also has featured under this concept as does, for example, the law in relation to work and young people or the law and the consumer, the law concerning alcohol, drugs and, in 2004, the new law on smoking in the workplace.

Development

This concept has declined in popularity over the years. A number of the titles recorded would indicate too an overlap with the concepts of community or stewardship. Typical actions would focus on recent transport initiatives, campaigns for resources, changing ways and mobile phones. Sometimes students have focused on the underdeveloped world while studying this concept. In 2002 the euro was especially popular.

Community

In some cases titles recorded have not been linked to an obvious concept but the focus has clearly been either the school or local community. Community is one of the four[3] domains in which the student explores the topic of citizenship, human rights and social responsibility. Typical examples of community-based Action Project titles that have been recorded would be 'The Local Credit Union', 'Attitudes in School', 'Amenities in Our Community'.

A community emphasis has also been included in other concept areas and it could be argued that most Action Projects have a community focus. Students are usually engaged with a community of some sorts in the course of the action they undertake. It could be said that, at a basic level, Action Projects involve students as a 'community of inquiry.'

---

[3] Under the Syllabus for CSPE, the four domains are The Individual and Citizenship, The Community, The State Ireland and The Wider World.

Interdependence

The uptake on this particular concept has been low over the years. The main categories explored here have been concerned with topics such as Fair Trade, logo/sweat shops and consumer issues. Other topics that come under this concept include Europe,[4] the United Nations and a few intercultural action projects.

Action Projects outside the syllabus

It is unfortunate that every year a number of Action Projects are presented around topics that are outside the CSPE syllabus. The titles recorded have been predominantly in the area of drugs, smoking, alcohol,[5] health and diseases such as cancer, meningitis, Alzheimer's and the like. In keeping with the key aim of CSPE, the participation of the students in authentic action only can be rewarded.

Human dignity

These Action Projects have been predominantly concerned with issues about treating people with dignity and have a particular focus on the area of disability. Typical topics/actions have been in the area of wheelchair access, contact with such communities as Camphill, L'Arche, St Michael's House and people with disabilities. In recent years the Special Olympics has featured largely in the Action Projects and this accounts for the increasing popularity of this concept as a focus for action. It will be interesting to see if the impact of the Special Olympics lingers as time passes.

Impossible to quantify

Sometimes students have given their Action Projects vague and general titles such as 'A Guest Speaker', 'Fundraising', 'A soccer match for charity', 'Remembering Hiroshima', 'Our aim to help others', 'Behind the Bars', 'Through Understanding We Offer Hope', 'A Visit from Tom Lyons'. Such topics as these are impossible to classify under any of the categories established and so fall into a separate category of their own.

Action Projects 2004

Having gathered information on the subject matter of Action Projects over a number of years, in 2004 the scope of the research was extended. In the 2004 CSPE examination the questionnaire completed by Assistant Examiners was re-designed to identify the nature or type of the actions being undertaken by students. Assistant Examiners noted both the title of the Action Project **and** the type of action in which the students were engaged.

---

[4] A Mock European Election would come under the concept of Democracy.
[5] Not applicable if an Action Project in these areas has a link to the course concepts

The results confirmed earlier impressions of what were the most popular types of action that students were undertaking.

Results: the nature of Action Projects being undertaken

Guest speaker	890	
Fundraising	662	
Combination	354	(where students both had a guest speaker and undertook fundraising for a particular cause)
Visits	364	
Survey	216	
Raising awareness	200	
Mock election	150	
Investigation	84	
Campaign	64	
Clean-up	31	
Recycling	30	
Protest/petition	10	
Publication	7	
Social event	7	
Exhibition	4	
Census	3	
Quiz	2	
In-School	1 each on	Drink fountain, Pedestrian crossing, School garden, Signs

The Action Project as a methodology

The evidence is clear: the nature of Action Projects seems to indicate that young people are engaging with the society in which they live. The central aims of CSPE are being met. Together with raising awareness and broadening knowledge, in the process, in the doing, students are developing the skills of engagement and participation; this enables them to develop a spirit of responsibility within a shared community. Significantly too Action Projects are leading students to reflection.

It is exciting to see young people involved in action that equips them for 'active, informed, critical and responsible citizenship' (Waddell and Wilson, 1999). Hart, cited in Osler and Starkey (1996), claims that if students are not given the chance to participate in their community, 'they will not gain the experience they require to exercise their rights and responsibilities as citizens'. 'The relationship between the individual and the community is a complex one,' argue Jones and Jones (1992) and so they maintain that 'the aims of active citizenship are to develop the confidence and values to engage at a national, European and global level'.

We live in an ever-changing world and authentic citizenship education, which both encourages and facilitates participation, will not leave students at the mercy of unpredictable, erratic and accelerated change but will equip them with the skills necessary to assess, reflect, understand, act and adapt to those changes. In meeting this challenge through citizenship education, specifically through CSPE in the Irish context, the Action Project is a very useful tool.

References

Council of Europe (2000), *Learning for Citizenship in the European Dimension – Orientations 2000: Toward a Europe of Knowledge*, Working Paper, DG XXII

Government Publications (1996), *Syllabus for Civic, Social and Political Education*

Groome, T. (1997), *Educating for Life*, New York: Thomas Moore Publishing

Heater, D. (1999), *What is Citizenship?* London: Blackwell Publishers

Jones, B.E. and Jones, N. (1992*), Education for Citizenship – Ideas and Perspectives for Cross-Curricular Study*, London: Kogan Page

NCCA (National Council for Curriculum and Assessment) (1993), *Civic, Social and Political Education*. Discussion paper, Dublin: NCCA

Osler, A. and Starkey, H. (1996), *Teacher Education and Human Rights*, London: David Fulton

Waddell, M. and Wilson, M. (1999), 'Educating the Citizen. Issues in Education', *ASTI Journal*, pp137-141

17

Living with contradictions: teenagers' experiences of active citizenship and competitive individualism

Majella McSharry

Notwithstanding the dramatic social changes that have taken place in the past half century, the theory of citizenship proposed by T.H. Marshall in the 1950s continues to make a significant contribution to current discussions. According to Marshall, it is the responsibility of the welfare state to ensure that citizens experience Civil, Political and Social Rights (1950). The global movement of people has heightened awareness of cultural diversity and this has given rise to the concepts of 'Cultural Rights' and 'Cultural Citizenship' which highlight 'the right to be different and to belong in a participatory democratic sense' (Rosaldo, 1994: 402).

Developing a coherent understanding of citizenship in a participatory democratic sense in Ireland is particularly important in light of the Government's 2006 call for a 'national conversation' (Report of the Taskforce on Active Citizenship, 2007) on participatory and active citizenship. The taskforce, established to promote greater participation, suggests that 'a healthy democracy relies on citizens who are well informed, interested and engaged. It is also linked to a shared sense of empowerment' (ibid:16). The taskforce highlights the promotion of participation among young people and indicates the family and school as two settings where young people should be regarded as citizens in a participatory democratic sense.

It is the purpose if this chapter to firstly examine how teenagers experience active citizenship in the home. The data are taken from interviews with thirty adolescents between the ages of twelve and sixteen, where they discussed social issues that affected them. The second and overarching aim of this chapter is to investigate how these young people experience active citizenship in their five respective post-primary schools. The chapter also explores the possibility that timetable and curriculum demands leave little opportunity for participatory democratic citizenship. It finally considers whether individualised success in examinations is seen to play a greater role in shaping citizens, than active engagement in the present.

Young people's active citizenship in the home

Democracy was certainly scarce in traditional depictions of the Irish family where children, and particularly teenagers, were expected to take on adult roles and responsibilities, yet unquestioningly succumb to authoritarian rules. Today many teenagers take on external adult roles and responsibilities within the workforce. According to McCoy and Smyth (2005), over 60 per cent of Irish Leaving Certificate students have regular part-time employment. However, unlike traditional motives, today's finance appears to arise out of a desire to fund a 'lifestyle' rather than arising out of financial need (ibid). Parents permit these lifestyles of work and pleasure, where young people actively participate in decision-making and autonomously engage in adult environments. From the second-level students I spoke with, it was apparent that responsibility, independence and freedom were fostered within many homes.

> *I'm very free. I know what's right and what's wrong so they trust me to do what's right. ... I work on Saturdays and I'm out on Sundays.* (Cian, age16)

> *I'm mostly out all the time. I go to work and when I come back I go to me club or I'm over with me friends.* (Caoimhe, age 16)

> *I've never been grounded in my life. I'd just laugh at my dad if he said I was grounded.* (Barry, age 16)

A significant number of interviewees described how decisions within the home were deliberated upon in a democratic fashion rather than dictated. Many of the teenage girls described relationships with their mothers that were based on mutual respect and equity of voice. Their mothers asked them for advice on clothes and exercise regimes and, in one case, for relationship advice. Some girls talked about how they and their mothers had gone on 'girlie' foreign holidays together. Some of the boys spoke of similar, equity-based relationships with their fathers, where they would enjoy a few beers together in the home, as an alternative to drinking irresponsibly outside the home. However, participants held quite a different opinion of their ability to actively participate in a democratic fashion in their school environments. Lynch and Lodge (2002) also found this mismatch between students' sense of autonomy inside and outside of school. They warned that teenagers:

Work in an adult world on adult terms; they have experience of exercising control over their lives, of being relatively autonomous, an experience that cannot be ignored when they come to school (Lynch and Lodge, 2002:155).

Perhaps students' experience of active citizenship in school is particularly confusing when school practices contradict the messages of democracy highlighted in the curriculum.

Young people's active citizenship in school

The concept of democracy is one of the seven pillars on which formal citizenship education is based in Irish second-level schools (NCCA, 1996). During their first three years in secondary education students should have attained some understanding of their right to express their views freely in matters affecting them, with their views being given due weight in accordance with their age and maturity (Article 12, UN Convention on the Rights of the Child). The curriculum encourages students to actively participate in their communities, particularly in their school community. Students learn that 'practising citizenship is about taking meaningful action' (NCCA, 2005:4) and that they 'must be given opportunities to become active citizens within their classroom, school, community and beyond' (NCCA, 2005:7).

In spite of such a strong message encouraging participation, the young people I spoke to felt that this focus on participation was often confined to CSPE and did not infiltrate other classes. A sense of frustration and confusion arose when their opinions were not listened to or taken seriously in school.

Outside school I'd say I have control but inside school I don't because the teachers are very cranky. The teachers say 'you're a child in primary school, you're an adult in secondary school.' They always say that. But then you can't express yourself because they say 'this is a school not a club or anything!' They always say things like that. You're not really heard and you're not really allowed to have your own opinion or anything. (Eve, 13)

My English teacher ... she doesn't like anyone talking. She's our strictest teacher. I think she should have a bit more communication. She doesn't listen to us. She just does her own thing. (Evan, 13)

You don't really have power in school because if you have an argument with a teacher, which is rare, but if the teacher is wrong, the teacher is always going to be believed over the student. Like in class you might be heard but it might go in one ear and out the other and not count. In some classes your point of view would be taken into consideration and a teacher might even say 'I've never heard that before.' That means a lot. (Andy, 16)

The data suggest that it means a lot to students when teachers acknowledge their contributions. Participation allows students to become active citizens in their school and the recognition of their contribution has an empowering affect.

It is only when educational settings practise active citizenship that students learn about living democracy in school. According to Banks, it is essential that students participate in democracy if they are to learn about it in any authentic and durable way. He contends that 'action without understanding can be mindless and often does as much harm as good,' and equally, 'understanding without action can be thin and inconsequential' (Banks, 2005:13). This of course reflects Dewey's emphasis on the importance of living democracy within education.

For Dewey, society must make provision for the participation of its members, and society must have an education system that gives individuals control (Dewey, 1916: 99). Schools working as democratic structures take the focus off learning for living in the future and focus learning on living in the present. 'It recognises them as citizens, rather than citizens in waiting' (Verhellen, 2000 cited in Banks, 2005:13). Many of the young people interviewed in the course of this study did not feel that they were given the opportunities to practise democracy through meaningful participation in their learning environments. Interestingly, however, while some criticised teachers for this, others felt that teachers did not have time to practise democracy, given the fast-paced and exam-focused nature of learning.

No time to participate actively

While much of society appears to have taken on the pace and dynamism of a 'runaway world' (Giddens, 1991:16), this is perhaps particularly evident within the rapidly timetabled structure of the secondary school. The pace at which these educational sites work is instantly recognisable. The sense of urgency connected with running from one class to another is evidence of what Adam calls the 'naturalisation of clock time'.

Unlike the variable rhythms of nature, the invariant, precise measurement is a human invention, and in our society it is this time created to human design that has become dominant to the extent that it is related to as time *per se*, as if there were no other times (Adam, 2003: 62).

Buzzers and bells ring every forty or forty-five minutes, to signal the end of one class and immediately the beginning of another. Some of the youths I spoke to felt that such strict timetabling, accompanied by formal curriculum demands, meant that teachers did not have the time to create classrooms based on active citizenship and democratic participation.

They need the work done. The teachers have so many different classes and they cannot really concentrate on just the one. You might only have them for forty minutes a day. ... You have to be more responsible and organised and start working as soon as you go into class because you only have the forty minutes and they have to try and get as much work as they can done. (Shannon, age14)

In many classes you don't have time to contribute because a teacher has like eight classes a day and only some teachers even get to know their pupils. (Mark, age 12)

You don't know them [teachers], like they just come in and teach your class and go out again and that's it. You don't talk to them. ... You can't because they just teach your class and there's so many of you in the class, then they just leave and that's the end of it. (Kevin, age 13)

The data describe a type and pace of work where 'children are subdued by curriculum requirements and discipline structures' (McLoughlin, 2004:131). Citizenship education encourages unity through interdependence and support, and diversity through freedom of voice and expression. However, it appears that the pace of learning fuelled by formal curriculum and examination demands renders this type of active citizenship virtually impossible. Perhaps this is not so much a case of citizenship being undermined by the practices and demands of the education system *per se*, but that it is undermined by globalisation and individualism and their proliferation within the education system.

Citizenship v. individualised success

Theories of citizenship promote connectedness, belonging, diversity and equality. Within these ideologies, terms such as 'first-class' and 'second-class' citizen appear bankrupt (Rosaldo, 1994). Nevertheless, their underlying meaning remains a strong social reality. Fundamentally individuals participate in society and are viewed by society at different levels. Those who demonstrate high levels of educational success are often afforded social positions that result in increased opportunities for participation in society.

As the global infiltrates the local, however, attaining such social positions becomes much more competitive. Therefore, while students are aware that they are globally interdependent and have responsibilities to support and respect their global neighbours, they are equally aware that they compete with these neighbours for coveted social positions as privatised individuals. The focus and pace of work in the school system is merely a display of competitive individuals (both students and teachers) seeking success within the system. Their likely quest is to attain superior levels of social participation in the future on the basis of their success.

There is limited opportunity for students to engage in critical reflection on their learning environment under an ethos of urgency and achievement. Students struggle to keep up on an individual basis. Privatised individuals grapple with the fear of failure while handling such fears: success 'becomes an *essential cultural qualification,* and the cultivation of the abilities demanded for it become an essential mission of pedagogical institutions' (Beck, 1992:76).

There is little time for unified supports or reflection on the diversity of learning within an exam-focused system, according to the young people interviewed in the course of this study.

I feel you have to keep up with the class or else you'll be pushed down. I wouldn't let that happen. I wouldn't let it get that bad. (Cian, age 16)

My English teacher tells us we're working towards the Junior Cert and we have to know our poems this year because we won't have time to do them again in second year and third year. (Evan, age 13)

My maths teacher has no patience if you hadn't picked something up after the first few times. (Ger, age 12)

It was the same when we went into second year, we got a new Irish teacher who was telling us what percentage was going for the listening comprehension. She was like 'come on girls, you have to do loads of listening'. We were like 'oh my God it's two years away'... It was very hard; all about work, work, work. After school study was good but when you're in there, it's 'come on, you have to study, no messing, no chatting down the back, no eating'. It's really intense. Yeah, there's an awful lot of pressure. (Gillian, age 16).

Our teacher does maths formulas on the board and if you say 'I don't understand that', it's just quickly explained without asking if you understand it and then he just keeps going and going and going. If you say it again they start getting narky because it's like you've accused them of not explaining it right. You just don't bother asking then. (Andy, age 16)

There was a palpable sense of frustration among these young people emerging from a perceived lack of control over their own learning. Even at primary school level, Devine made similar observations where control over the pace and content of learning, as well as the physical school space, was deemed by students 'to be firmly in the hands of adults, justified in the main by adult ownership of the school and classroom' (2004:118).

There appears to be a genuine academic consensus that becoming an engaged and knowledgeable citizen is a process that needs to be practised and lived (Banks, 2005:5). There is now a more general awareness that:

Schools and colleges are places where people learn about behaviour, dialogue, decision-making as well as a range of skills, knowledge and attributes that enable people to act as thinking, critical, responsible and caring citizens in a democratic society (Report of the Taskforce on Active Citizenship, 2007:21).

There is an acknowledgement that schools should be the type of democratic structures in which participatory citizenship is played out (NCCA, 2005:7). There is, therefore, an unquestionable emphasis being placed on the importance of shaping citizens through inclusive and diverse participation in the learning environment. However, for the students interviewed this was overshadowed by an educational focus on shaping individuals for success in the future. Students learned to associate success in school with the outcome of examinations, rather than with their democratic participation in education. 'Doing well in school' was directly linked to success in examinations.

If I don't do well in school, in my exams, that's the rest of my life down the drain. (Mark, age 12)

The Leaving Cert ... it's not going to decide your life but it'll go a long way towards it. (Andy, age 16)

It's so difficult for 16 and 17-year-olds to make a decision on subjects that are undoubtedly going to affect the rest of our lives, with whatever points you get. (Brian, age 16)

These students associated education with preparation for success in examinations and the importance of this in influencing who they become as individuals. Life opportunities and social participation were essentially dependent on the academic achievements of each individual.

Conclusion

This chapter has highlighted a rejuvenated emphasis on understanding citizenship and encouraging active citizenship in Irish society. A message outlining the importance of empowerment through active participation in democratic structures is extended to young people through government reports and through their citizenship education curriculum. According to the young people who contributed to this chapter, however, there is often a mismatch and contradiction between the level of engagement and empowerment they experience inside and outside of school. Students described their schools as environments where the push for democratic participation found in CSPE class did not always flow into other classes. Nevertheless, many students did not blame teachers for this, rather the demands of a highly exam-focused curriculum.

A significant number of these young people were willing to accept their learning environment being dictated by exam-focused learning if it led to success in future examinations. However, what is most worrying is that students associated empowerment with individualised success in examinations. Examination points measured self-worth for many. In order to challenge such attitudes it is essential that self-worth and empowerment are linked to daily democratic participation. It is vital for students to see, in the daily practices of their schools, that self-worth and empowerment emerge from the freedom to participate in diverse ways and to have such participation promoted and applauded.

References

Adam, B. (2003), 'Reflexive Modernization Temporalized', *Theory, Culture and Society*, Vol.20, No.2, 59-78, London: Sage Publications

Banks, J.A. (2005), *Democracy and Diversity*, Seattle: Center for Multicultural Education

Beck, U. (1992), *Risk Society: Towards a New Modernity*, London: Sage Publications

Devine, D. (2004), 'School matter – listening to what children have to say', in J. Deegan and A. Lodge (eds), *Primary Voices: Equality, Diversity and Childhood in Irish Primary Schools*, Dublin: Institute of Public Administration

Dewey, J. (1916), *Democracy and Education: An introduction to the philosophy of education*, New York: Macmillan

Giddens, A. (1991), *Modernity and Self-Identity*, Cambridge: Polity Press

Lynch, K. and Lodge, A. (2002), *Equality and Power in Schools: Redistribution, Recognition and Representation*, London: Routledge Falmer

Marshall, T.H. (1950), *Citizenship and Social Class*, London: Pluto Press

McCoy, S. and Smyth, E. (2005), *At Work in School: Part-Time Employment Among Second-Level Students*, Dublin: Liffey Press

McLoughlin, O. (2004), 'Citizen child – the experience of a student council in a primary school', in J. Deegan, D. Devine and A. Lodge (eds)*, Primary Voices: Equality, Diversity and Childhood in Irish Primary Schools*, Dublin: Institute of Public Administration

NCCA (National Council for Curriculum and Assessment) (1996), *Civic, Social and Political Education syllabus*, Dublin: NCCA

NCCA (2005), *Civic, Social and Political Education, Guidelines for Teachers,* Dublin: NCCA

Report of the Taskforce on Active Citizenship (March 2007). http://www.activecitizen.ie/

Rosaldo, R. (1994), 'Cultural Citizenship and Educational Democracy', *Cultural Anthropology*, Vol.9, No.3, 402-411

Taskforce on Active Citizenship (March 2007), Background working paper. http://www.activecitizen.ie/

United Nations Convention of the Rights of the Child (1989). http://www.unhchr.ch/html/menu3/b/k2crc.htm

18

Some educational issues raised in response to the Taskforce on Active Citizenship

Tom Healy[1]

This chapter explores the relationship between education and active citizenship, taking account of the work of the Taskforce on Active Citizenship in 2006. It identifies a number of key areas that require further examination in the context of expectations that education – at least formal and school-based learning – can make a vital contribution to renewing and sustaining civic engagement and awareness throughout life. In discussing active citizenship it is necessary to spell out the meaning of terms such as 'active' and 'citizenship' as well as their relationship to learning in various contexts. It is also necessary to avoid compartmentalising active citizenship as if it were a completely self-contained sphere of analysis and response, separate from wider concerns about the future of democracy, society, politics and economy.

The Taskforce on Active Citizenship

The Taskforce on Active Citizenship was established by the Taoiseach in April 2006. The Taskforce was required to 'recommend measures which could be taken as part of public policy to facilitate and encourage (i) a greater degree of engagement by citizens in all aspects of Irish life and (ii) the growth and development of voluntary organisations as part of a strong civic culture'. Following a series of meetings and consultations at regional and state level, a report was submitted to Government in March of 2007. Following acceptance of its recommendations by Government, the report was published on 28 March 2007 and the Taoiseach announced, at its launch, the establishment of an Implementation Group to be chaired by Mary Davis who had chaired the Taskforce.[2]

[1] This chapter has been written in a personal capacity and does not reflect the views of the Department of Education and Science.
[2] Refer to http://www.activecitizen.ie/index.asp?locID=12&docID=63

Education as the silver bullet for active citizenship?

While the final report of the Taskforce (available at http://
www.activecitizen.ie) covered a very wide range of public policy issues,
from support for voluntary organisations to local democracy and
integration of newcomers, education featured as a major topic. This
reflected the prominence given to it in the various regional seminars – a
summary of which is contained in a Report entitled 'Report on Active
Citizenship Consultation Process'.[3]

The Report of the consultation process stated:

> A clear and unanimous view to merge from the consultation was that
> active citizens are 'not born but made'. In this context, education
> generally, and formal education in particular, was seen as having a key
> role to play in the development and promotion of an ethos of civic
> participation and voluntary activity. However, there was substantial
> criticism of the education system as it is currently operating as being
> overly concentrated on the production of 'workers' rather than 'citizens'
> (p.24).

Learning – inside and outside the formal education process – is seen by
many as a key element in promoting civic values, trust and participation.
Other contributors to this volume have referred to the high levels of
expectation accorded to institutions of formal education to provide civic
knowledge, skills and values. Yet, the experience in the Republic of Ireland
and elsewhere cautions against too high an expectation that education (or,
to be more precise, schooling) can be necessarily the main or sole answer.
There are three essential reasons for this:

- Education is more than schooling, curriculum and teaching – important
  as these are
- Learning *for* citizenship is more than learning *about* citizenship
- Citizenship, itself, is a contested term.

Citizenship – a contested term

Taking the latter reason first: 'Citizenship' may be understood as implying
some or all of the following – active participation in volunteering, legally-
recognised membership of a nation-state, compliance with public order

---

[3] The full report of the consultations can be downloaded at: http://www.activecitizen.ie/
getFile.asp?FC_ID=16&docID=49

and the common good and adherence to democratic principles and values. Indeed, 'citizenship' may act as an exclusive and excluding term, implying that some are 'in' and others are 'out' in terms of rights and responsibilities. Likewise, 'active' citizenship may be directed to any number of ends including ones that promote sectarian, racial, political and social interests of some to the detriment of others. The location of social housing in 'my backyard' or 'your backyard' may be a more effective agent of 'active citizenship' than any number of moral tracts or good citizenship programmes in schools.

Hence, we need to be discerning with respect to both language and meaning when we discuss citizenship and, for that matter, democracy. The Taskforce explained the concept of active citizenship in the following terms:

Active citizenship is about engagement, participation in society and valuing contributions made by individuals, whether they are employed or outside the traditional workforce. In practical terms, this engagement and participation may mean membership of a resident's association or political party or lobby group, or volunteering to help out in a local sports club, or caring for a family member or neighbour, or simply being active and caring about the local neighbourhood, the environment as well as larger global and national issues (p.2).

Although the above definition did not explicitly mention democracy, it is clear from a reading of the entire report that active citizenship as understood by the Taskforce is about positive, active, democratic citizenship and, furthermore, is not confined to acts of volunteering or informal good neighbourliness. It is all these things and more. Taken to its logical conclusion, active citizenship would challenge existing structures and institutions by creating space for partnership, dialogue and sharing of decision-making at various levels and on various matters of public concern.

Consideration of active citizenship inevitably raises the question of how learning relates to engagement in society. The Report of the Taskforce states that:

Active citizenship will not achieve its full potential without a concerted and consistent effort to address current obstacles to it at political, governmental, sectoral, community, organisational and individual levels. Education, both formal and non-formal, and capacity building is key to this, through a system of lifelong learning opportunities in the community, classroom and workplace (p.18).

Learning for citizenship

Much of the debate about education and (active) citizenship centres around the role of curriculum in relation to transmission of civic skills and knowledge. There has been a number of important and valuable developments in this area in schools in the Republic of Ireland in recent decades. For example, the development of the Transition Year at the beginning of senior cycle (upper secondary level) is unique by international standards and offers nearly a half of all students in the relevant age-cohort an opportunity to develop and experiment with a range of practical skills in various settings including in many cases volunteering and participation in civic projects. Other examples include the work of Cooperation Ireland which has brought students and schools together across the island of Ireland in applying knowledge and skills in very practical ways to help communities and foster civic learning.

At primary level a broad, child-centred curriculum has an important contribution to make along with areas in the primary curriculum such as Social, Personal and Health Education (SPHE) or Social, Environmental and Scientific Education (SESE). Also, the intercultural guidelines at both primary and second level provide an important reference for educators in facilitating integration and mutual respect in an increasingly diverse society.

The introduction, in the 1990s, of a new subject in Junior Cycle (lower secondary education) – Civic, Social and Political Education – placed a greater focus on active learning and project work as well as knowledge of politics, society, the European Union and global issues. The subject is mandatory for all students in Junior Cycle and leads to a written examination as part of the Junior Certificate at age 15/16. CSPE also includes an action project undertaken in the third and final year of Junior Cycle.

While the development of CSPE is a significant advance on the teaching of civics in the 1960s and 1970s, the following should be noted:

- CSPE typically takes one class period per week, only, in most second-level schools.
- CSPE has to compete with other subjects in the curriculum. Its status and perceived utility may be judged by the length of parental queues leading to the CSPE teacher at the once yearly parent-teacher meetings.
- Currently there is no universal provision for a follow-on programme of studies in political and civic education at senior cycle (upper secondary education) although the National Council for Curriculum and Assessment (NCCA) is currently examining and piloting work in this area.[4]

[4] http://www.ncca.ie/uploadedfiles/publications/SPEd_Report.pdf

- It is difficult to measure or assess the quality of learning and teaching in regard to CSPE across different schools and classes.
- Judging by the findings of research elsewhere (OECD, 2007), it is likely that young people learn just as much from actively applying civic knowledge and opportunities as from instruction in knowledge about political participation, institutions and current political issues.

That said, the vital role of schools in promoting social engagement and knowledge through subjects such as CSPE as well as more broadly should not be underestimated. From history to English literature to religion to Social, Personal and Health Education, students are provided with opportunities to learn about a range of issues including human rights, ethics, the global community and the responsibilities of individuals and communities. An interesting finding to emerge from the most recent OECD Programme for International Student Assessment (2006) was that students in the Republic of Ireland had the highest average score among OECD countries in a measure of environmental awareness. Fifteen-year old students here were more familiar than their counterparts elsewhere with issues such as deforestation, acid rain, greenhouse gases and nuclear waste (Eivers *et al*, 2007).

Aside from curriculum, assessment and teaching – vital as these areas are to the development of civic attitudes and skills – there is an 'elephant in the parlour'. It is worth quoting in full the notes of a round-table conversation held with a range of education stakeholders on 12 October 2006 as part of the Taskforce consultation process:

Active citizenship sits within a wider social and economic context. If we practise inequality in the way schools are organised and in the way people are channelled – especially in the cross-over from Primary and Post-Primary – we are sending powerful signals that reinforce existing social inequalities and discourage inclusion and active engagement in society from a very early age. It is not enough that schools be asked to fix social problems or encourage active citizens. Our housing policy, social programmes, tax-benefit system and spatial/transport planning all impact on schools, equality and active citizenship. Hence, school admissions policy and practice is a vital area to be examined and acted on.

The above point was captured, too, in the final Report of the Taskforce:

A strong theme that emerged in our consultations was that, beyond any specific programme or intervention to enhance Active Citizenship, the role of school ethos and social equality were crucial in providing the right context (p.21).

If schools and policies around schools *practise* democracy and inclusion, there is a fair chance that young people will get the message. Civic values are caught more than taught. But they need to be taught, assessed and valued too.

Learning is everywhere

Learning to be active, engaged, informed, inclusive, tolerant and vigilant to promote societal good is a civic habit and virtue cultivated in a wide range of settings from home to school, community, youth organisation, parish and workplace. School is just one place where learning occurs. Since schooling accounts for around 15 per cent of young people's total waking time during the years of compulsory education,[5] and since subjects specifically focused on civic education and knowledge account for a much smaller proportion of this time, schools need to be very smart and efficient in the way they help young people to develop their civic skills and knowledge. Young people may be learning more about social engagement and civic values from Utube and Facebook. Informal learning inside and outside formal education settings is vital.

In many cases, the impact of informal learning is positive and complementary to that of formal education. However, in other cases, to some extent, and in some parts of the world, schools may need to counteract negative influences from other sources. In yet other cases, the challenge is to build on, and complement, the influence of out-of-school sources. Unlike other areas of the curriculum, learning about social engagement, rights, responsibilities, democracy and sustainability deals with issues that are often contested, vaguely defined and open to different viewpoints and interpretations. Care is needed in avoiding an excessively authoritarian approach. Learners must discover their own path while respecting that of others.

History, especially but not exclusively in the twentieth century, is full of many examples of various institutions using formal education to propagate very particular sets of beliefs, identities and values. In some cases, this reinforced ignorance, exclusion and mutual distrust. The state and other public institutions, in the twenty-first century, need to be vigilant in striking the appropriate balance between assumed public

---

[5] The average annual total of hours of instruction at ages 7-8 and 15 across OECD countries is, respectively 769 and 911 (Education at a Glance, OECD indicators, 2007: 370).

values and goods on the one side, and individual, family, community choices on the other – some of which may not be entirely compatible with the former.

Practical steps and challenges to develop active citizenship through learning

The Taskforce made a number of specific recommendations. It is worth summarising and considering those that pertain to education and formal education in particular:

Use of school facilities

... that better use should be made of schools at evening and weekend time to act as community hubs – facilitating, for example, adult education, literacy programmes, various community activities and services (p.21).

Curriculum development

... the expansion of education for citizenship in the school system and in the youth and adult education sectors, and in particular:

– ensure that every Transition Year student has the opportunity to take part in an active learning community-based project, building on existing programmes such as the Young Social Innovators (YSI). To contribute to this, participation in YSI should be increased incrementally to make it available to a larger percentage of Transition Year students

– strengthen the status and role of the CSPE programme in the junior cycle and introduce a citizenship programme as an exam subject at senior cycle

– include workshops on Active Citizenship/Voter Education as a constituent element in Adult/Community Education Programmes (p.21).

Certification and recognition of civic learning

... the development of a certificate/award (complementing Gaisce awards) which would be earned through completing at least three months volunteering or community involvement activity (in Ireland or overseas). This could be done, for example, through a 3-month/year 'civic engagement' gap during further education or the early stages of working life (p.22).

Student Councils

The Taskforce, therefore, welcomes the progress in rollout of Student Councils and supports their extension to all second-level schools by

2009, with more effective support to ensure that they are enabled to have a real influence on decision-making (p.21).

Higher education

… that the Higher Education Authority (HEA) should lead an initiative, with appropriate resources, to promote, support and link together citizenship initiatives across the Higher Education sector, including 'service learning' and volunteering by students (p.22).

Voter education programmes

Establishment of an independent Electoral Commission with a mandate to … support voter education programmes (i) through the formal education system and (ii) in community, adult education and other settings, with special priority for persons in disadvantaged areas, young people and the growing ethnic and cultural diversity in Ireland (pp 16-17).

Educational support for newcomers

The Taskforce therefore supports, in line with commitments in *Towards 2016*, development of a comprehensive policy on integration of migrant communities to Ireland, in consultation with relevant stakeholders. This should include specific measures to promote and support their involvement in civil society. This will need to address issues such as language training and should also explore innovative measures like mentoring by people from the local community (pp 22-23).

Moving to a focus on 'citizenship' understood as legal belonging to the nation state, the Report goes on to recommend:

… that a formal ceremony should be introduced which would mark someone's admission to Irish citizenship and allow them to publicly demonstrate their commitment to Ireland and that information material and short education courses should be developed on Irish citizenship, which would encompass Irish history, democratic institutions, culture, language and traditions, and be made widely available (p.23).

In many respects and detail, the above list of recommendations reflects what was already recommended in the Report of the National Economic and Social Forum, *The Policy Implications of Social Capital* published in 2003 (NESF, 2003). The broad thrust of the recommendations on education including use of school facilities and curricular reform were echoed in the OECD publication *The Well-Being of Nations* published in

2001 (OECD, 2001). It is also worth noting that the recommendations of the Taskforce overlap with some of the recommendations in *The Report of the Democracy Commission* (Harris, 2005)[5] among others, in highlighting the role of schools, youth organisations and other centres of learning in the promotion of civic awareness, values and behaviour.

Two key conclusions on educational research and active citizenship emerged in the Taskforce Report that had not been referred to in the NESF Report:

> 1 In the course of its work, the Taskforce has come to the conclusion that there is a need for more ongoing analysis and research on civic engagement in Ireland. This will facilitate better monitoring of progress and trends, which will in turn allow policies to be developed and refined. This should include development of new statistical sources. To contribute to this, it is recommended that Ireland should participate in the 2009 International Association for the Evaluation of Educational Achievement (IEA) Civic Study (p.26).
>
> 2 ... the establishment of a National Observatory on Active Citizenship to act as a focal point for such research, drawing together key research findings, statistical trends, new indicators and qualitative research and community-based action research – locally, nationally and internationally including EU. It would also seek to engage in a more collaborative and mutually beneficial way with various communities (p.26).
>
> ... Such an Observatory could be located within a lead Higher Education institution. It would be based on a network of communities, researchers and higher education institutions. It would identify emerging issues of public concern in relation to Active Citizenship and commission independent research and public information dissemination. It could also assist in the development of new forms of scholarship and research partnerships directly relevant to Active Citizenship. It would operate in an all-island and European context (pp 26-27).

The first recommendation referred to an upcoming study of 14-year-olds. Arising from this Report, the Republic of Ireland is participating in the *International Civics and Citizenship Education Study* (ICCS), along with 37 countries including the bulk of EU member states. The survey will focus on civic knowledge, dispositions and attitudes among 14-year-olds, typically in the second year of lower secondary education. There will be a strong European component to the Survey addressing knowledge and

6 http://www.tascnet.ie/upload/Democratic%20Renewal%20final.pdf

attitudes in relation to European affairs and institutions. The European Commission, which is supporting the survey, is endeavouring to develop a series of indicators of education and active citizenship as inputs to the EU core indicators. ICCS 2009 builds on previous international studies of civic education conducted in 1971 (in which the Republic of Ireland participated) and 1999 (CIVED – in which the Republic of Ireland did not participate).

An important policy-related conclusion of earlier research is the finding of David Campbell in an analysis of CIVED data that the existence of an 'open classroom' dialogue was among one of the most statistically significant explanatory factors related to positive measurable civic outcomes among 14-year-olds. An open classroom climate is one in which debate and critical thinking about civic and political issues is fostered. Campbell's finding echoes others including those of Whiteley (Whiteley, 2005:20).

The second area of educational research mentioned was the establishment of an Observatory on Active Citizenship. While the report did not go into detail on how such an Observatory would operate, some clues are given to suggest that it might involve:

- networking and partnerships across different fields, disciplines and jurisdictions
- an all-island and European focus and cooperation
- policy analysis and relevance
- new forms of scholarship and research.

Perhaps, given the complexity around education and its contribution to active citizenship, the establishment of such a research approach is timely and urgent.

References

Eivers, E., Shiel, G. and Cunningham, R. (2007), *Ready for Tomorrow's World? The Competencies of Irish 15-year-olds in PISA 2006, Summary Report*, Dublin: Educational Research Centre

Harris, C. (ed.) (2005), *The Report of the Democracy Commission: Engaging Citizens, the case for democratic renewal in Ireland*, Dublin: TASC and Democratic Dialogue

Healy, T. (2005), 'In Each Other's Shadow: What has been the impact of human and social capital on life satisfaction in Ireland?' Doctoral Thesis, University College Dublin. http://www.socialcapitalgateway.org/Final TH PhD 9 Feb.pdf

NESF (National Economic and Social Forum) (2003), *The Policy Implications of Social Capital. Forum Report No. 28*, Dublin: Government Publications

OECD (Organisation for Economic Co-operation and Development) (2001), *The Well-Being of Nations, The Role of Human and Social Capital*, Paris: Centre for Educational Research and Innovation, OECD

OECD (Organisation for Economic Cooperation and Development) (2007), *Understanding the Social Outcomes of Learning*, Paris: OECD

OECD (2006), Programme for International Student Assessment, available at http://www.erc.ie/documents/tomorrows_world.pdf

Whiteley, P. (2005), *Citizenship Education – Longitudinal Study. Second Literature Review – Citizenship Education: The Political Science Perspective. Research Report No. 631*, University of Essex. http://www.dcfs.gov.uk/research/data/uploadfiles/RR631.pdf

Index